HC
427.92   Wang, Hui, 1958-
.W37718   The gradual
1994   revolution.

$39.95

DATE			

BAKER & TAYLOR BOOKS

The Gradual Revolution

The Gradual Revolution

China's Economic Reform Movement

Hui Wang

Transaction Publishers

New Brunswick (U.S.A.) and London (U.K.)

Library of Congress Catalog Number: 93-36079
ISBN: 1-56000-169-0
Printed in the United States of America

Library of Congress Cataloging-in-Publication Data

Wang, Hui, 1958-
    The gradual revolution: China's economic reform movement/Hui Wang.
    p.   cm.
    Includes bibliographical references and index
    ISBN 1-56000-169-0
    1. China—Economic policy—1976- 2. Central planning—China.
3. China—Economic conditions—1976- . Title.
HC427.92.W37718   1994
338.951—dc20   93-36079
                                                             CIP

This is a RAND study.

RAND books are available on a wide variety of topics. To obtain information on other publication, write or call Distribution Services, RAND, 1700 Main Street, P.O. Box 2138, Santa Monica, CA 90407-2138, (310) 393-0411, ext 6686.

To Chun

Contents

Acknowledgments

This book is expanded from my Ph.D. dissertation completed at the RAND Graduate School. I would like to take the opportunity to thank those institutions and individuals that supported me in this endeavor, namely, The RAND Graduate School, which provided a nurturing environment for my work; also, the 1990 Bradley Fellowship of the American Institute for Strategic Cooperation that supported me during the early stages of my research. I am likewise indebted to the Asia Foundation, which provided financial support while I completed my research. I am also grateful to the Ford Foundation for its earlier support. I particularly want to thank Cindy Kumagawa, RAND book program director, for her enthusiastic support of the project. In addition, I would like to express my appreciation to Sabra Feldman, who patiently read and edited the manuscript. And, I wish to thank the RAND library staff for their services.

My greatest debt is to my dissertation committee: Jonathan Cave, Jonathan Pollack, and K.C. Yeh of RAND. They generously offered their knowledge, insight, and inspiration throughout the writing process. Moreover, I owe a special debt to Charles Wolf, Jr., dean of the RAND Graduate School. His support, guidance, and faith in the outcome of my efforts were invaluable during the course of my study.

Despite the nurturing environment, this book still might not have come into existence without the essential help and support of my colleagues, friends, and family. First, Kirsten Speidel, Darlene Thomson, Manbing Sze, Loren Yager, and Roger Benjamin, of RAND; and my highest regard to Albert and Roberta Wohlstetter for their encouragement and support and for sharing their wisdom with me. I am also appreciative of the comments on many of the ideas in the book offered by my friend, Qiren Zhou. Finally, I thank my family members, particularly my wife, Chun Li, who gracefully shared with me all the pressures and joys of the past few years and who uniquely contributed to the accomplishment of the project. I dedicate this book to her.

HUI WANG

1

Introduction

China's economic reforms since the late 1970s have transformed it from a centrally planned to a market economy. What follows is an inquiry into the institutional changes brought about by this transformation, with an emphasis on the process of institutional selection and the rationale underlying it. This study reveals the critical importance of human factors to specific institutional changes, as well as the transformation as a whole.

The recent period of economic reform within China is noteworthy for its strong impact on the country's economic performance. Due to the reform process, China has moved steadily toward a market-oriented economy. More than a fifth of the world's population is participating in a historic transformation of its economic institutions, and the enormous momentum that is now building within the Chinese economy will be felt around the globe in the decades to come.

A Focus on Human Factors in the Reform

More interesting still is China's persistent search for the path that might enable it to transform its centrally planned economy (CPE) in accord with specific circumstances that related to its human characteristics, institutional and cultural setting, and economic development level. It is a search that has combined both deliberate choices and the spontaneous evolution of economic institutions.

Institutional selection occurred, developed, and functioned within a certain institutional and human environment. At the beginning of the reform process, the varied elements making up the existing environment were the legacy of the centrally planned system. China's CPE created and left behind fundamentally different economic institutions than those of a market system, because under a CPE mandatory planning and its accompanying administrative order pervaded all economic activity.

The centrally planned system exerted a long-lasting influence on the behavior patterns and knowledge and skill levels of groups of people, as well as on other fundamental traits, such as values. It molded and shaped people, forcing them to specialize. Therefore, what really faced the reformers of China's CPE were not only the planning apparatus and the state control machines, but also a whole set of CPE-specific human factors. During the reform process both the institutions and the human factors involved underwent dramatic and continuous change, taking on new forms that differed from theoretical models based on either competitive markets or a pure CPE. Even though the question of whether China's CPE should be reformed no longer seems to be a major issue, existing knowledge — theoretical and empirical — provides few miraculous prescriptions for successful change. Since the importance of human factors in institutional transformation seems not to have been fully realized, it is worth pointing out that the most profound changes in China's reform relate to the economic system's human assets. (This term encompasses both the human constituents — reform decision makers and other government officials, enterprise owners and managers, workers, peasants, and other individuals, such as teachers and doctors — and their experiences, knowledge, skills, values, and habits.) From a certain perspective, human factors contributed most to defining the specific circumstances of a reform.

For China's economic reformers, the delicate task of searching for the path of transformation lies in a selection of institutions that is appropriate to the country's specific circumstances. Their recognition of the importance of the relationship between economic institutions and circumstances is not new. Nearly fifty years ago, Friedrich A. von Hayek observed that the "economic problem of society is mainly one of adaptation to changes in particular circumstances of time and place." Here, in analyzing China's reform process, we will emphasize specific circumstances of recent economic reform in China and the importance of economic institutions, particularly as viewed in terms of human factors.

As China's reform experiences indicate, the nature of the human factors inherited from the CPE determined to a large extent what institutional arrangements would work effectively and what kind of institutional selection there should be. Human factors were not only the variables responsible for initiating reform and determining how it proceeded, but also the major constraints upon the reform. How successful institutional selection would be largely depended on whether there was a fit between any given institutional arrangement and the related human factors. Further, differentiation of human assets among into different groups of people contributed to variations within the reform process and discrepancies in the success of institutional selection. Moreover, as the human factors evolved during the reform, the constraints upon the reform slackened, and new institutional arrangements were called for.

Interests and Issues

Chinese economic reform offers a unique case study in the gradual transformation of a centrally planned economy into a market economy. Among the various economies currently undergoing or that have undergone parallel transformation, China so far seems to present a more incremental and cumulative pattern of institutional change. Incremental development often appears less appealing than dramatic change. China's experience deserves scrutiny for the information it provides about the relationship between the reasons for reform, the social and economic context of the changes, and the pace of this transformation. Indeed, at least as significant as speculation on the existence of hidden trends underlying changes in the economic and political apparatus of a society is an understanding of the intrinsic and spontaneous forces for institutional change, and the mechanism for implementing change that is embedded in a given institution. Examination of recent Chinese economic reform touches upon the fundamental questions of how the transformation of economic institutions effectively promotes economic development and how that development may lay the foundation for further reform. Understanding such a gradual reform process can help to explain further the primary factors of economic performance both in China as well as in other reforming countries.

China's reform of its economic system reveals the dynamics behind many aspects of institutional evolution: the goals, definitions, content, and constraints, which were subject to continuous change and variation throughout the movement. In terms of the process and progress of reform, the effects of the evolution of the economic system have been cumulative. They have also been psychological, emotional, and material in nature.

A gradual revolution produces many puzzling structures. For example, during the reform, both institutional forms and human factors evolved, creating a great variety of differentiated economic institutions.

Further, although most people were attracted to the reform by its promise of a better life, it was not entirely clear to them that with reform would come new discrepancies in the distribution of income, wealth, and even opportunity. This gap between perception and reality resulted in shock, dissatisfaction, pain, and a sense of loss. It would have been better had the reform been understood as a long-term investment entailing risk and an uneven distribution of the benefits. From a certain perspective, reform can be seen as an investment (with attendant risks), and its benefits regarded as the return on that investment. However, the return must be appreciated as being both unpredictable and highly differentiated.[1]

Thus, paradoxically, economic reform is claimed to be in the people's interest, but there is no effective mechanism for the people — either as individuals or as groups — to express preferences in matters of reform. What we do know is that the great social and economic change inherent in reform results in a net gain overall and an improved living standard for most; however, the possibility that some might suffer cannot be ruled out, and the long-term outcome of reform for different generations over time is unclear. Change or movement within China's economic institutions has appeared to be contingent on and related to the expected versus actual capability of people, technology, and which functions of certain institutions have been involved.

The majority of the people in China who were affected by the economic reform movement were not active participants in it and had no way to influence its course, although they had to live with its outcome. This is at the heart of the paradox that exists between interest and representation. Reform was appreciated quite differently by the general population than by the movement's decision makers, and its future benefits were discounted or valued in a variety of ways at different levels and in different sectors of Chinese society.

In terms of the transformation from a centrally planned to a market economy, there are three plain but essential issues: What are the connections between institutional change and economic development? What influences the choice between a relatively gradual and a dramatic reform process? and What are the factors determining institutional selection in a transition?

With China's reform, the following broad questions arise: What were the original goals of the reform movement when it started in the late 1970s? Did they change? If so, how and was the result the dissolution of the centrally planned system and the move to a market system? What was the mechanism by which China's incremental reform made fundamental changes? What prevented the transformation from stopping somewhere between a CPE and a market system? What direction is China's economic reform taking, and what drives it?

On more specific issues of China's reform, questions include: How did China reform its agricultural system, why was it so successful, and what distinguished it from other reforms? To what degree were the experiences of agricultural reform helpful in carrying out other reforms, and why? How did China deal with its state enterprises and state ownership? What did China really want to gain from launching its special economic zones, how did these goals evolve, and what kind of impact did the zones have on the reform as a whole?

In addressing these issues, this study, while covering the period from the late 1970s to 1992, focuses on the first decade of the reform:

from the end of the 1970s to the end of the 1980s. Almost all major changes were made in this first decade of reform, and this period representative of the reform movement as a whole. In this inaugural decade, a series of dramatic changes occurred in what had long been a stagnant economy. Economic reform — focused on decentralization, privatization, and the development of markets — radically changed the overall performance of the Chinese economy. In particular, economic reform enabled 800 million Chinese peasants to break away from the bonds of the commune system. State-owned industry steadily diminished from a virtual monopoly to its present position, accounting for less than half of China's total industrial sector.

The revitalization of the Chinese economy due to this first decade of economic reform is clearly demonstrated by its strong performance. As a result of reform, agricultural production increased by an average of 6.2 percent (excluding price changes); during the period 1953 to 1978, agricultural production increased only 2.6 percent.[2] China's import-export values rose from $20.6 billion in 1978 to over $100 billion in 1988; China's export position jumped from thirty-second worldwide in 1978 to fourteenth a decade later.[3] In the last four fiscal years since 1989, due to the tremendous economic momentum built by the reform, China's exports have continued to increase more than 15 percent annually, much faster than the worldwide average.[4] From 1978 to 1988 the real Gross National Product (GNP) of the Chinese economy increased about 1.52 times, with an average annual growth rate of 9.6 percent.[5] China's achievements in the last decade represent a major success in attaining a high growth rate and rapid development while gradually but significantly transforming the institutions of a CPE to a more market-oriented economy.

Shadows

At the same time, however, various economic, political, and social problems emerged, frustrating and challenging the reforms. These problems included inflation, corruption, deterioration of public services, and some failures in providing appropriate social policies. On the one hand, many of the problems posed by the transformation from a CPE to a market economy in China were quite unprecedented, and the society's institutions may have failed in some way(s) to adjust and adapt. On the other hand, the uncertainties embedded in the transformation to a fundamentally different system caused even more pain, tension, conflict, and losses in the Chinese economy as well as in the lives of some individuals that had initially been foreseen.

From the first day of China's reform, there were shadows surrounding it. From a broader perspective, two historical and generational legacies — China's population[6] and the Cultural Revolution — stood out as constraints to the economic reform. China began and conducted its economic reform with a heavy population: over 22 percent of the world's people lived on less than 8 percent of the world's arable land.[7] At the time the reform was started, according to a report by Li Xiannian at a central meeting in early 1979, not only did the rural people not have meat or extra grain to sell, but "peasants in many areas simply don't have enough grain for themselves to eat, and, in some areas, peasants are *seriously* short of grain."[8] Second, the economic reform was launched when the nation was still under the shadow of more than a decade of disastrous destruction of economic and human capital due to ideological radicalism from 1966 to 1977. For example, colleges and universities were essentially shut down during those eleven years, standard curricula in primary and high schools were replaced by political propaganda programs and ideological education schemes, and respect for traditional civilization and knowledge was demolished, all of which caused a human capital shortage for economic development in the years that followed. This perhaps was the only time in China's long history that the traditional search for knowledge and respect for learning were abandoned for ideological reasons.[9]

More important, the centralized communist political system provided the primary institutional setting for the reform. Indeed, the group of pragmatic leaders, represented by Deng Xiaoping and Chen Yun, who reemerged in the late 1970s, played a crucial role in breaking away from the previously ideology-guided strategy of development and in initiating the historic reform movement. They advocated a more practical economic strategy that included opening China to the West. They took the lead in critiquing the radical economic policies of the past few decades. Consequently, there was widespread decentralization accompanied by a substantial increase in economic freedom, a significant diversification of economic decisions, and somewhat loosened political control. China opened her door(s) to the world. All of this, however, occurred under the same one-party political system and was not accompanied by real, essential, or large-scale change in the main characteristics of the Chinese political system. During the decade of reform this system was still the Communist one-party control structure that allowed the 1989 tragedy in Tiananmen Square to happen. Economic reform, especially in its later years, was often in conflict with the existing political system and had to yield to politics. Indeed, economic reform did not alleviate in any way the demand for political reform and could not serve as a substitute for the reform of China's political institutions. The discord between the economic and political movements grew, and this imposed a major limitation on the development of economic reform, particularly after the influence of agricultural reform spread throughout the economic and social systems. The failure to conduct corresponding substantive political reform left China in a state of high uncertainty. The continued delay of appropriate political reform — ultimately characterized as the introduction of a system of freedom and democracy — seemed to put China in a position of fewer alternatives and ever high stakes for systemic political change. Little progress in political reform and even less tolerance for political pluralism indicated a rigidly constrained and institutionalized setting for economic reform and further revealed the complexity of the transformation in China.

When the Reform Started

The Chinese economic reform was initiated against a background of widespread dissatisfaction brought about by radical, ideologically guided economic policies, the return of pragmatic leaders and economic thought, rapidly improving relations with the West (and the United States in particular), the increased flow of information from the outside world, and the pressing challenge from the world's then fastest-growing economies (particularly those of Hong Kong, South Korea, Taiwan and Singapore) which share cultural and historical roots with China.[10]

Most scholars, including Harding (1987), Liu (1988), and Perkins (1988) agree that Chinese economic reform occurred chiefly in the years between 1977 and 1979, and centered around December 1978, when a plenary meeting of the Chinese Community Party's Central Committee made a landmark decision on China's strategy of economic and political development.[11] This meeting was characterized by the adoption of the pragmatic slogan Seeking Truth from Facts, and it demonstrated the leadership's willingness to reevaluate the policies of economic development followed during earlier decades. More specifically, this meeting indicated the prevalence of practical thinking and marked a break from the traditional understanding of social economies. At the meeting, such economic views were criticized for "overcentralization,"[12] ideological dogmatism was denounced, and emancipation of thinking was advocated. Behind all these changes were significant personnel reshufflings, among which the reemergence of Deng Yiaoping into China's top leadership circle was to have the most far-reaching impact on the reform movement. This meeting laid the foundation for new, reformist economic strategies.

Because of the significance of this December 1978 meeting and, more importantly, what actually happened in 1979, I will argue that the year 1979 marked the true start of the reform. Apart from the meeting just prior to the beginning of that year, several major reforms suggest 1979 as the actual starting point for Chinese economic reform.

At a central working meeting held in Beijing in April 1979, the need to reform industrial and overall economic management was voiced. In particular, four major issues of economic reform were brought up for "serious study": market function and mechanism, autonomy for enterprises, more authority for local governments, and the use of economic levers instead of administrative instruments in economic management.[13] Raising these issues represented an important step forward from the consensus at the central meeting at the end of 1978 which had focused on what parts of the economy to reform.

On 4 April 1979, the central government released a document spelling out, for the first time, an agricultural reform strategy and introducing responsibility systems on an experimental basis.[14] This experiment tried to introduce relationships between an individual's work and his reward, and hence posed the initial challenges to the traditional organization of production and distribution of the commune system. The "commune" system of agricultural production was gradually dismantled over the next four years, and a new agricultural system with the family as its basis was established in its stead. This institutional reform initiative in agricultural production started the movement that finally brought about an end to central planning in agriculture.

On 25 May 1979, a bold attempt to reform the system of state enterprise was launched with eight pilot projects in three major cities (Beijing, Tianjing, and Shanghai).[15] On 13 July 1979, Beijing released five major documents on enterprise reform that requested that all the provinces conduct their own similar experiments.[16] On the same day, a decree announcing a new incentive-based distribution of income between central and local governments was released that provided local governments with the motivation to increase local income through a system of shared interests with the central government.[17]

Furthermore, on 15 July 1979, two reports from Guangdong and Fujian Provinces were endorsed by the central government; they proposed implementation of a special opening-up policy, of which the keystone would be the inauguration of special export zones — the embryonic form of the now-famous "special economic zones" (SEZs) adjacent to Hong Kong.[18] Apart from the SEZs, these two local reports bearing the central government's endorsement provided a working model for fostering greater economic autonomy at the local level.

In addition, two important price adjustments in 1979 broke the mandated frozen price structure and indicated the partial recognition of a price mechanism in the economy. For many years before these price adjustments, prices had been fixed and the impact of price on production and consumption ignored and denied. In March 1979, the purchase prices of 18 kinds of agricultural products were raised.[19] A more comprehensive price adjustment involving grocery prices and wages took place later in September of the same year.[20] These price adjustments were based on the perceived failure of fixed prices to reflect costs incurred in production. They did not, however, allow the market to decide the price of a product; they merely reduced the gap between production costs and selling prices. Nevertheless, the price adjustments of 1979 turned out to be the beginning of further experiments in price reform during the following decade.

Thus it was during 1979 that the existing centrally planned system was challenged and a broad range of changes in the economy started to take place. The reform movement that got underway in 1979 covered many of the major aspects of the economic system, including price, enterprise structure, agricultural production, the economic relationships between the central and local governments, and policy. As 1979 stands out in the history of China's reform movement, 1978 was also important for the preparation leading up to the ground-breaking meeting held at the end of the year, at which basic order was restored to the economy after Mao Zedong and the Cultural Revolution. There were even some initiatives in overhauling the economic system by, for instance, sharing marginal profit between the government and enterprises.[21]

While this study extends its discussion of China's economic reform to the early 1990s, the prime period covered lies between 1979 and 1989. Choosing the beginning of 1989 or the end of 1988 as the close of this period is admittedly rather arbitrary. The decision was made essentially to avoid complicating the study in order to address the issues of reform in as straightforward a way as possible. What happened in Tiananmen Square on 4 June 1989 and in the following months brought extraordinary factors into play that influenced and disturbed (at least for a certain period) the development of economic reform. Although this single variable alone does not explain the variability of China's economic development in 1989 and 1990, the fluctuations reflected by both the policies and major indicators immediately after the tragedy would seem to be unusual, and could create confusion in assessing the outcome of the reform process. In fact, both the economic reform policies and the people's confidence in them halted after the dramatic event.[22] Indeed, the democratic movement in Tiananmen Square should, to a large degree, be attributed to the prior decade's economic reform. Economic reform cultivated both the atmosphere and the institutions of free economic choice and competition among equals, which are in accord with the principles of political democracy. The market economy is, indeed, the natural cradle for freedom and democracy. In essence, there is no physical or mental confinement that can prevent free choices and voting processes (by selecting certain products rather than others) in the market from spreading throughout the social and political life of a society. The Tiananmen Square event itself reflected political, social, and economic problems and frustrations related to reforms. For example, corruption and unequal opportunity raised the questions of both fairness and efficiency, and were at that time among the most pressing issues for Chinese society. Nevertheless, given the intention of this book, I have elected to focus on issues before the Tiananmen Square episode. Of course, a clear understanding of the ten years of economic reform prior to the summer of 1989 is of considerable value to anyone interested in evaluating the Tiananmen Square protest and its aftermath in the context of the reform movement as a whole.

There have been, indeed, differences between regions in economic development and reform practice. In addition, more and more interactions between the central and provincial governments have been taking place in shaping reform policies in recent years. Despite these facts, there is little argument that the decisions on the Chinese economic reform in its first decade were, with few exceptions, made in Beijing. The central government dominated both the initiation and development of the reform during the period 1979 to 1989. This study seeks to explore and to explain how the transformation from a centrally planned system to a more market-oriented economy took place.

Relying on increasingly available data about the reform movement and using a case study approach, this book will analyze the process of reforming China's economic system, with emphasis on economic behavior and institutions, to discover the institutional dynamics at work and to identify the underlying assumptions that have influenced the reform movement's path.

Collecting information for this study was a particularly difficult task. While it is true that more and more data have become available for the study of China's economic policy and economic development, there are often difficulties and unexpected obstacles in gaining access to the officially available data, not to mention the problems of definition and interpretation. Since many documents and records of reform experiments and policies were distributed directly to government offices and enterprises through administrative channels, they were readily available in libraries. In the past, mainly due to the central bureaucracy's practice of applying arbitrary controls on information, government documents on reform and economic development were distributed only to certain levels in the administrative hierarchy; as a result, many documents could be found only in highly specialized publications. It is my particular intention to use data from published sources so that others may conveniently examine these same works.

In general, there are three kinds of data used in the study.

Documentary information: Mostly issued by the central government in Beijing, containing data on the reform movement from 1979 to 1989; a few documents relate to the economic system and economic adjustments in the 1950s, 1960s, and just prior to the onset of reform in the 1970s. These papers include important regulations, policies, instruction, memoranda, speeches, proposals, reports, announcements, and other communiqués. In China at the time, some of the speeches by top leaders would often be regarded as guiding principles for policy design and implementation, even though they were not yet set down in formal policies or regulations, and before an important conference officially confirmed or altered them. Formal documents like the no. 1 decree of 1986 issued by the central government, "Arrangements for Agricultural Work in 1986," and important informal documents like Chen Yun's speech outline "On Issues of Plan and Market," written on 8 March 1979, are all included in this study. Limited interviews with participants in policy formation at that time were utilized to confirm or clarify some interpretations of documentary sources.

Statistical data: Sources include *Almanac of China's Economy, Almanac of China's Statistics,* and other survey statistics released by the Chinese Statistical Bureau or its local branches.

Professional literature: These secondary sources mainly cover the debates and discussions on the decade's economic reform and economic development in both Chinese and English.

There are primarily two limitations on using the documentary information. The first is in interpretation. Many documents were drafted in the process of political compromises and therefore are vague and/or ambiguous. Some of the compromises were made, in the Chinese way, not in the form of concessions, but in the form of coexisting, essentially conflicting items in the same document. In other words, some of the compromises were made not be identifying and agreeing on common principles, but by retaining differences of opinion less noticeably or by couching them in deliberately ambiguous language. For example, in a document of 1 January 1984 issued by the central government on agricultural reform, it was said that subcontracting would be allowed but subleasing would not.[23] No definitions of "subcontracting" or "subleasing" were given. A deed could be categorized as either a subcontract or a sublease, leaving the interpretation and implementation of the policy dependent upon local officials.

The second limitation of the documentary information is in measurement. Even though a document may be clearly written, there is considerable room for interpretation, which makes it difficult to measure the effects of a policy. Whether a reform policy or regulation led to some change in economic or institutional behavior or within an institution will not always be clear. It is not uncommon for several policies to be contradictory. Moreover, the effect of a reform policy might well not be apparent for some time. In the short run, fluctuation could cause "noise" to interfere with assessing and measuring its effect.

As will be discussed in chapters 2 through 5, the Chinese economic reform has essentially experienced two distinct phases of development in the last decade. The first phase was from 1979 to 1984 and the second from 1984 to 1989. In general, the economic reform of 1979 to 1989 was incremental, and there might not be a clear-cut indicator to differentiate the first stage from the second. Many reform policies continued to be effective across the years, and some measures were adopted and adjusted from previous ones. Nevertheless, the goals and definitions of the economic reform in its early and late years are substantially varied, and the contents of reform also differ. As will be suggested later in this study, the major characteristics of the early and late reforms are different, and an awareness of these differences is crucial for understanding what really happened. There were some jumps in the evolutionary reform process, and 1984 was the time when some relatively major changes occurred. What happened in 1984 serves to separate the two phases somewhat better than events in other years. Most important, 1984 is the year urban economic reform was formally launched. It is the time when agricultural reform achieved genuine success and the battle against the old mandatory, centrally planned system clearly shifted from an agricultural economy to a national economy. The hold of orthodox economic thinking had been broken by the success of the new system in the agricultural sector; by 1984 or so, Chinese reform had achieved enough momentum to encompass the whole economic system with its agenda of change.

In the remainder of the book, I draw a model for each of these two phases of reform. Each analytic paradigm comprises four basic elements: dominant belief, approach, chief concerns, and proposition.

Dominant belief is defined as the belief that sets the direction and intent of reform. Dominant belief is assumed to be the most important factor underlying the primary origin and concept of economic reform; it provides the foundation for the goal and definition of the reform. In this regard, to understand the reform's purpose, the way it proceeded and why, and its crucial constraints, we have to examine the reform's dominant belief. Dominant belief is the primary assumption for understanding and analyzing the Chinese economic reform.

Reform *approach refers* to the intended strategy to execute the reform. In general, the Chinese implemented their economic reforms in an incremental and cumulative way. More specifically, they adopted an experimental approach called "keep touching stones while walking across a river," an old Chinese phrase that will be discussed at greater length in chapter 2.

Another important element of this paradigm, *chief concerns,* is the major criterion used explicitly or implicitly to judge and adjust the direction and pace of the reforms. Chief concerns are the factors that reveal why reform policies and measures are chosen to be one way or an other. As we will see, the reform is part of a historical transformation of the economic system, and chief concerns relate to the factors that drive the process of selection and innovation of economic institutions. Chief concerns reflect these factors in reviewing and comparing the performance of different economic systems and policy arrangements.

Propositions are the major constituents of the reform decision makers' understanding of the reform. In other words, the role of propositions in the paradigm is to present the dominant interpretation of China's economic reform on the basis of the paradigm's models. These propositions will be tested with evidence of the reform movement.

This book consists of six chapters. After this first chapter of introduction, which lays out the background of the reform movement in China and the method of this study, chapter 2 presents the first model and uses it to analyze the early reform (1979-84). Chapter 3 is devoted to understanding and explaining this first-phase economic reform in China. Chapter 4 studies the second analytic model and analyzes the reform of the second phase (1984-89). Chapter 5 endeavors to explain this later period of economic reform. Chapter 6 offers conclusions on the record of Chinese economic reform during the decade as a whole.

Notes

1. It might be interesting to raise the following questions: Who makes the investment and how much? Who gets the returns and how? What did or does the reform mean to different groups of people as far as differing expectations, experiences, opportunities to enjoy the outcome of reform, and current status? I intend to discuss some of these questions in follow-up studies.

2. Also see *A Statistical Survey of China 1989* 1989, 9-10; Wang Mengkui, "Economic Construction of Ten Years," in *Almanac of China's Economy 1989*, II.30. In calculating the average growth rates for 1978-88 and 1953-78, I have used Total Agriculture Product Value, which was the principal unit used to measure agricultural development in China.

3. Ji Chongwei, "Ten Years of Opening-up," in *Almanac of China's Economy 1989*, II.47; Wang Mengkui, "Economic Construction of Ten Years," in *Almanac of China's Economy 1989*, I.48.

4. This figure is based on China's official statistics for 1989, 1990, and 1991, and a projected annualized estimate based on the statistics for the first half of 1992.

5. Wang Mengkui, "Economic Construction of Ten Years," in *Almanac of China's Economy 1989*, II.30.

6. Many factors, including population policies, tradition, and social and economic development, contributed to the rapid population growth of the 1950s, 1960s, and 1970s that resulted in the lagging momentum of population growth in the 1980s and beyond. The first and most important factor was the population policies in the 1950s and 1960s. Since China was a centrally planned economy, its population policies greatly influenced and even determined the pattern of population development. In the 1950s and 1960s, the Chinese government considered a large

population a sign of national power and strength and strongly encouraged its people to have more children, ignoring China's basic living conditions in addition to a number of the major consequences of such policies. One of the primary consequences was that the rapid population growth made scarce resources even scarcer and social conflicts more complicated. Under the policies for population growth there was even a movement in the 1950s based on the concept of the "heroic mother" and "model family" to advocate higher birth rates. This movement encouraged each family to have five or six children as a contribution to society. Even worse, opposing opinions were severely repressed and some outspoken scholars (such as economist Ma Yingchu) were criticized in the nationwide government-run media for being "reactionary Malthusist's." The direct consequence of these population policies was an increase in population of 20 million per year for most of the 1960s and early 1970s, after which the government installed an abrupt reversal of its population policy by implementing a mandatory birth control program. Undoubtedly, this serves as an example of the potentially high social cost(s) of such decisions and of how important it is to be cautious in making any such move.

The second factor contributing to this rapid population growth in the 1950s, 1960s, and 1970s was that social policies and economic development after 1949 contributed to a decline in infant mortality and an increase in life expectancy.

The third factor appeared to be the long-standing Chinese tradition favoring large families, particularly among agricultural families, in which the number of men in a family is seen as an indication of prosperity. The age-old land distribution system of the agricultural Chinese economy, frequently influenced by the egalitarian demands of peasant uprisings and the redistribution of land by new dynasties, also implicitly endorsed a relationship between more people and more land. In the end, population size had been and would continue to be important to the development of China's economy.

7.   According to the World Bank's 1981 report *China — Socialist Economic Development* (Washington, D.C.: World Bank, vol. 2), China provided food for about 22% of the world's population on less than 8% of the world's arable land.

8.   Li Xiannian, "Report at the Central Working Meeting of the CCP," in *Collection of Documents on Economic Reform 1977-1983* 1984, 9. At the working meeting, which was held in April 1979 and focused on eco-

nomic problems, Vice Premier Li Xiannian made this remark on agriculture as part of a comprehensive criticism of the existing economic strategy.

9. From 1966 to 1977, China's economy, education, and social life were in disorder. Normal college and university education, for example, was cut off for more than ten years, and high school graduates were sent to communes and factories to be reeducated. The idea that knowledge was useless was pervasive, and students who submitted blank test sheets were sometimes treated as heroes. Zhang Tiesheng from Liaoning Province was one of these national heroes in the 1970s. Most often, some political or ideological reason would be the true motive.

10. Information from the so-called Four Dragons (Hong Kong, Taiwan, Singapore, and South Korea) was particularly compelling and threatening. Because these economies had been similar in some respects to China's back in the 1950s and 1960s, comparative data on these economies was deemed especially meaningful. In the early 1980s, there was widespread discussion within China about the fundamental crisis that the Chinese were facing.

11. Among the representative opinions on when the reform began, are the following:

In his 1988 study on models of Chinese economic reform, Liu Guoguang (1988, 667-68) set the meeting of December 1978 as the starting point for the reform and made what happened from 1979 onward the subject of this study.

Dwight H. Perkins (1988, 607, 621, 629) observes that the Chinese rural reform basically started in 1979 and, since "opening up actually began even earlier," 1977 and 1978 should be viewed as part of the reform years' period.

Harry Harding (1987, 71) contends that "China began experimenting with economic structural reform soon after the reformers achieved dominance over the restorationists during the Third Plenum at the end of 1978."

12. After more than one month of preparatory meetings, the Third Plenum of the 11th Party Congress was officially held during 18-22 December 1978. Even during the preparatory meetings, the debates on political policy, economic strategy, and personnel organization were long, intense, and heated among the modest and pragmatic people, represented by Hua Guofeng, and the fundamentalist pragmatic leaders, represented by Chen Yun and Deng Xiaoping. For more detail about the decision to change

the economic and political development strategy see "The Communiqué of the Third Plenum of the 11th Party Congress of the CCP," in *After the Third Plenum — Selection of Important Documents* 1982, vol. 1., pp. 1-2, 4-8, 12.

13. Ibid., p. 6.
14. The meeting of the Central Committee was held in April 1979 and focused on economic problems. Details are contained in *After the Third Plenum — Selection of Important Documents* 1982; and *Collection of Documents on Economic Reform 1977-1983* 1984, 178-81.
15. "Memorandum of the Meeting on Agricultural Work," in *Collection of Documents on Economic Reform 1977-1983* 1984, 95-96.
16. *Collection of Documents on Economic Reform 1977-1983* 1984, 178-81. The trial of enterprise reform was launched in May 1979 with eight enterprises in three cities (Shanghai, Beijing and Tianjing), and the trial was publicized nationwide. A serious preparation meeting for the experiment was held and sponsored by China National Economic Committee in April 1979, and participants included representatives from the eight enterprises, government officers from related ministries and cities, and professors and research fellows.
17. "Regulations on Expanding the Autonomy of the State Enterprises," in *Collection of Documents on Economic Reform 1977-1983*. 1984, 182-89.
18. "The State Council on Experimenting with New Financial Management Methods," in *Collection of Documents on Economic Reform 1977-1983* 1984, 803-7.
19. "Endorsement of Central Committee of the Chinese Communist Party (CCCCP) and China's State Council (CSC) on Guangdong Province's and Fujian Province's Reports on Special Policies and Flexible Measures (extracts)," "Guangdong Province's Report on Expanding Foreign Trade, Economic Development (extracts)," and Fujian Province's Report on Using Overseas-Chinese and Foreign Investments to Speed-up Socialist Construction (extracts)," in *Collection of Documents on Economic Reform 1977-1983* 1984, 471-80.
20. Zhou Taihe 1984, 172. In March 1979, the Chinese central government decided to raise the prices of 18 categories of agriculture products, including grains, cotton, vegetable oil, sugar, meat and dairy products, fish and water products, etc.
21. "Major Points of the National Meeting on Prices and Wages," in *Collection of Documents on Economic Reform 1977-1983* 1984, 921-28.
22. "CCCCP's Decisions on Speeding-up Industrial Development (draft extracts)," in *Collection of Documents on Economic Reform 1977-1983* 1984, 171-75.

23. Policies toward private industry, for example, shifted sharply from encouraging to containing its development. Loans and credit to private industry were cut or stopped, and a massive shut-down of private business followed, although policies toward private industry shifted back little more than one year later toward greater tolerance.

For example, there are questions such as how much contribution the economic reform really made to the development and growth of the Chinese economy considering factors such as technological progress, what kind of relationships and interactions between political and economic reforms the Chinese were exposed to, and how reform decisions were affected by the roles of specific individuals or organizations. Specific problems of how the market was gradually developed, how the private and non-state economies emerged as both the planned and market economies were functioning, and how the monetary system was reformed, will not be explored in detail.

For this specific problem, I had to call one of the people who was directly involved in drafting the document and consult on the meaning of the two concepts, as well as the political compromise behind them.

2

Early Reform
(1979 to 1984)

When the early reform movement first surfaced, the world was still engaged in the Cold War, and transformation of the Chinese centrally planned economy (CPE) did not seem inevitable. Many aspects of China's early reform reveal an intuitive search and exploration for a new and better economic system. Even though the early reform's concerns and measures differed largely from their counterparts later on, there is nonetheless a certain consistency throughout China's economic reform process, and economic reform constituted an integral part of the whole revolution. Reform during this period was comparatively primitive, and constraints it encountered were typical of a metamorphosing CPE. During this period, the basic CPE elements were still dominant, even though the elements of a market economy were growing rapidly.

Initiation of the Reform

At the beginning of the reform, China's economic strategy largely reflected the state of the CPE in the late 1970s. At the time, Chinese economic strategy could be characterized as ideologically radical, physically and mentally closed, organizationally centralized, and economically quantity oriented. Mandatory political education, isolation from outside information and contacts, ideological self-content, and centrally controlled distribution of income and rationing had kept the economy, including living standards, stagnant. In particular, technological progress in the economy as a whole was slow except for that of military-related industries. Moreover, the annual population growth of 12-14 million ate up most of the economic growth.[1] Production was not adjusted by consumption but by a rigid, compulsory plan. Factories and enterprises strove to meet the quotas of the central plan, ignoring both the costs of production on the supply side and consumer need on the demand side. There were constant gaps between supply and demand because of the centralization of authority, information, and production, and because of poor incentives.

The failure of the existing centrally planned system and the emergence of pragmatic leaders were the prime catalysts for the initiation of China's historic reform movement at the end of the 1970s. From the economic perspective, fixed wages and the decline of real income, shortages and poor quality, unemployment, and an increasing number of peasants living in poverty and hunger presented an undisputed picture of an economic system in deep crisis. This crisis presented challenges to the existing radical economic strategy and the centrally planned system, and resulted in demands for a profound reform of that system. China's economic reform had its origin in this demand for systemic change. From political radicalism and political prosecution, Mao Tzedong's death in 1976 led to a wave of appeals for political reform across China's whole political spectrum. The change in the political climate paved the way for a group of pragmatic leaders who came to power in response to the tremendous ground swell for political change in the late 1970s. Under their leadership, the reform movement began — and it evolved into a revolution beyond anyone's imagination.

A Devastating Economy

Under the central planning system, widespread shortage and overproduction coexisted in the Chinese economy prior to reform. By the end of the 1970s, shortage had become widespread in China. In his book, *Economics of Shortage,* Hungarian economist Janos Kornai explains the phenomenon of shortage and the mechanism that creates it in a centrally planned socialist economy. Kornai and others[2] have suggested that shortage is inherent and rooted in the central planning system and directly related to its budget system; it is also linked to state ownership. As a CPE before the reform, China was obviously no exception. In shortage situations, however, many products were overproduced or never used. Implementing the mandatory, centrally directed plan, factories often produced goods for which there was no consumer. Even when there was a consumer, the supply and demand often broke down. Under the central planning system, manufacturers might never contract with their customers, actual or potential. There was no real market. Instead, the allocation of production and goods was designed and controlled by the planning bureaucracy. As a result, on the one hand, supply often did not meet demand in terms of quantity, quality, specification, and response time. On the other hand, information from the demand side could not go directly to the supply side, but rather went through a long bureaucratic process that drastically reduced the information eventually communicated to the production sector. Without even taking into account other important factors, such as the incentive structure and technological progress, the coexistence of widespread shortage and overproduction created some bizarre economic situations. For example, even while the central planning agency was claiming a "serious shortage" of steel in 1979, according to a report of the central government there was a huge overstock of 17.1 million tons of steel (about 54 percent of China's total steel production in 1978).[3]

Even worse, there was no proper incentive or mechanism for the conduct of internal trade. Even when demand was communicated, producers did not have the incentive to adjust production and products to the needs of consumers. Under central planning, state enterprises had no alternatives for implementing the plan. More often than not, these state enterprises were not much concerned about the consequences of inappropriate supply because there was no incentive to adjust. For both producers and consumers, the only mandate was satisfaction of their direct responsibilities to government agencies by fulfilling the requirements of the state plan. Thus, ordinary consumers were at odds with the state enterprises in their pursuit of quality and value in the products they used. But consumers had no access to and no power in the planning process, just as they had no choice in the goods and services assigned them by the plan. Therefore, by eliminating incentives and relegating to itself economic control, the central planning system resulted in a hopeless deterioration in China's economic performance prior to reform.

Further, lack of a mechanism and incentives for trade reflected problems in ownership structure and overall contractual relations. Because of the vertical integration of the planning system, enterprises were controlled by separate government departments and ministries and did not have the authority to trade with one another. This problem could be attributed to contractual relations in the CPE. Because of state ownership and the overall reward mechanism based on existing contractual relations, enterprises did not have incentives to trade their surpluses.

As a result of the inefficiency of the CPE and the continuing deterioration of economic performance in China before reform, life for its people became increasingly grim and hard. As queues on the street were getting longer and longer, many commodities were divided among store employees and their associates before reaching the shelves. The number of mandatory quotas on goods and services, including most necessities, increased relentlessly. Quotas expanded from rice, vegetable oil, and clothes to meat, eggs, milk, bicycles, watches, radios, etc. Sometimes, one had to accumulate quota allocations for years to be able to buy certain items. A bicycle, to take one example, required several years' worth of the industry's quota units allotted each person; so family members were often forced to pool their individual quota units in addition to committing financial resources in order to make such a basic purchase; this in turn severely restricted their purchase of other items for years to come. In addition to the problems of long queues and crippling quotas in daily life, the quality of products and services declined steadily. People considered themselves fortunate to obtain anything at all when most people got nothing, so quality became a luxury. Those who did demand quality in goods and services had to bribe those who produced or otherwise had access to what they wanted. Since all prices were set officially and no market mechanism was allowed, paying in kind became widespread and made the situation even worse. A doctor's prescription of expensive free-of-charge medicines, a butcher's access to good cuts of meat, an official's power to assign a good job to someone's son or to provide a more spacious apartment, and so on, all became means of exchange for high-quality and/or scarce commodities. Quotas holdings were also exchanged. There was no officially recognized market for this kind of exchange, and these exchanges were mostly not admitted. This could be called "implicit exchange." Implicit exchange existed in situations of both shortage and poor quality. Implicit exchange was in fact an exchange of power, privilege, access, and social connection. All implicit exchange took place on a contingency basis, and transaction costs were usually high. Further, implicit exchange was not only ineffective but also accelerated the decline of moral and professional standards in both production and commercial transactions. Worse still was that the peasants, who could barely keep enough of their crops for their own consumption, had no access to the power and privileges necessary to conduct implicit exchange but had to suffer from the planning bureaucracy's policies and the deterioration in the quality of goods and services. The deterioration of China's economic performance and the its serious consequences for people's lives by the end of the 1970s favored the rise of an economic reform movement.

Pragmatic Leadership

The reemergence of pragmatic leaders who had been dismissed or deprived of real power during the Cultural Revolution in the vanguard of economic reform is especially noteworthy. At the end of the 1970s and in the early 1980s, this group of leaders openly committed itself to putting the Chinese economy on the fast development track by means of sweeping changes in its economic development strategy, thus boldly expressing its ambition to modernize the nation's moribund economy.[4]

Given that authority and power in China at this time were highly centralized and concentrated in the hands of a few top leaders, some of these pragmatists' characteristics would be instrumental in decision making and would be reflected in the processes of reform. Although various domestic and international elements also contributed to the birth and subsequent development of the reform, this small group of leaders and what lay behind their decisions merit special attention. As reform gradually decentralized the economy in its later years, local governments and newly freed sectors of the economy contributed increasingly to shaping the path of reform. Particularly after 1984-85, when the Chinese reform movement entered its second phase, diversified and decentralized processes of reform became ever more important. However, the development and results of the reform in its early phase were integrally related to the characteristics of this group of leaders operating under these conditions.[5]

These pragmatic leaders were basically lifetime veterans of the Communist one-party system. They tended to emphasize the equitable distribution of commonly held property; they insisted on the necessity of stability and unity, and tolerated no political pluralism; and they perceived political diversification as a danger.[6] Even though certain members of the group later tended to tolerate (to a certain degree) some substantial changes in economic institutions as reform proceeded, the overall limitations of these leaders as a group would be noticeable in the future. In the early stage of the reform process though, they were by no means prepared to compromise on matters pertaining to the communist belief system, and the principles of communism were enunciated explicitly from time to time, even as reform gained momentum.[7]

Still, this group of leaders differed from its predecessors in its pragmatic approach to the economy's problems. It appeared to be more willing to admit the failures and inadequacies of the existing system. From the beginning, it strongly advocated making economic development the priority of the party and of the nation.

Recognizing the importance of both the state of the Chinese economy in the late 1970s and the characteristics of this group of resurrected, more pragmatic leaders for understanding the reform movement's pattern and path, I will now discuss the economic reform of the early years by examining its dominant belief, approach, chief concerns, and three propositions.

Belief in Improving the Centrally Planned Economy

The dominant belief in this period could be described as follows: The CPE should be able to function more efficiently and the system should be reformed so as to bring out its potential efficiency. Originally, the economic reform had been officially announced as an effort to reform the "economic management and business operation systems" of the centrally planned Chinese economy, and this had set the basic tone for the early reform.[8] Obviously, in the beginning, China's decision makers did not see reform as the far-reaching transformation of the market that it later turned out to be.

The failure of the economy was attributed by the early reformers primarily to the radical, ideologically based economic strategies and policies of previous decades, instead of to shortcomings within the CPE system itself, as they came to believe in the reform's second phase. The problems were attributed to the "overall management system, overcentralization, severely rigid planning, and mandatory even distribution." The central government at the time also realized that as a result of this economic system, governments, officials, enterprises, and individuals did not have the incentives and motivation needed to take the initiative and to increase production.[9] "Overcentralized control" was pronounced a serious defect of the socialist planning system.[10] Allocation by the "overcentralized" system, as understood at the time, led the economy into an even worse mess: factories kept producing what might never be sold or consumed, while severe shortages prevailed. Specifically blamed were those decisions implemented since 1966, when the Cultural Revolution started and most of the pragmatic leaders, for instance Deng Xiaoping and Chen Tun, were ousted.[11] Censuring the radicals and their strategies may also have served the political purposes of the reemerging leaders as they sought to take over full control of the nation. The differences between the radical and pragmatic strategies were obvious and profound. It wouldn't be surprising to find that the new leaders were attempting to accelerate the transfer of power out from under Mao's shadow in the person of his hand-picked successor Hua Guofeng (then the general secretary and premier) and into their own hands. In other words, political motivation might have influenced the pace of economic change. Their ideological consistency throughout the decade of change, both prior to and after they successfully completed the transfer of power, suggests that political motives did not prevent the newly dominant leaders from arriving at better-informed conclusions about the economy's problems. In addition, records of these leaders in the 1950s and 1960s also bespeak a consistent advocacy of a more pragmatic strategy. Chen Yun, for example, was in charge of the committee that formulated the first revisionist document on China's CPE. This document introduced into the system for the first time many measures for building incentives into the system, such as reducing mandatory quotas and experimenting with a profit-sharing mechanism.[12] This attribution of the economy's failure to the radical regimes of the 1950s, 1960s, and early 1970s held until the mid-1980s, when an influx of new experiences and information started to shake the ideological foundations of the CPE itself.

Attribution of Economic Failure to Radicalism

This aspect of the dominant belief reflected the intention to improve the CPE, which also laid down the primary constraints on the early reforms. On the one hand, the new leadership wanted to maintain the dominance of the state economy. From the beginning of the reform period, new mechanisms for incentives were intentionally introduced in reform programs and, at the same time, spontaneous initiatives for new incentives implemented by government agents and other individuals were tolerated and sometimes openly accepted. There was, however, no intention in the early phase to replace the dominance of the state economy with that of the private sector. Instead, the leaders wanted to combine the centrally planned and market mechanisms while subordinating the market to a planned economy.[13] Even though some freedom in the economy was allowed and decision making was opened up, central planning remained the main mechanism for resource allocation and the core of the Chinese economic system.

One important aspect of the belief was maintenance of the CPE within the orthodoxy of socialism's superiority to capitalism. At the time reform was launched the entire capitalist world was believed to

be in deep trouble. It was described as characterized by such features
as business cycles and fluctuations, inequities of income and wealth,
mass unemployment, and monopolies — all problems that could be
avoided by adopting a centrally planned and publicly owned economic
system.[14]

Intention to Improve the CPE

The persistence of the dominant belief was rooted particularly in
three factors. The first was that the reform leaders were a special
generation of career revolutionaries. After nearly thirty years of
communism[15] and more than twenty years of fighting before that, all
of their achievements, the values they fought for, and the meaning of
their wartime sacrifice were embedded in the dream of an ideal
communist society. In addition, all their political privileges and
economic interests had been built on and associated with the existing
communist system. "Any challenges to the system were taken
personally." This dominant belief was also strengthened by their
leaders' direct experiences and constrained by their limited knowledge
about communism and capitalism. Capitalism was associated with evil
and sometimes identified with the precommunist Kuomintang era;
hence, the widespread corruption and misallocation of resources under
the Kuomintang comprised the communist leaders' only notion of
economy and society under free market capitalism.

Second, the leaders' experience with governing in the 1950s and
1960s, when the CPE had occasionally operated in a more pragmatic
way and had adjusted to solve its (primarily bureaucratic) problems,
exerted a strong influence. By the early 1980s, almost all of the high-
level officials in the government and the planning bureaucracy had
participated to some extent in the 1950s industrialization movement
and the introduction to China of the planning system from the Soviet
Union. The mid-1950s[16] was thought by many people to have been an
era of superior economic planning and efficiency compared to the late
1970s, which suggested great potential for economic improvement
through reform within the existing system. In the early stage of the
reform process, the mid-1950s were invoked paradigmatically and
cited as the golden age of the Chinese CPE. Moreover, a sense of
personal and even generational glory might also have led many of

those who had recently reassumed important leadership to draw comparisons between their personal experiences in the 1950s and 1960 and the present, since their own lives under communist ideology and central planning during that era were the primary sources of experience for those carrying out China's economic reform.

The third factor determining the dominant belief was the insularity of the Chinese populace. When reform started, the capitalist world was still pretty much unknown to the Chinese, whose exposure to modern political theory was confined to what Marx and Lenin had written about the European economy sixty or more years previously. It was impossible for most Chinese to get a full picture of capitalist society and to understand the basic concepts of today's noncommunist world (such as competition, free prices, insurance, and social security). The hostile international environment of the 1950s and 1960s ruled out any Chinese attempt to take an objective look at the capitalist economies, let alone to adjust old perceptions of them, thus depriving the country of external stimulus toward social progress and the evolution of its economic institutions. Indeed, substantially improved relations between the United States and China were a crucial condition for China's cautious emergence from its self-imposed isolation since the end of the 1970s. But the policy of openness to the West did not mean that China had relaxed its vigilance against the West or accepted the West's capitalist economic system. Ever since the Opium War had forced China's closed door open in 1840 and obliged the Chinese to learn from the West, the idea of[17] accepting and embracing the market system after the end of the 1970s grew only gradually as the Chinese had more and more direct experience with and knowledge of the market economy.

Ironically, although the experiences of the mid-1950s were brought up as examples of a well-functioning CPE in the early days of reform, the Chinese had actually conducted their first serious criticism of their economic system in 1956 and 1957. The point is that the centrally planned system was found to have serious problems even during the First Five-Year Plan (which officially spanned 1953 to 1957).[18] In other words, even before the radical Great Leap and Cultural Revolution, the problems of the CPE had been noticed. The Great Leap was a national movement to boost the economy between 1958 and 1959, guided by a radical strategy of "surpassing Britain in five years and America in 15 years." The commune system was initiated at this time. The movement was followed by the collapse of the economy in 1960-62. Leaving this topic for discussion later in this chapter, here I want only to point out that the problems of the CPE appeared to have been ignored, overshadowed by problems of ideological radicalism during the late 1960s and most of the 1970s that became disastrous. Prior to economic reform, economic discourse had become radicalized, overwhelmed by such slogans as, "we would rather choose proletarian grass than a bourgeoisie crop." This kind of ideologically radical slogan filled textbooks and movies alike, especially in the early 1970s. Ideological radicalism exceeded rational bounds in both production and consumption. For example, during the Cultural Revolution, workers and peasants had to read Mao's quotations and political propaganda every day before starting production. Once a new political document was released by the central government, all production work was stopped so that everyone could be educated and committed to the lesson. To a certain degree, the widely spread inclination to attribute economic problems to ideological radicalism diverted attention from the central planning system itself. Obsolete knowledge, biased information, and limited experience with different economic systems all contributed to the allocation of economic blame.

Wisdom of the Special Economic Zones

Even though the experiments with special economic zones (SEZs). started in 1979, represented a breakthrough from the previous logic of closed-door changes and adjustments, the early policy of openness still had obvious limitations, and these were consistent with the dominant belief. The original intention of the SEZ experiment was to learn from the West (mainly in technology), to improve China's exports so as to enhance its ability to import advanced technology, and to use imports from the West to help modernize the economy.[19] Actually, at the outset of the experiment in 1979, Shenzhen and other zones in Guangdong and Fujian Provinces were officially proposed as "special export zones" instead of "special economic zones."[20] The special export zones originally resembled manufacturing export areas in Singapore, Taiwan, and elsewhere. To the assertion that SEZs were promulgated to introduce a free market that would replace central planning is, however, questionable. According to early documents on the SEZs, their primary goal was to attract foreign investment and to promote exports.[21] Speculation as to other possible motives for the establishment of SEZs is unwarranted. The goals and operations of SEZs have evolved ever since the program began, and their functions differ in many respects from what they appeared to be in the later days of the reform movement. The SEZs themselves served as ongoing laboratories, providing empirical information that facilitated the adjustment of outmoded expectations to the realities of international trade and economic institutions around the world. The SEZ experiment told people much that was unexpected, and it bridged the information gap created by ideology. The significance of SEZ experiments was far-reaching and revealed the wisdom of the reformers' policies at the time. Indeed, the policymakers demonstrated a sensitivity to subtle but pertinent information; an ability to think unconventionally, going beyond the bounds of ideology and experience; and a healthy tolerance for diversity and diversification, even as the outcome of the new idea was still uncertain and its impact unknown. In summary, the dominant belief of the first-phase reform consisted of three basic elements: recognition of the troubles and problems in the existing CPE, maintenance of faith in the feasibility of the CPE, and intention to improve the CPE.

"Touching Stones While Walking Across a River": Approach 1

From the beginning, the Chinese economic reform was not guided by theory. Instead, it benefited from increasingly diversified economic experiments that permitted continuous adjustment and selection of appropriate economic institutions in a process called "keep touching stones while walking across a river."[22] Throughout the reform, China retained this experimental approach and pursued institutional change incrementally. The "touching stone" approach offered a way to create, accumulate, and test the new centrally planned system, whereas the Chinese approach did not necessarily imply such a restriction. Even though the reform approaches of both the early and later phases fit this category of "touching stone," we find upon close examination that there were significant differences in the approaches to reform in the two phases.

China's General Experimental Approach

In the "touching stones" approach — moving across a river by keeping in constant touch with the rocks and stones on the river bottom — movement should be cautious. In other words, one should avoid losing contact with the ground or falling into a trap while taking an overly adventurous journey. Another often-used phrase to describe reform in Chinese is "one step go, one step watch," which conveys a similar idea.[23] The "touching stones" approach contains a mechanism to handle uncertainty with a feedback and adjustment process ruling out the possibility of jumps or dramatic development at some point. To some extent, this Chinese approach appears to be akin to the Western concept of trial and error, which strives for incremental and cumulative progress instead of dramatic change. The "touching stones" approach, however, does not imply a clear and specific target, as trial and error usually does, and bears no relation to the method O. Lange (1936) used to reach the market equilibrium price in his model of market socialism.[24] While the trial and error approach applied by Lange refers mainly to the technical process employed to arrive at the equilibrium point between supply and demand, the "touching stones" approach, in contrast, implies a philosophical methodology for the entire reform of an economic system. In addition, the trial and error approach suggested by Lange would actually confine the search and its experiments to setting price targets within the framework of the centrally planned system, whereas the Chinese approach does not necessarily imply such a limitation.

The "touching stones" approach reveals the determination to control the process of change, the presumption of uncertainties in the course of reform, the importance of processing interim information, and the willingness to respond to any pertinent signals. Under this approach, uncertainty is treated not as something rare, but rather a routine encounter in the reform process. "Touching stones" thus fosters an open-ended search — itself a learning mechanism — that is part of the process of incremental reform.

By "touching stones," the progress of reform relied heavily on feedback from ongoing experiments in economic performance. Whether a reform should continue or be terminated, whether or not a regulation should be adjusted, and whether and how a problem-solving technique was effective, were tested and examined with the ex post facto outcome of a given policy. With this approach, China's reform went forward with cautious steps, constant assessments, and continual adjustments. In a more general sense, "touching stones" seemed to be a vehicle by which the reform movement went beyond the constraints of prejudice, ideological commitment, and limited knowledge. Particularly in the early years of reform, this approach helped overcome the barriers of orthodoxy and encouraged rational decision making. Moreover, although criticized both inside and outside China, the open-ended "touching stones" approach seemed to allow the Chinese great flexibility and creativity in their selection of and innovation in economic institutions.

From the perspective of cognitive process, this approach allowed learning by doing and often helped to introduce elements of new institutions successfully. This was especially true of the formative stage, when there was little knowledge and the direction of change was not so clearly perceived. At the time when orthodox ideology still pervaded China's decision-making processes, formal confrontations with or theoretical challenges to orthodoxy would often escalate political resistance. This is not to argue that political clarification was not necessary, but rather that attempts at consensus building could sometimes be both time consuming and ineffective in this climate of entrenched belief. Given the limitations of their experiences and knowledge, the reformers themselves may not really know much more than their opponents about the outcome of a proposed experiment. What the reformer needed most was evidence from new experiments. The worst thing for simply quarreling on a policy issue was subsequent killing or unlimited postponement of a proposed experiment. Both supporters and opponents could learn form a successful experiment and gain knowledge about a new system or business. Particularly, the "touching stones" approach emphasized process and evolution. It allowed alternatives to compete and to be compared. This approach might have lessened the chances of falling into a trap of an elite's design or any one-step grand plan that assumed knowledge of the future of the economy and the world.

As the economic reform developed and its policies kept pace, China persisted with this principle of experimentation characterized by the "touching stones" metaphor. In the second phase of reform, this approach came to incorporate new elements.

Closed Sources Experiment

One such distinguishing feature of the early reform process was its dependence on so-called closed-source (in contrast to "open source") information, meaning that the early reform generated its experiments through and drew its doctrine from a critique, to a large extent self-referential, of China's own experiences. Put a different way, the sources of experiments and policy alternatives were largely limited to what direct experience and intuition could suggest. For example, in a representative document dating from early 1979, the criticisms of the existing economic system and policies were based mostly on comparisons with the country's economic performance during the 1950s and the mid-1960s.[25] Problem areas identified by means of these comparisons included distortion of the economic structure, stagnant agricultural production, declining productivity, and the low profitability of industrial production. In general, the closed approach was adopted in an implicit pattern in which references to and comparisons with the past were first derived to identify and sort out problems, followed by suggestions for experiments based on these observations. The closed approach is in contrast with the open approach, which draws its references and models from all forms of economics, including capitalist ones. The open approach naturally assumes the importance of theory; it will be discussed in detail in chapter 4.

Limitations of the "Touching Stones" Approach

While this approach led to the logic of open-ended and performance-driven reform, it also placed restrictions on the reform due to its obvious reliance upon first-hand demonstration. It created a demand for immediate and positive feedback, which may sometimes be too strict a standard for economic and social experiments. The demand for short-term results appears to be the common limitation of both the open and closed versions of the "touching stones" approach because such an approach sometimes prevents an experiment from undergoing a necessary maturation process to allow its mechanism to function to full advantage. In other words, the demand for short-term results could eradicate those experimental alternatives that took longer to achieve success or exhibit even slight fluctuations in their performance. In addition, the closed approach has the obvious limitation that experiences provide only a small portion of potential alternatives and information, thus narrowing the path to the goal of faster development and modernization. This constriction of options means slowness in getting to the core of the problem and thus the solution.

In practice, for the Chinese, dependence on closed sources of experiments in effect meant attempts to adjust and select China's economic institutions in the recent past — that is, the experiences of 1956-57 and some of those in 1963-65. These experiences included a series of efforts to revise the typical version of the Soviet-style CPE. Particularly, pragmatic efforts to decentralize the CPE and introduce profit incentives in the 1950s seem to have had great influence, as we will see, upon the reform strategies and policies in the early phase of reform that started in 1979.

Experiences in the 1950s and 1960s

In early 1956 the newly established, centrally planned system was found to have more and more problems, and pressure was mounted for change.[26] Before the centrally planned system became fully institutionalized and gradually eradicated the elements of incentive, these problems were understood to be related to the system's perceived lack of responsiveness and flexibility.[27] At first, when problems were found, they were handled ad hoc. Later. it became increasingly clear that such problems were no longer sporadic but widespread. Concern with the need to adjust the economic system was expressed in the report of the central government on the Second Five-Year Plan, which pointed out for the first time the problems of rigid control and overcentralization in the Soviet-style economic system.[28]

Then, after one-and-one-half months of intensive deliberation involving representatives from various industries and local leaders,

Mao Zedong voiced explicit criticism of the consolidation of authority in the hands of the central government and the attempts to simply duplicate the Soviet model.[29] In his report *On Ten Relationships,* issued in late 1956, Mao expressed this concern by claiming that "it seems problematic to centralize all authority in the central government and to leave no authority to local government and to enterprises." He went on to point out that "we could not do exactly as the Soviet Union does in centralizing all authority in the central government." Mao raised further questions about how to allocate more authority to local governments.[30] In terms of decision making, he emphasized finding some appropriate balance between centralization and decentralization. As a follow-up development, there was a series of discussion meetings from May 1956 to October 1957 that resulted in "Regulations on Improving the Industrial Management System,"[31] an effort to address these problems. The new policies focused on decentralization of central control over the economy, leading the modern world's first movement to revise and adjust a typical CPE. Over two decades later, the first phase of economic reform had many similarities with this effort to revise China's CPE in the 1950s, and the first-phase reform of the early 1980s implemented in several areas similar policies to those of the adjustment of 1957. Chief among these were the following.

1. *Reallocating financial authority by allowing local government to dispose of any budget surplus.* The policies and regulations for adjustments to the economic system of 1957 no longer compelled local governments to surrender their surplus to the central government but allowed them to dispose of it themselves. In addition, the new regulation said the surplus of overfilled export quotas would be divided proportionately between the central and local governments. These changes in distribution policy were intended to provide incentives for local governments and factories to lower costs and increase profit.
2. *Allowing more autonomy for enterprise by reducing mandatory quotas.* In 1957, mandatory quotas were reduced from 12 to 4,[32] and the state enterprises were allowed to share in the state's extra profit.

3. *Allocating more authority for managing enterprises to local governments and allowing local governments some authority in deciding the price of small commodities.* Authority over many factories and production units in, for example, the food industry and the textile industry, was almost completely passed down from the central government to the local level.

Apart from the experiences of the 1950s, some of those of the 1960s (after another round of centralization during 1960-62)[33] included the following two adjustments to management hierarchy, agricultural organization, and allocation of profit between the government and enterprises.

1. *Conducting industrial reorganization and reintegration in an attempt to reduce the inefficiency of the planning hierarchy and administrative bureaucracy.* Giant corporations and industrial organizations in the form of trusts were created to replace administrative management based on ministerial organization. Transaction costs across ministries and regions were reduced as a result, and more were allocated with fewer restrictions from vertical planning control.[34]
2. *Reducing the size of work and distribution groups in agriculture so as to increase incentives for production.* In limited areas, dividing the land of communes among families, or allowing some families to be responsible for a piece of land, were also experimented with. It turned out to be obvious in some places that production under the commune system simply could not provide enough grain and under other agricultural products, and going back to production on the basis of single-family units or small groups of fewer families became the last resort to boost agricultural productivity during this period.

The closed "touching stones" approach permitted the Chinese to search pragmatically for solutions to their economic problems, drawing from their own experience and breaking away from the bonds of ideologically binding orthodoxy. With its emphasis on information collection, feedback, evaluation, and selection of responses on the information process, this approach enabled open-minded policymakers to learn from the prior experimentation in the early phase of economic reform, when the direction of that reform was still highly uncertain.

The experiences of the 1950s and 1960s constituted an important resource for reformers in this initial stage. First, they were better equipped to overcome ideological difficulties: while there was a recognition the system was in deep trouble, any modification of the *status quo* still caused resistance in the prevailing climate of radicalism. As long as a change had been allowed and tried before, however, it tended to face less resistance. Second, the experiences in the 1950s and 1960s helped to alleviate decision makers' worries over the uncertainty they faced by providing, derived models. Fear of the unknown is often exaggerated and biased due to prejudice and lack of knowledge. Using relevant experiences, one could shorten the process by selecting an appropriate institutional arrangement and bringing about the benefit of a new system, and build up confidence for reform. Of course, the experiences of the 1950s and 1960s might also have been of negative value to reformers by confining them to old paths. But, by and large, the past experiences in adjusting the Soviet-style central planning system appear to have been a positive factor in the initiation of the reform because these earlier experiments tended toward decentralization and diversification.

Shaping Existing Human Assets

The adoption of this closed approach to reform should not be seen simply as a conscious decision on the part of the nation's leaders, but rather as the outcome of the many social and economic factors operating at that particular time in China in the late 1970s and early 1980s, all of which, seen or unseen, contributed to the adoption of the reform approach. Above all, the nature of the available human assets (i.e., participants in the reform process on all levels) — experience, knowledge, learning, and the ability to process information — has been most significant. Human assets affect the ability of decision makers to form policies as well as their preferences for certain policies and, at the same time, affect other reform participants' spontaneous selection of institutions to reform initiatives. Since the early phase of reform operated principally in a top-down fashion, the qualities of the decision makers had a more direct impact on the course of reform. Thus, the reformers' experiences in the 1950s and 1960s contributed more than other factors to shaping the closed-source approach to reform.

From this perspective, human assets could be divided into two categories: (1) comparatively fixed and (2) more marginal. Experience, knowledge, and skills belong to the former group; learning capability and information processing belong to the latter. After years of living under the CPE and communist revolution, China's human assets were strongly colored by these phenomena and had been, to a large extent, specialized by the existing system. Leaving discussion of the most specialized of these elements to later on, here we will discuss only information processing. The way in which the reformers processed information determined in part what alternatives would be available to them. In the early days of the reform movement, conscious and unconscious barriers, both in society as a whole as well as in the minds of individuals, created a special information-selection mechanism. These obstacles worked to block some information processes and let others through. Those that got through the filter were accepted and tolerated on the basis of ideology, prejudice, and past experiences. This filtering mechanism was strong when the reform started because of China's highly centralized control system and long-closed society. Centralized control tended to exclude information that related to the way of life and socioeconomic institutions of the West and to allow in only information that related to science and technology. (Information on these subjects was considered to be institution-neutral and less threatening to the existing economic system.) Such a selection process effectively excluded some reform alternatives that could otherwise have been considered. The hesitation and resistance to outside information typical of isolationist societies existed in attitudes not only of the Chinese government and planning bureaucrats but throughout the Chinese people as a whole. As more information gradually builds up a more comprehensive picture of the West, the hesitation and resistance are evaporating in a self-perpetuating process. Therefore, China's adoption of a closed approach to reform in its early phase was closely linked to its contemporary social and political context and may well have precluded some other path of reform.

Chief Concerns

Chief concerns are criteria used in assessing an experiment. As discussed above, the development of Chinese economic reform and the evolution of China's economic institutions largely depended upon a continuous process of evaluation and response. In this process, decision makers and other reform participants applied chief concerns in adjusting, selecting, and restructuring economic institutions.

In the early stage of reform, the chief concerns were apparently functional efficiency and the principle of the CPE. The first of these, efficiency, is theoretically stated in terms of economic effect of limited input. In reality, efficiency of an experimental system was reflected in economic performance, and was usually measured by comparing the effects of certain economic activities. In agriculture, for example, given the same village or county, the efficiency of one of its responsibility systems would be measured by comparing the output of that system before and after an experiment. Choosing between two alternative systems, one would simply compare the output of the two systems.

The second chief concern, the principle of the CPE, is the wish to preserve the CPE system and to abide by its constraints (namely, state ownership and the mechanism of central planning). This chief concern, which could be equated with the doctrine of socialism, was used to judge whether an experiment would be acceptable.

Concern from Efficiency

From the beginning, China's economic reform was closely related to its concerns with efficiency. Its starting point was recognition of the poor performance of the economic system, which was judged mainly by measurements of its efficiency. In an important meeting of the Chinese Communist Party (CCP) in early 1979 on reform and the national economic strategy, serious instances of low efficiency were aired in an attempt to criticize and reconstruct the economic system.[35] The report at the meeting, given by Li Xiannian, pointed out some major problems in economic performance regarding efficiency: 24.3 percent of state enterprises were in deficit; the ratio of output versus input for capital investment was about 69 to 1 (as compared to 84 to 1 in the mid-1950s); and about 20 percent of industrial capacity was idle due to lack of electricity.[36]

In the reform process, efficiency was the number one concern in initiating a new experiment or in judging the effect of a new policy, as seen from an examination of very early experiments with enterprise reforms. In a report endorsed by the State Council one year after the enterprise reform experiment was launched in mid-1979, the reform policies under the experiment were evaluated in terms of efficiency. Based on records of more than 6600 enterprises under this nationwide experiment, the report found that "the output of the enterprises that were part of the reform experiment in 1979 increased 11.6 percent over 1978; the profit of these enterprises in 1979 increased 15.9 percent over 1978." The report also concluded that, in general, the enterprises in the experiment achieved higher rates of output increase, value increase, and profit increase *during* the experiment than *before* the experiment, and the rates were higher than those *not* in the experiment.[37] After its positive evaluation of the experimental policies, the document endorsed their broader adoption throughout the country. Since the early enterprise reform did not touch the issue of ownership and maintained the dominance of central planning, only efficiency was examined. Even though the two concerns of efficiency and control of ownership both applied to the assessment of an experiment, efficiency was deemed more important, whereas the quest for improved efficiency generated experimentation, conformity to the CPE principle alone did not.

In practice, the concern for efficiency in agricultural activities was mainly related to land yield, and for nonagricultural activities was usually reflected in direct budgetary and other financial measurement and comparison. In theory, when measuring the efficiency of agricultural activities, both labor and land, the two primary factors in crop production, should be considered. In practice, however, the total output and the output per unit were the measurements used; input was not considered. This method was used because a large labor surplus was built into China's agricultural system. Since agricultural reform had reapportioned land to each family, it was quite understandable that the quality of agricultural labor improved. But whether the total amount of labor used in agriculture increased depended chiefly on whether labor flowed into or out of agriculture. In the first few years of reform, liberated peasants focused on conversion to the new system and a few peasants left agriculture; thus there was no significant change in the total size of the agricultural labor force. Therefore, given the reality that large amounts of surplus labor existed and peasants did not have many employment alternatives, increases in output could reflect changes in efficiency. In terms of the total amount of land under cultivation, any change would have reflected the encroachment of urbanization and industrialization on arable land.[38] While it was true that some unused hill and riverbank land was better used after the reform, this did not constitute a true increase in available land, but only the return to use of land that had been abandoned due to the lack of incentives under the commune system. Basically no substantial land acreage was developed for agriculture. Based on the existing technology, after thousands of years of intensive cultivation, China simply did not have much land available for new development.

The way in which efficiency criteria were applied to assess agricultural experiments can be illustrated by the following example. In an important document from Beijing the central government in 1983 fully acknowledged the reform of the responsibility system, specifically the "family responsibility system," by listing the improvements in agricultural performance and declaring that "it breaks through the situation of our long-stagnant agriculture production."[39] Using 1952 prices, agriculture productivity increased 20.6 percent in a 21-year period, from 1958 to 1978; however, it increased 22.8 percent in the four-year period from 1979 to 1982. In terms of agricultural commodities provided by each peasant, the efficiency increased only 19.4 percent from 1957 to 1978, but it increased 34.9 percent from 1979 to 1982. In nonagricultural enterprises, greater efficiency was usually indicated by increased profit or decreased demand for subsidies. Similarly, greater efficiency at the local level might be indicated by more local surplus and/or increased financial contribution to the central government. The policy of separating local and central budgets was inaugurated in 1980 in an effort to reform the financial relations between central and local governments, and was tested in 1981 and part of 1982 mainly by measuring economic performance as reflected in the budget situation.[40] The results led to continuation of the policy for the next couple of years.[41]

Concern for the CPE's Principle

It was the second of the two chief concerns — the principle of CPE — that primarily established the parameters for the reform and its experiments. The orthodox values of socialism included the concept of common or public ownership, even and controlled distribution of income, and state central planning. Even though its ideological concern was usually not very clearly defined or expressed, particularly as the reform as yet posed little challenge to the CPE system, it was substantive and could not easily be compromised.

There is plenty of evidence that the CPE principle was a chief concern. As the family responsibility system gradually came to prevail in agricultural production by the end of 1981, Chen Yun, one of the top decision makers, warned that "after adopting the family responsibility system, it should still be clear that the state plan will persist," and "in the end, peasants in the new economic system should conduct their economic activities under the state plan."[42] Clearly, the new family-based system was considered to be still under socialist central planning, rather than operating independently. Another case in which this concern was explicit was in the reform policies for the private sectors. In a 1981 reform to encourage the development of the private sector, there was a clear restriction on the number of apprentices and employees, which was limited to five, in effect severely curtailing growth of this kind.[43] Even though private and family businesses in urban areas were recognized and encouraged to develop at this time, they were still required to apply to local governments for permits. Additionally, in policy documents, the government still had to label those who owned or worked for small private businesses "socialist labor"[44] to maintain consistency with the doctrine of socialist economy. About two years later, in a renewal of the reform-oriented policy governing private industries (specifically for the cooperative economies developed from private family businesses), the employee limitation was increased to ten and a rate of 15 percent was set as the ceiling for the annual dividend.[45] When the government resumed its policy of encouraging private and family business, it still had to impose some restriction on its scale by saying that this part of the economy would be "supplemental to the public or the state economy."[46]

The Planned Economy as a Big Corporation

In this analytic paradigm, three propositions are important for understanding first-phase Chinese economic reform. The first of these three reflects the core of the policymakers' perceptions of the Chinese economic system and the essence from which they derived their economic reform. It can be called the "big corporation proposition" because it equates the CPE with a large scale commercial organization.

This proposition includes the following three major aspects:

Common interest. According to the big corporation proposition, the socialist economy was like a huge corporation, in which each unit and individual in the economy ultimately had a common interest.

Dominance of capital planning. According to this proposition, the plan should be dominant and the market supplementary in the economy. The common interest was to be taken care of by the central planning mechanism, and the market was to be allowed to play a supplementary role to planning in the economy.

Internal relations. Derived from the big corporation proposition, this tenet held that all economic relations in the system were internal, and the performance of the overall economy largely depended upon their alignment.

The three aspects of the big corporation proposition reveal that early reformers were still on the old track of a CPE, in keeping with the economic thinking of the time. However, real change did occur from within this system.

The Common Interest

The common interest of the planned economy — in the guise of a big corporation — was represented by the state and the government. In reality, "the state" was only nominally a separate entity, and the government actually functioned as the state. The state took care of the common interest by planning for production and other economic activities and by redistributing income and wealth among the members of the economy. Evidence of these assumptions can be seen, for example, in Chen Yun's remarks at the end of 1981 and in early 1982, that while each was getting a better life, the state should still reserve substantial resources and national income to make investments based on the state plan in order to take care of the national economy as a whole.[47] He particularly warned of the danger of ignoring the necessity for the state to control some national income on behalf of all the members of the economy.

This attitude is also evident in a number of other regulations and policies of this time. In an official document used to interpret and explain the policy of enterprise reform, it was made clear that the state felt that it represented the common interest. Granting enterprises 40 percent of the increased profit was already substantial, argued the authors of this paper, since the state had to take care of many other aspects of life in the common interest of the whole economy.[48]

More specific evidence for the big corporation proposition is contained in foreign trade policy, where the state represents the common interest. The central government had repeatedly emphasized that the benefits of composition should be shared internally and kept within the centrally planned system.[49] This premise justified control of exports under the state plan so as to protect against the national interest's being compromised from outside. It was assumed that if someone within the system lost, then someone else in the system must gain, and the system itself lost nothing. In other words, if loss could be contained within the system, then the issue would become the allocation of surplus or of entitlement among members of the system. This self-contained model was challenged in the early 1980s when, as local governments and enterprises were granted more autonomy, each strove to gain access to the world market and competed against the others to sell its products there. The resulting export price wars aroused serious concern about preservation of the common interest.

The lowering of selling prices due to competition was a concern in light of the break-up of the central government's control of exports, and it was seen as a net loss to the system, a system whose interests should presumably be represented by the central government. If the monopoly collapsed, the profit generated by it would disappear. If the price elasticity proved smaller than one, then lowering prices would only reduce the producers' surplus. In general terms, if lowering prices resulted in less producer or seller surplus and more consumer or buyer surplus, it would be seen as harmful to the CPE.[50] In this situation, competition among Chinese sellers might lower prices and transfer surplus to foreign buyers. The central government held that all the economic activities of and competition among provinces and enterprise under the centrally planned system and state ownership should ultimately serve the common interest. Therefore, the central government intervened in late 1981 and tried to raise prices again by reducing the number of Chinese sellers who were granted access to the world market. By designating some agents rather than others, the policy might have hurt the market. But it was believed that if the state had to risk losing something, it would be better to lose it to one of its members instead of to an outsider, thereby serving the "common interest." In December of 1981, the central government issued a regulation restricting export permits to eleven categories of products.[51] The application for these permits became a control mechanism to avoid competition among Chinese sellers.

In early 1982, in another attempt to control exports and prevent "others" from benefiting from the competition, one more comprehensive foreign trade management regulation was issued. This required all foreign trade products to be strictly classified; only designated organizations and agents were allowed to trade certain commodities.[52] As a result, even though economic reform had already brought rapidly increasing diversification and competition to the domestic market, Chinese foreign trade lagged far behind other aspects of reform and continued to be monopoly dominated and plagued by distribution problems. While price controls meant more profit for the planning system, only the designated seller could get the profit; other sellers were excluded. More profit for the "corporation," or the centrally planned system, did not necessarily mean more profit to nondesignated producers. Moreover, since the designated seller might not be the most efficient one, such a policy of export monopoly would create inefficiencies through centrally planned misallocation while protecting less efficient producers. In the long run, it could result in low economic efficiency and stagnation of technology and economic organization. In handling problems of foreign trade, the concepts of "big corporation" and "common interest" became explicit in decision making. When the common interest of the CPE was uncertain, the boundaries for reform would emerge and reform would be halted.

Dominance of Central Planning

The second aspect of the "big corporation" proposition is the dominance of central planning. A representative view of the relationship between the planning and market mechanisms was that a socialist economy should have two parts: the planned economy, which was the system's principle component, and the market or spontaneous economy, which was secondary and supplementary.[53] The basic understanding at the time among policymakers was that "the state combines both the planned balance and market supplement to guarantee a healthy and appropriate development of economy."[54] The principle was that the market economy could be allowed and even developed in most economic sectors as long as the planned economy still dominated and was able to control the production and distribution of key products and resources.

The relationship between the plan and the market was consistent with the chief concerns of deficiency and the preservation of the CPE. It was recognized that the introduction of market factors could improve the efficiency of the economy, as the plan obviously failed to take into account information on the entire economy and failed to respond to the needs of (all) individuals and the national economy as a whole. Central planning, although it had serious shortcomings, was still seen as the key mechanism and economic institution to promote economic development and social welfare. Furthermore, apart from their negative perception of the market, it was always difficult for those who were used to centralized control and political domination to accept diversification and the spontaneity of decisions embedded in the market. The institutions associated with centralized control and political decentralization accompanied the market and economic reform.

Internal Relations

The third aspect of the "big corporation" proposition concerns economic relations within the CPE. In essence, these were considered to be internal relations. They included relationships between the central and local governments, between the government and enterprises, between the government and individuals, between enterprises and individuals among enterprises, and among different groups of people. With its central planning mechanism, the government system, in the name of the state, distributed and redistributed income and wealth, assigned vertical and horizontal relations, and issued instructions on carrying out economic activities. State ownership legitimized the central planning mechanism. Most importantly, the central government was seen as the final authority in the economy's hierarchy.

From the standpoint of internal relations, economic malfunction could be solved by adjusting the economy's internal relationships. Bureaucratic problems, the planning system's lack of flexibility, poor incentive mechanisms, etc., all fell under this heading. In line with the first proposition, the government was supposed to handle these and other problems within this "big corporation."

Focus on Incentives

The second proposition concerns incentives under the Chinese CPE and understanding the problems with the economic system in the first phase of reform. It holds that all the problems of the CPE were related to the lack of an incentive mechanism in the hierarchical system. Since there did exist some other incentives, such as political or even spiritual, this incentive proposition could also be stated in a slightly different way: namely, that all the problems of the CPE were related to the lack of an *appropriate* incentive mechanism. The two statements mean the same thing in practice.

Lack of Incentives: The Early Diagnosis

To early policymakers, the Chinese CPE's lack of production incentives was related to, among a host of other factors, the ownership structure, contractual relations, and the decision and information processes. The inappropriate incentive mechanism was mostly part of the centrally planned distribution process.

The central planning system was designed to encourage free riding: according to the central plan, one could be assigned little work to do for substantial reward. Income, wealth, and opportunities were distributed and redistributed among individuals, economic units, industries, regions, and even generations according to state plans. The means of distribution and redistribution included the assignment of quotas, planned incomes for individuals, state-controlled investments, and planned budgets for production units and local governments. There was little connection between how much one produced and how much one earned. Each unit was expected to share ownership with others and did not have an independent interest. In practice, each unit and individual saw all the others as free riders and, at the same time, enjoyed free riding while simply doing what the plan assigned and taking whatever it distributed. In the eyes of the Chinese, the root of all the problems with the CPE could be found in the incentive mechanism; consequently, the establishment of incentives for each individual member, unit, and level of the system appeared to be the starting point for reform.

Mandatory redistribution, in particular, eliminated the separation of economic interests that in turn caused the elimination of incentives. As a CPE, the Chinese economy before the reform lacked an institutionalized incentive mechanism to promote economic development. Under this system, private ownership and long-term contractual relations were destroyed, and incentives and rewards, if any, were ad hoc. There was no stable, guaranteed institution for separation of interests which were entirely subject to the dictates of the plan. Sometimes, when it was found that there was too much control and too few incentives and motivation, a policy would be formulated to establish a correlation between effort and return, but these were always temporary; institutional intervention to create incentives based on entrepreneurial self-interest was rare and inevitably followed by a reactionary return to tight control to allay fears of instability.

Incentive Problems in Three Major Relationships

During the first phase of reform, it was recognized that in the previous CPE the vertical hierarchy had dominated, the economy had operated on the basis of mandatory instructions, and incentive mechanisms had been ignored or dismissed. In line with this proposition, incentive problems were particularly involved in three kinds of relationships: those between local and central governments, those between the government and enterprises, and those between the government and individuals.

First, because of central control and the lack of separate budgets, local governments had scant incentives to improve their local economies. In the relationship between central and local governments, it was the central government that made decisions and gave instructions for local governments to implement. Local governments were an extension of the state and part of the centrally planned system; they were not expected to have independent interests, and, not surprisingly, their budgets were planned by the central government and central planning agency. If a local economy performed better and created more profits, it would not reap rewards. Prior to the reform movement, local governments surrendered all income to the central government, which then redistributed this aggregate income among China's regions. Shanghai's income and expenses in the late 1970s will serve as an example. Prior to economic reform, Shanghai, the largest and most developed industrial city in China, was required to surrender about 95 percent of its local income to the central government. This mechanism seriously undermined its motivation to improve its economic performance.[55]

Second, because of central planning and full surrender of profit to the Beijing government, enterprises had no incentive to increase production or seek efficiency. The central planning system determined what to produce, how much to produce, and how the products would be counted or priced. Apart from such production decisions, the state also required enterprises to turn over all of the profits and products to the state for distribution by the planning system, with no assurance whatsoever that there would be any clear correlation between contribution and "return."

Third, because of even distribution and the centrally planned wage system, individuals had nothing to gain from additional effort or innovation. In the relationships between the state and individuals and between enterprises and individuals, individuals could not expect a correlation between their contributions and the income and benefit derived. Since wages and salaries were set by the central government and had to be implemented by each level and unit in the CPE, any wage and salary increase would be due only to some change in a person's compensation score, calculated on a basis of factors such as seniority.[56] There was no definite rule on when a pay increase or pay-related review should be made or when the state should issue a decree for a pay hike. During the eleven years of the Cultural Revolution, for example, wages stayed the same for everyone. In the relationship between the state and the peasants, the state and the planning system decided how much grain and other agricultural products peasants should surrender and how the products would be counted or priced. Just like workers in enterprises and factories, peasants did not have any sense of the correlation between contribution and income. In particular, since the prices of agricultural products were kept very low, much agricultural production was unprofitable no matter how much was produced. As a result, peasants simply went to the field to put in an appearance, and collect a share of what the commune or production team distributed.

In addition, since the CPE relied upon centralized, bureaucratic decisions rather than diversified, individual choice, there was a lack of responsiveness in decision making and information processing to changes in the economy. Centralization of the decision process created inefficiency and indifference among individuals and economic units alike regarding their economic activities, choking the motivation to respond swiftly to events by initiating changes. Even had the central planning system wanted to collect suggestions from the lower levels of the social organization, the long vertical and bureaucratic process of communication, the sense of superiority and inferiority, the differences in information interpretation at different levels and positions, all might reduce the motivation to take action beyond one's assigned duties.

At the famous meeting at the end of 1978, it was concluded that "only by adopting all the measures (of reform) would we be able to raise the levels of initiatives, enthusiasm, and innovation of central ministries, local governments, enterprises, and individuals."[57] It was understood that the key problem was with the system's incentive mechanism, and economic reform began from there.

Realignment of Internal Relations

The third proposition of the paradigm, the realignment of internal relations, provides the core understanding of the rationale underlying the early economic reform. With the first proposition stating what the economy was, and the second proposition speaking to what was wrong with the economy, this third proposition addresses what made the early reformers act to solve problems in the economy. The proposition states that economic reform was intended to realign and rearrange the overall internal relations of the CPE so as to motivate each level and each unit of the economic hierarchy, and to improve the efficiency of economic organization.

This third proposition leads to the following three subpropositions:

Subproposition of independent budget. Many problems with the distribution system in the communes and the overall economy were attributed to the lack of incentives: there was no clear connection between what one contributed and what one got in return. Reform decision makers tried to remedy this situation by establishing and institutionalizing independent budgets for both organizations and individuals. The concept of an independent budget arose from the recognition of differentiated interests among organizations, various levels of the government and the planning hierarchy, and individuals. The effort was based on the simple logic that, with relatively independent budgets, local governments would work to keep them in balance by many means, including boosting local economic development.

Subproposition of price. Price was seen as an accounting unit in the corporation and was mostly a means to adjust horizontal internal relations between different industries, between producers and consumers, and between regions; and prices were set by the plan rather than by the market.

Subproposition of profit sharing. Profit sharing between the state and enterprises and between the central and local governments was designed to redistribute interests among the different levels of the big corporation. While the price subproposition emphasizes adjustment of the horizontal interest arrangement, the profit-sharing subproposition concerns the adjustment of the vertical interest arrangement in order to increase incentives.

Separation of Budgets as a Motivational Tool

With regard to the first subproposition, a relatively independent budget was advocated early in the reform process so that each level, unit, and individual in the economic system could expect both revenue and expenditure to be within its own budget. This first subproposition provides the foundation for the second and third subpropositions since budgetary independence, raising prices, or lifting price controls would mean changes in the accounting system but would produce no incentives. Likewise, if sharing meant merely that an enterprise had to surrender all its income to the state for redistribution, it would be meaningless as an incentive. This discussion pertains to Chinese economic reform in its first phase, when the economy was still seen as a big corporation with a central planning mechanism. It was only in second-phase reform that issues of ownership, privatization, markets, and withdrawal of the government from the economy were addressed. But returning to the topic of budgetary independence, "independence" was not understood as defining property rights and legal guarantees but was meaningful only in a relative sense. By the time of the early reform, property rights were not recognized and a real legal system was not assumed, so that budgetary independence was strictly relative in this context, and there was no institutional force to prevent reversal of the reform. Real independence of budget is predicated on the existence of property rights, as well as a set of rules and institutions governing relations among parties. Such rules and institutions make a contract implementable, return for effort expended predictable, and controversies negotiable.

There is evidence of attempts to implement separate budgets in the early efforts of decentralization. From as early as 1979, the Beijing government tried to encourage local governments to be more responsible for the development of their local economies and social welfare by detaching their budgets from its own. (Chapter 3 will provide more detail on this subject.) The existing system was understood to be over-centralized, giving local governments insufficient authority and incentives to respond to the needs of local economic development. This trend toward greater fiscal autonomy was evident within the corporate hierarchy, as well. Prior to reform, enterprises operated under the control of a series of complicated criteria and quotas. Under reform, enterprises were granted the authority to dispose of their extra funds and surplus goods on their own.

Adjusting Prices to Reallocate Surplus and Increase Production

With the second subproposition, price adjustment was used to reallocate surplus and to make production profitable so as to increase production. Price adjustments specifically functioned to distribute profits and therefore interests among sectors, industries, and enterprises. Before reform, higher or lower prices had been purely an accounting function: if the price of a product was set too low (as was common) and the producer was in deficit because production costs were higher than the selling price, then the problem was solved by subsidizing the producer. Under that system, a deficit implied nothing about management and income. When the planning price of goods was lower than their cost, then the higher the production the greater the loss. Thus, even though there was demand for a product there was no corresponding increase in production to meet the need. Price adjustments were intended to correct this situation of negative incentive and to spur production by making it profitable.

Price adjustments served as a means of realigning internal relations. Higher prices led to the transfer of profit from producers to consumers; lower prices led to the reverse. All such transfers were within the corporation. Adjusting prices and therefore reallocating surplus among different groups of people and organizations was expected to improve the economy's convoluted internal relations.

Early agricultural reform raised agricultural prices in an attempt to give peasants more incentive(s) to increase production and to leave them in control of the resulting surplus. The reform leadership acknowledged peasants had been squeezed too much in the effort to industrialize because comparatively low prices for agriculture products and high prices for industrial products set by the state redistributed assets between and among rural and urban areas. Before reform, China's priorities had been heavy industry and the defense sector; much less was invested in agriculture and the consumer products industry. The long-standing sacrifice of peasant interests led to agricultural stagnation in terms of overall output and even a steady decrease in the production of some major agricultural products (including necessities such as cotton and oil) per capita, as the population maintained a high growth rate.[58] In contrast, however, from 1979 to 1981 there were three increases in the prices of agricultural products, making increased production profitable to peasants and contributing to the rapid growth of agricultural production.

The Government's Concession of Profit-Sharing

The profit-sharing subproposition was one of the most popular of the early reform measures. It occurred at the level of enterprise reform, when in 1979 a mechanism for sharing extra products and profits with the state was installed. A commission mechanism was embedded in the profit-sharing institution that was designed to promote production and increase the wealth of the state by "combining the interests of the state, enterprise and individual."[59] A policy similar to profit sharing was also tested in the relationship between the central and provincial governments. In an experiment conducted in July 1979, one of the principle measures implemented was to share local revenue on the basis of a fixed proportion, which would be set jointly by the two sides.[60]

In summary, the three measures in concert served to rearrange China's internal economic relations. As components of the third proposition, these three measures (each of which corresponds to a subproposition) were applied to solve the major problems of incentive by adjusting and realigning internal relations in the economy. Budgetary separation worked through decentralization and was intended to motivate every unit and individual to improve economic performance by enabling each to pursue its own interests. Price adjustments changed the distribution of profits and surpluses between demand and supply sides and were intended to increase production, particularly where there were shortages. The concept of sharing profits changed the customary understanding of the CPE and the relations between the government and producers it imposed or created. A new mechanism resulted from profit sharing through which increases in production and improvements in performance came about because individuals and enterprises actively pursued their own interests rather than simply met raised central planning quotas.

Concluding Remarks

The first proposition — that of the big corporation — describes how the CPE was operated before and during reform's early stages; the second proposition — that of incentive — states what the reformers and decision makers understood to be the cause of the problems with the CPE; and the third proposition — that of realignment of internal relations — laid the foundation for the policies of the Chinese economic reform in its first phase. The "big corporation" proposition relates to and is consistent with the dominant belief in improving (rather than abolishing) the CPE. Even though the second proposition points to the problem of the lack of incentives under the CPE, the reform was still conducted by way of realigning internal relations with the CPE structure. This realignment could improve the incentive mechanism, but it left many problems unsolved. Particularly, while economic reforms did improve incentive mechanism, and while increased efficiency moved into its later years, they also exposed the more fundamental problems inherent in the CPE which will be discussed in chapters 4 and 5. The next chapter continues the analysis of the first phase of Chinese economic reform.

Notes

1. *Almanac of China's Statistics 1986*, 91. In the seven years from 1976 to 1982, the Chinese population increased by 11.5 to 14.7 million each year. The population growth rates of the early 1970s were even higher.
2. Economists who were actively involved in the debate on the socialist planned economy include Fred M. Taylor, Oskar Lange, Abram Bergson, H.D. Dickinson, Abba Lener, Maurice Dobb, E.M.F. Durbin, James A. Yunker, Ludwig von Mises, Friedrich A. Hayek, Lionnel Robbins, Peter Murrell, etc.
3. According to the report by Li Xiannian at the working meeting of the Chinese Communist Party (CCP) on 5 April 1979, in addition to a 10 billion-yuan shortage of daily-use commodities, "the supply of steel, timber, and cement could not meet the demand of 45.7 billion yuan for capital construction" (*After the Third Plenum — Selection of Important Documents* 1982, vol. 1, p. 118.)
4. Ibid., p.115.

5. *Almanac of China's Statistics 1981*, 223.
6. For example, there was a call for "a new Long March" to realize modernization in "The Communiqué of the Third Plenum of the 11th Party Congress of the CCP," in *After the Third Plenum — Selection of Important Documents* 1982, vol. 1. Ye Jianying (1979) spoke of "the dream for more than half a century" being to build a prosperous and strong China (*After the Third Plenum — Selection of Important Documents* 1982, 5, 247).
7. I don't have any intention to attribute the occurrence of the reform to any specific person; instead, I would attribute it to a group of pragmatic leaders. It might be true that some specific person — e.g., Deng Xiaoping, showed some insight and wisdom during the reform. But in essence, an economic and social reform, one way or another, was bound to happen as the result of widespread dissatisfaction over the existing economic and political system, burgeoning access to information, as well as human nature. There was a veritable explosion in the availability of information, which carried new knowledge. Both absolute and comparative inspiration, as well as the dissemination of information, has accelerated in the last couple of decades as a result of the rapid development of information in science and technology. Human nature has prompted the reforming impulse in the guise of the Chinese people's endless quest for something "better."
8. The speech, "On Four Cardinal Principles," by Deng Xiaoping on 30 March 1979 was typical in its attitude toward any political uncertainty and instability. See Deng Xiaoping. "On Four Cardinal Principles," in *After the Third Plenum — Selection of Important Documents* 1982, vol. 1, pp. 80-108.
9. Deng Xiaoping, "Implementing Decisions of Adjustment and Guaranteeing Stability and Unity," in *After the Third Plenum — Selection of Important Documents* 1982, 627-48; CCPCC 1982, 1285-87.
10. "The Communiqué of the Third Plenum of the 11th Party Congress of the CCP," in *After the Third Plenum — Selection of Important Documents* 1982, vol. 1, p. 6.
11. Ibid., pp. 1-15.
12. Before the Cultural Revolution, Chen Yun and Deng Xiaoping were both vice premiers of the Chinese State Council. Even though Chen still nominally held positions in the State Council during the Cultural Revolution, he again came to be in charge of the economy after 1978. Deng was ousted at the beginning of the Cultural Revolution before he was formally removed from the position of vice premier in 1967. He was called back to Beijing and recovered his official rank in 1973 before losing it in 1976.

13. For a fuller account see Zhou Taihe 1984, 51-63.
14. Hu Yaobang, "On Creating A New Situation of Construction of Socialist Modernization," in *Collection of Documents on Economic Reform 1977-1983* 1984, 65-67.
15. Ibid.
16. Li Xiannian, "Report at the Working Meeting of the CCP," in *After the Third Plenum — Selection of Important Documents* 1982, vol. 1, p. 140.
17. For example, one of the most popular textbooks at the time embodying views of capitalism was *Political Economics* (Su Xing, Yu Guangyuan) published by the People's Press. The Chinese media also selectively covered the phenomena of economic crises, unemployment, monopoly profits, business closings, strikes, and street crime. Political economics classes based on this kind of textbook were required, and debate or even doubt about this view of capitalism was not allowed.
18. The term "communism" here is used differently than is usual in China. Here it is employed to avoid confusion with the term "socialism" as commonly used in the West. In China, communism was perceived as the goal of socialism, and the Chinese called their economy a socialist economy or socialist system. But in the West, the economies of the communist totalitarian countries are usually referred to as communist economies or communist systems.
19. Some might also include one or two years in the mid-1960s when production and the economic order had substantially recovered after the Great Leap of the late 1950s and the collapse of the economy in the early 1960s.
20. For example, in Ma Hong 1982 (43), when discussing economic development during the First Five-Year Plan in the mid-1950s, Ma says that "the new socialist system demonstrated a tremendous advantage." This was especially so since after that time the Chinese economy was frequently disrupted by this or that political movement: the anti-rightist movement of late 1957; the "Great Leap" and "People's Commune" movement(s) of 1958-59 and the subsequent collapse of the economy from 1960 to 1962; "Four Clean-up," in 1964-65; and the Cultural Revolution from 1966 to 1977. As these political movements ran their course, economic order was ravaged. In fact, 1956-57 was the time that the problems with the CPE were, for the first time in China, discovered, examined, and criticized.
21. The Opium War against China was launched by Britain in 1840 and is one of the most notorious wars in modern history.
22. The problems of the centrally planned system — e.g., inflexibility, bureaucracy, and misallocation of resources — were aired for a

comprehensive investigation in 1956, and some measures were adopted to solve them.

23. The inspiration for special economic zones seems to stem from the examples of Singapore, Taiwan, and Hong Kong, which opened some special areas for improving exports through a "free port" or some other special conditions such as tax exemptions for foreign investment. Yuan Geng, acting chief of Zhao Shang Ju, a large corporation from mainland China headquartered in Hong Kong, was named to set up the first such special zone in late 1978 in She Kou, which later became part of the Shenzhen special economic zone.

24. See the proposal to the Beijing government by Guangdong Province in June 1979 (abstract) in *Collection of Documents on Economic Reform 1977-1983* 1984, 474-75; the proposal to the Beijing central government by Fujian Province in June 1979 (abstract) in *Collection of Documents on Economic Reform 1977-1983* 1984, 479; and the document containing the central government's endorsement of these two proposals in *Collection of Documents on Economic Reform 1977-1983* 1984, 471.

25. Ibid.

26. "One step go and one step watch" is translated from the Chinese phrase *zou yi bu kan yi bu.*

27. Lange 1936.

28. See Chen Yun, "Economic Situation and Lessons," in *After the Third Plenum — Selection of Important Documents* 1982, vol. 1, p. 604.

29. Li Xiannian, "Report at the Working Meeting of the CCP," in *Collection of Documents on Economic Reform 1977-1983* 1984, 9-12.

30. See Chen Yun, "Economic Situation and Lessons," in *After the Third Plenum — Selection of Important Documents* 1982, vol. 1, p. 604.

From 1953 to 1956, The Chinese central government tried to copy the Soviet economic model and adopted its centrally planned, state-owned economy. This period, known as the First Five-Year plan period, was when the Chinese first put all the economy under a mandatory, centrally controlled plan and converted private ownership to state or public ownership. The Soviet-style compulsory planning system was installed with the hands-on help of hundreds of specialists from the Soviet Union numbering over a thousand at the peak of support in the early and mid-1950s.

31. Li Xiannian, "Report at the Working Meeting of the CCP," in *Collection of Documents on Economic Reform 1977-1983* 1984, 9-12.

32. Two schematic examples drawn from real situations will illustrate some of problems with the centrally planned system.

Case 1: A construction team (from ministry A) had completed its work ahead of schedule in Luoyang and did not have new work assigned. In the same city, another project should have been started but no construction team (from ministry B) was available at the time. Repeated efforts failed to coordinate the replacement of the available labor force.

Case 2: One summer, the government requested factories to install fans in offices and workshops because of health concerns. But the current plan had not budgeted for purchasing the fans and all a factory could do was apply for a contingency permit. The summer was already over when the factory finally got the permit. The story appeared in a newspaper. Many such cases were used to attack the centrally planned system at the time.

33. At first, the system was criticized for its lack of responsiveness and flexibility when people were still trying to deny the validity of the newly duplicated system. But later, as the system became institutionalized and insensitive problems became inevitable under it, people began to look for the underlying causes of the problems.

34. Chow En-lai 1956, 61.

35. Ibid., 11-12.

36. Zhou Taihe 1984, 57-60.

37. Surplus was defined as the difference between how much the plan required and how much actually had been produced, instead of the difference between expenses and revenues. Specifically interesting experiments included changing the adjustable budget based on the previous year's expense to a fixed, quantitative relationship between the central and local (i.e., provincial-level) governments. Under the centrally planned system the central government functions were divided among its administrative units, such as the State Council, or its various departments, such as the Ministry of Textiles.

38. The twelve mandatory planning quotas were the value of total products, the quantities of main products, the new experimental products, the technical rates or input and output, the rate of decreasing costs, the volume of decreasing costs, the number of employed workers, the number of workers at the end of a year, the volume of wages and salaries, the average wage, labor productivity, and profit. Of these, the last four were truly mandatory. The first eight were reduced to the status of guidelines. (See Ma Hong 1982 and Zhou Taihe 1984.) There were other related experiments, such as converting free interest to charging interest through banks.

39. Even though the regulation moved in the direction of decentralization, it focused on decentralization from the central government to local

governments, with much less emphasis on decentralization from the government to factories, so that more enterprises were placed under the authority of local governments rather than the central government in Beijing.

40. Before discussing the economy of the 1960s, we should review the radical movements from 1958 to 1959, the Great Leap, and the Commune Movement. The mass economic chaos of 1958-60 led to another of centralization in the early 1960s followed by relative decentralization in the mid-1960s. The nationwide campaigns of the Great Leap and the Commune Movement left a series of disastrous consequences in their wake. From 1958 to 1959 there was an interesting combination of changes in the economic system. As in architecture, the commune system was chosen as the sole form of economic institution in the rural areas, and almost all the incentive mechanisms of private ownership were dismantled. As a result, unrestricted demand for and consumption of goods by commune members far surpassed the capacity of the supply system defined by the commune mode of production. This was exacerbated by the collapse of Chinese agriculture at the end of this period. As in industry, controls over agricultural production units were either passed down from the central government to provincial governments, or from government to the units, causing production units to try to increase output to fulfill and surpass planned targets with no consideration of costs. There was no change at all in the mechanism of resource allocation. Unfortunately, these disasters in the late 1950s were, however, wrongly attributed to the loss of planned balance through decentralization, and more central controls were requested. In the early 1960s some centralization measures were adopted. These largely reversed the 1957 reforms. In some fields controls were even tighter than they had been before 1957, including the setting of quotas, the strict application of approval procedures for new projects, and the canceling of profit-sharing policies. Then, beginning in 1964, the central government again started to rethink decentralization due to growing conflicts and more evidence of low efficiency under "overcentralization."

41. Zhou Taihe 1984, 11-117, 296-97.

42. Li Xiannian, "Report at the Working Meeting of the CCP," in *Collection of Documents on Economic Reform 1977-1983* 1984, vol. 1, pp. 10-12.

43. Ma Hong 1982, 414. The ratio of the effective asset completed versus the total investment was a criterion used to assess the efficiency of capital construction. For example, if in a five-year period the total investment was 100 billion yuan and the completed and delivered project worth 80 billion yuan, then the value of the ratio is 80%.

44. "National Economic Committee's Report on the Experiments of Allowing More Autonomy to Enterprises and Further Suggestions," in *Collection of Documents on Economic Reform 1977-1983* 1984, 209-14.

45. Ibid., 209-10.

46. "CCCCP on Issues about the Current Agricultural Policies," in *Collection of Documents on Economic Reform 1977-1983* 1984, 159.

47. See Zhou Taihe 1984, 187.

48. The financial reform in 1980 of the relationship between the central and local governments was focused on separating their budgets in an attempt both to impose more pressure on local governments to economize spending and to introduce new incentives for them to increase profits. The reform allowed local governments to spend more if they earned more. (This will be discussed further in chapter 3.)

49. Further reform began in December 1982 and was guided by the document called "Announcement on Improving the Financial Management System of 'Separating Income and Expense, Clearing-up at each Level' by the State Council." See this document in *Collection of Documents on Economic Reform 1977-1983* 1984, 841.

50. Chun Yun, "A Couple of Viewpoints on Economic Work," in *After the Third Plenum — Selection of Important Documents* 1982, vol. 2, pp. 1057-95.

51. "The CST's Principal Regulations for the Non-agriculture Private Economy in Urban Areas," in *Collection of Documents on Economic Reform 1977-1983* 1984, 629.

52. "CCCCP and CST on Creating More Opportunities, Liberalizing Economy, and Solving Urban Employment Problems," in *Collection of Documents on Economic Reform 1977-1983* 1984, 634-35.

53. "The CSTs Announcement of its Regulations on Urban Cooperative Businesses" and "Supplemental Regulations on the CST's Principle Regulations for Non-agriculture Private Economy in Urban Areas," in *Collection of Documents on Economic Reform 1977-1983* 1984, 664.

54. See the policy document on private business in *Collection of Documents on Economic Reform 1977-1983* 1984, 645.

55. Chen Yun, "A Couple of Viewpoints on Economic Work" and "On Strengthening the Planned Economy," in *After the Third Plenum — Selection of Important Documents* 1982, vol. 2, pp. 1057-58.

56. "Interpretation and Explanation on the Draft Regulation of Profit-sharing Between the State and Enterprises," in *Collection of Documents on Economic Reform 1977-1983* 1984, 810-12.

57. Chen Yun, "Economic Situation and Lessons," in *After the Third Plenum — Selection of Important Documents* 1982, 605.

58. The calculation of producer's surplus and consumer's surplus and the transfer of surplus between the producer and consumer is treated in texts such as Hirshleifer 1980, Varian 1987, and Friedman 1984. In the theoretical model, one side is called the producer and the other side is called the consumer. In applying the model, the seller would be the producer and the buyer would be the consumer.

59. "Report on Adopting a Permission System on the Export of Certain Nonplanned Products and Materials," in *Collection of Documents on Economic Reform 1977-1983* 1984, 569-73.

60. Chen Yun, "On Problems of the Plan and Market," in *After the Third Plenum — Selection of Important Documents* 1982, vol. 1, pp. 68-71. Hu Yaobang, "The Report at the 12th Party Congress," in *Collection of Documents on Economic Reform 1977-1983* 1984, 66. *Shanghai Statistics, 1981-1985*, Shanghai Statistical Bureau.

    For example, China used a universal wage scheme which comprised eight grades for all kinds of industrial employees. "The Communiqué of the Third Plenum of the 11th Party Congress of the CCP," in *After the Third Plenum — Selection of Important Documents* 1982, vol. 1, p. 7. *Almanac of China's Statistics 1983*, 103. Li Xiannian, "Report at the Working Meeting of the CCP," in *Collection of Documents on Economic Reform 1977-1983* 1984, vol. 1, p. 9.

    The profit-sharing mechanism was similar in part to a commission scheme, in that both worked on the basis of a contract for the allocation of profit. The purpose of this profit-sharing policy was briefly described in the document "Regulation on Profit-sharing in the State Enterprises," in *Collection of Documents on Economic Reform 1977-1983* 1984, 184. See the temporary regulation on the financial relationship between the central and local governments issued by Beijing on 13 July 1979, in *Collection of Documents on Economic Reform 1977-1983* 1984, 182-88.

3

The First Phase: Reforming China's Centrally Planned System

During the first phase of reform, China primarily tried to adjust its economic system within the framework of the centrally planned economy (CPE). While many major aspects of the CPE were challenged, the basic institutional characteristics remained. The reform extended into agriculture, enterprise, and the relations between the central and local governments, as well as into industrial organization, price controls, and the overall hierarchy of the central planning system. Secondary aspects included rapid development in such areas as the private sector and the bold experiments of the special economic zones (SEZs). However, the basic institutional characteristics — the central planning allocation system and state ownership — were still dominant, and the market was introduced mainly to supplement and improve the central planning mechanism.

I will begin with a general review of where the first phase of Chinese economic reform came from, to lay down a foundation for a more detailed discussion of the substance of the early reform. It is particularly important to note the initial state of the prereform Chinese economy in understanding this whole movement. When reform started, the Chinese economy was trapped in irrational, radical, and orthodox ways, and its inefficiency was blindly ignored. The state plan consisted of a collection of quantity-based assignments and quotas. In practice, the mandatory goals and quotas drove enterprise to pursue quantitative expansion completely in the dark, with little or no consideration of demand, quality, and efficiency, undermining the fundamental economic relationship between cost and benefit. This indifference to economic efficiency was coupled with a deteriorating work ethic and entrepreneurial spirit. Because markets and free exchange were officially prohibited, individuals sought access to resources and opportunities through politics, nepotism, bribes to officials, and all other possible means outside the system. This kind of corruption further worsened the allocation of resources under the central planning system and left the economy to stagnate. Furthermore, the dominance of politics, with its ideological weapons, over the economy and other parts of life drove officials to follow ideological codes mindlessly and to concern themselves only with their political careers. As a result, the criterion of efficiency for economic performance was abandoned. Therefore, prior to reform, the Chinese economy was seriously ill with a combination of diseases: mandatory planning, corruption in access to resources and opportunities, and replacement of economic concerns with political pursuits. The sacrifice of efficiency in the interest of equity might have been justifiable, but this was not the case. Efficiency was simply viewed as irrelevant and was abandoned. Organizational and institutional selection and innovation ceased. Efforts to economize the use of resources were not appreciated; words such as "profit" and "revenue" were distasteful; and voices of complaint were stilled. The only growth in the economy was in the size of the quotas in the mandatory plan. In sum, Chinese economic reform began with an economy that lacked the basic concepts of efficiency, quality, and creativity and with little but mandatory quotas in their stead.

Where, then, was the Chinese economy after it had gone through its first phase of reform? There are three factors to which, in answering this question, I will refer repeatedly. The first is the concern for efficiency. The second is the process of experiments and selection. The third is the constraint of traditional thinking on which the CPE was founded. The discussion in this chapter will focus specifically on agricultural reform, the reform of relationships between the central and local governments, and enterprise reform using the analytic paradigm of the realignment of internal relations that was developed in the last chapter.

Returning to Family-Based Agriculture

During the first period of reform, agricultural reform was the most significant and far-reaching. The introduction of the "family responsibility system" actually led to dissolution of the rural commune system (which had been in existence for more than two decades throughout China's rural areas), whose evident failure by the late 1970s served as a call for reform. Agricultural reform began in 1979 with the goal of introducing a new incentive mechanism by experimenting with a variety of responsibility systems. Although the establishment of the family-based responsibility system represented a milestone in China's economic reform, it was consistent with the dominant belief of improving the existing planned system, and was thus characteristic of the early reform movement.

Even though four to five years appeared to be short for such profound reform, close examination reveals that an experimental and incremental approach did not necessarily mean a lengthy search for appropriate institutions. The success of China's agricultural reform policies could not, however, easily be duplicated in most other economic sectors. Why? What distinguished it lay in the special characteristics of the agricultural system's human assets in the selection of the family-based responsibility system.

Irrational Commune System

Before the reform, peasants had worked in the commune system, which operated under the control of the central plan and a "big-bowl" distribution mechanism. The "big-bowl," or *da guo fan,* is a metaphor whose primary meaning is that a group of people share food in a big bowl no matter how much each person has contributed to the production of the food in the bowl. There is thus no relationship between production effort and consumption entitlement.

Agricultural reform became urgent when production simply could not provide enough food to feed both peasants and city dwellers. Although successive political and ideological movements attempted to boost agricultural production, the grain production could hardly keep pace with population growth.[1] Even the slow growth of grain production was achieved only by sacrificing the production of meat and fruit and by turning forests and grassland into grain fields. The poor performance of agriculture under the commune system already threatened the survival of the nation. The most devastating problem with the commune system was, as discussed earlier, its lack of incentives.

First, the "big-bowl" distribution policy and the commune production system allowed and, in effect, encouraged, freeloaders, and it lacked appropriate incentives for peasants to increase production and improve efficiency. Under a big-bowl system, there simply is no relationship between how much food someone produces and how much one can consume. As long as a person maintains membership in the group, he is allowed to take and eat from the big bowl, no matter how much he contributes. The big-bowl system does, however, provide a guarantee of food for every member as long as the big bowl has something in it to be eaten. Entitlement is based on group membership, which is highly inclusive and extremely tolerant of substandard levels of individual contribution. In this kind of group there is a propensity for harmony — at least, apparent harmony. In the marketplace, an enterprise increases its input only with the expectation that the consequent increase in revenue will be larger than the increased input cost. In the big-bowl group, on the other hand, the benefit created by an additional member could actually be substantially lower than the added cost. To a rational economic organization, marginal cost in relation to marginal benefit is the critical concern for decision making at the input, versus output, level. The big-bowl system's mechanisms are similar, to some degree, to those of the "commune" described by Alchian and Demsetz[2] in which a member's sole concern is maintaining the minimally acceptable (threshold) amount of contribution. Peasants before the reform got their income in cash or in kind at the end of each year, calculated on the basis of how many days or how many "points" each of them had worked. In some areas, a day was used as the unit by which work contribution was calculated; in most areas, though, peasants used a point system. Points were assigned to each person with or without relation to his productivity, depending on locale. Certain villages, for example, would assess an individual's productivity based on experience, age, gender, and past record; other villages used only a schematic accounting method: 5 points for a juvenile and 10 points for an adult. In general, among adults, the number of points assigned to each person, from the productive to the lazy, was the same or nearly so. Adding up all the days for each peasant and then dividing the total income of the village or production team in a year would be the income per unit day for a peasant.

Second, since peasants were often excluded from making decisions on agricultural production and had to follow the instructions of the state plan, they were deprived of the opportunity to make rational choices. Under the commune and central planning, decisions such as what and when to plant on a given plot, even what kind of fertilizers to use, were often dictated to a production team. Quotas specifying quantities of agricultural products to be submitted to the state and acreage to be devoted to each crop were handed down from a superior planning committee to a county, from a county to a commune, and from a commune to a brigade and a team. As a result, land that was naturally better suited, for example, for cotton or vegetables by climate, soil, or geographical location, might have to be planted with grain. The degree of control by the plan varied from place to place.

Hence, prereform Chinese agriculture combined the big-bowl and central planning mechanisms. The big-bowl eliminated incentives for improving production; central planning replaced rational choice in determining the operation of the agricultural system.

Family Responsibility System

After 1979, the reformers experimented with various systems of responsibility that tried to build up a direct relationship between what a peasant or a family could produce and what it might expect to get in return. After several years of diverse experiments, one of these — the family responsibility system — prevailed over the other available alternatives, including the commune system.[3]

The family responsibility system, briefly speaking, is an economic institution in which each agricultural family performs as a basic unit and is responsible for the leasing of land, production, the distribution of income, and for contributing a portion of its agricultural products to the state (the last of which could be seen as a sort of leasing cost or tax). The family responsibility system got underway with each farming family receiving land by signing a land lease contract with the local production team or a committee in the village, in exchange for which each family made a commitment to the state to deliver specific amounts of grain and other agricultural products. The contracts also granted each family seeds, tools, cows, and tractors, all formerly the property of the collective production team. Contracts were usually created through collective consultation and bargaining within a production team which, at the time, typically coincided with a natural village. The production team divided the amount of grain and other agricultural products, which related to the quotas of the state plan, into shares directly attached to each piece of land. Farmers called these shares "responsibility grain (or other products)" and "contribution grain (or other products)," depending mainly on whether they were required or not.[4] After they delivered or sold certain required amounts of grain or other products, all that remained belonged to the peasants, who could keep or sell it on the market at will. Given the fixed amount of land under their control, peasants would try every way possible to increase their output per unit of land. Theoretically, peasants would increase the input of labor until the marginal product equaled the cost of labor,[5] and, in fact, idle and deceptive work under the communes did automatically disappear under the new agricultural system. In the early reform period, peasants in most areas did not have many alternatives other than farming; therefore the alternative cost of labor was fairly low, and peasants under the new system tried to take better care of their fields and to increase output from the land. Later, as more opportunities emerged, such as construction and manufacturing, the family-based system also allowed peasants to allocate their labor between farming and nonfarming production. Clearly, the adoption of the family responsibility system served to improve efficiency.

First-Phase Model Considered

The establishment of the family responsibility system reflected the dominant belief that it would improve the existing system and satisfy the chief concern of the CPE principle. The family responsibility system was based on land leasing rather than privatization, and the lease terms at the time were usually three to five years in the first phase of reform. In early 1980, when responsibility systems were permitted officially, the document that endorsed the various responsibility experiments contained an additional qualitative statement that they should be considered in every respect part of the socialist economy.[6] Even as late as 1982-83, when the family responsibility system prevailed and the commune system was, in effect, dissolved, it was still claimed that the family responsibility system was part of the socialist, collective operation.[7] This claim, apart from possible motives of political compromise to divert ideological confrontation, was mainly based on two criteria: first, the essence of the system was land leasing, in contrast to privatization; second, the required amounts of products to be sold to the state were mainly decided according to state planning. Agricultural reform, therefore, was originally geared toward improving instead of replacing the CPE.

Agricultural reform also demonstrates the early Chinese approach to economic reform — the closed approach of "touching stones." The selection of the family responsibility system was not accomplished in one step, nor was it by any means predesigned. There were several steps that led to the dissolution of the commune and the establishment of the new system. During the multiple stages of early reform, experiments with a variety of other alternatives were also conducted, affording opportunities for comparisons. Significantly, most of these experiments were related in one way or another to certain past experiences and emerged as the peasants' spontaneous choices.

The agricultural reform, which became a nationwide movement, was born in a small village in Anhui Province in 1978. What happened in this village literally ignited what later came to involve 800 million Chinese engaged in agriculture. That year, Xiaogang, a village in Anhui's Fengyang County, was experiencing a serious shortage of food due to the commune system and bad weather. Everyone in the village faced hunger, and many peasants might have had to choose between staying to die and leaving the village to beg for food. One day, the production team chief of Xiaogang called together two peasants to discuss a way out of the situation. At this secret nighttime meeting, the three reached a consensus: that only apportioning the commune lands to individuals could save villagers from hunger and beggary. They then went to the most senior and respected member of the village for his endorsement. When this secret decision, which involved a prohibited and extremely risky action, was announced among family representatives, support was unanimous, but they were overwhelmed by worry over its potential consequences. The three decision makers, in particular, were risking prison, and the family representatives pledged that, should anything happen to them, they would take care of the three men's families. Distributing the commune's land to each family immediately resulted in changes in the peasants' behavior and increases in annual output. The decision of the Xiaogang peasants was later endorsed by Wan Li, the province's reform-minded governor. [8]

From then on, agricultural reform spread from Anhui Province to the whole country, and various responsibility systems were tested and put into place. By the end of 1979, over 50 percent of the collective production teams in the country had adopted one or another form of responsibility system. [9] Among these were systems that divided workers into groups of smaller size for some work only; systems that did so for all production tasks, each small unit responsible for the outcome, good or bad; systems that divided work among individual families; and systems that divided total production among families, which eventually evolved into the family responsibility system.

Gradually, the family responsibility system demonstrated its advantages, mainly in terms of organizational stability and strong incentives, over the old system and most of the alternatives, and thereby, through a process of comparison and selection, became China's dominant agricultural system. At the end of 1982, Beijing issued an important document, "On Issues of Current Agriculture Policies," in which the family responsibility system was fully endorsed. By late 1983, 98 percent of production teams in the country had adopted the family responsibility system. [10] As a result of the reform, agricultural production grew from 1979 to 1984 at a sustained annual growth rate of 7.98 percent. [11]

From the perspective of the relationships between these agricultural reform experiments and the earlier efforts of allocating land to families in the late 1950s and early 1960s, it is worth mentioning again the closed-source "touching stones" approach. The process of trying out and then selecting the family responsibility approach illustrates in part how this reform approach was applied. Reform was instituted to solve problems in the commune system. When reform experiments were being considered, people first tried to find ideas from their own experience, and the mode of family-based production was familiar to peasants. Despite the fact that the family-based responsibility system demonstrated its advantages over the other responsibility experiments developed during the reform process, this system was still several steps away from achieving dominance.

Apart from the family responsibility system, agricultural reform also included a series of coordinated price adjustments and policies designed to allow a free market to develop, which reflected an understanding of incentive problems and of the reform of institutional relations. In 1979, the prices of agricultural products were raised after having been frozen for a long period. Prices of agricultural products were raised 20.1 percent in 1979, and, after 1980, farmers were allowed to sell their extra agricultural products at market prices.[12] At the same time, prices of some products mainly sold to peasants, such as plastic film and diesel fuel for tractors, were lowered. As discussed above, the price adjustment was not intended as an introduction of the market system in order to allocate resources, but instead as an adjustment of the internal relations of the "big corporation." Allowing peasants to sell their products on the free market also worked to bring in new incentives, since market prices were usually higher than planned prices. It was, however, true that as agriculture developed rapidly and the proportion of products sold on the market kept increasing, the market developed into a major mechanism in the allocation of agricultural resources.

Peasants' and Officials' Institutional Memory

The responsibility systems, as experiments or as a sort of economic institution, could be traced back to the 1950s and 1960s. After the commune system was established across the country in 1958 and the subsequent immediate agricultural failure occurred, Jiangsu and Henan provinces tried in 1959 to divide the land and collective production among families in an effort to increase production. Again in 1961, when agriculture was on the brink of collapse under the commune system, family responsibility systems were tried in more areas, including Anhui, Guangxi, and Hunan Provinces. By the spring of 1961, 40 percent of commune production teams in Anhui Province, which went farthest in this direction, had adopted some kind of family responsibility system. In addition, in 1964, Yunnan and Guizhou Provinces also had some production teams that had adopted family responsibility systems. [13] In the twenty-year history of the commune system in China, there had been many efforts by peasants and local officials to diverge from the commune and to return to a family-based production system. Such examples of diversion from the commune system would become particularly prevalent whenever agricultural production was declining and could not provide enough food. Unfortunately, each of these experiments was shut down and peasants were forced to return to the commune system. Thus, the emergence of the family responsibility system and other experiments at the end of the 1970s had its origin in the peasants' experiences in China's recent history.

It is important to point out a connection between these isolated experiences with agricultural reform and a smooth institutional transformation. Institutional transformation refers to the transition from one specific economic institution to another and occurs when an organization's or system's institutional characteristics are fundamentally changed. The reform that changed agriculture from the commune system to the family responsibility system was a huge institutional transformation. Although the family-based production experiments in the 1950s and 1960s were short-lived and some officials who permitted or supported these experiments were dismissed, they provided memorable experiences for the peasants and local officials involved, who recalled important details regarding the circumstances that had prompted their past choices, how the two different systems had compared, and how to switch from one system to another. In many other cases of institutional change, people did not know much about the new systems, were too uncertain during the transition, and were not confident about their ability to adapt to the new system. In those cases, friction arose and the costs of transformation correspondingly increased. In contrast, peasants and local officials had some specific experience in transforming the system and had confidence in their ability to manage farming operations on their own. Peasants remembered how to cultivate land, arrange production activities seasonally, and use labor and technology in ways appropriate to single family units. To a certain degree, these direct experiences of past family-based production constituted a preparatory and implicit institutional element for the introduction of the family responsibility system.

This experience-related institutional element or "institutional memory" relates to certain human assets. In the abstract, institutional memory refers to the institutions and associated behaviors, experienced by some portions of society in a substantial way, that could still be retrieved. This institutional memory embedded in the special human assets provided institutional and behavioral clues for initiating experiments and selecting an appropriate replacement for the system. Institutional memory often entails strong personal preferences on the basis of tested experiences.

Specifically, with regard to China's reform, Chinese peasants of the late 1970s had institutional memories about family-based production in the late 1950s and the 1960s and extending back even further, to the early 1950s and before. Prior to the communist takeover, Chinese peasants had worked mainly on the basis of family units, either on their own land or for a landlord. After the communists came to power and redistributed land to every family during the land reform of the late 1940s and the early 1950s, the family-based production mode was dominant in agriculture. These precommune experiences were still alive for a majority of peasants at the time. This is to say that although only a few provinces' (e.g., Anhui) peasants had the memories about going back to family-based production from the commune system, a majority of peasants still could remember the experiences prior to the commune system.

Those local officials who first endorsed and supported the introduction of a new agricultural system were chiefly those who had already done so in the 1950s and 1960s. Those officials who had been dismissed for their earlier support of land distribution schemes were usually most enthusiastic in endorsing the new experiments with family responsibility systems, in their desire to vindicate both the reform itself and their own support of it before. When China's system was still characterized as a planned one, the role of the local officials who had experience was important. Their sensitivity to the new experiments and their inclination to accept it reduced the threshold for entering the state where a conflicting system, the commune, was still operating. Anhui Province provided evidence for the relationship between institutional memory and the initiation of a certain institutional experiment. As the province that had become most involved in the late 1950s and 1960s, Anhui was the starting place of the agriculture reform of the late 1970s as well.

These institutional memories also helped peasants to adapt to the new system; although such a profound transformation inevitably entailed costs in converting existing human assets, the disruption was significantly lessened by this familiarity. Because of various differences between the methods of family-based versus collective production, some existing skills were no longer needed and other new skills were required. In this situation, with direct experience of production under the family-based system, peasants needed only to draw from their own experiences rather than to learn all over again. Direct experience thus certainly helped China's peasants to adapt in less time and with less cost. Further, institutional memory helped to reduce fluctuations in production levels due to the transformative changes taking place.

Adjusting Governmental Relationships

The reform of the relationship between the central and local governments was part of the overall first-phase economic reform. The change in relations between the central and local governments was the transfer to the provincial governments of some of the authority and responsibility for making decisions about planning, production, resource allocation, and investment that had heretofore rested with the central government. This was seen as linked to the overall reform not only because the major reform measures proposed by the central government had to be implemented through local governments, but also because local governments (mainly the provincial governments) increasingly influenced the central government in developing the reform and shaping its policies.

Provincial Government

Provincial governments played a critical role in promoting the reform, which was by and large initiated by the central government in

Beijing. Given the dimensions of the economy and the population of China, on the one hand, it was difficult and ineffective for the central government to bypass the provincial governments to control the national economy and to direct the economic reform. On the other hand, provincial governments were the most visible force in the critique of the centrally controlled policy and often the most aggressive bargainer with the central government. Particularly, provincial governments could always argue with the central government for special rationing on the basis of local and specific circumstances, taking advantage of information about local economies.

In this traditionally centrally controlled country, the balance of relative control and freedom for provincial governments had long been one of the most sensitive issues for the central government. Even under the central planning system, the importance and sensitivity of this matter were still crucial. Change in the central government's economic strategy altered the relationship between the central and provincial governments. In the adoption of the Soviet-type economic system, the Great Leap Forward, the adjustment in the early 1960s, and the Cultural Revolution, there had been significant changes in the arrangement of this relationship.[14] The reform of this time was no exception. When pointing out the actual importance of provincial government to the CPE as a whole, I do not want to ignore the roles played by city and county government. But by any measure, provincial governments were far more important in linking a central policy with its actual economic impact.

The central government allowed and even encouraged provincial governments to take the lead in reforming local economies, thus spearheading a decentralization process. The central government incrementally increased the freedom and authority of the provincial governments, enabling them to be more and more active in promoting reform and development. In some cases, provincial governments also pressed for specific freedoms and authority. The demand from local governments for more authority and rapid decentralization was often used by the central government to promote the economic reform against the wishes of the bureaucratic apparatus of the central planning agencies and ministries. When reform began, the central planning offices controlled most of the large- and medium-sized enterprises, and any trade and cooperation among these enterprises had to be applied for and assigned by these agencies. Hence the economy was separated into many practically disintegrated parts by the planning bureaucracy, and an efficient use of resources was arbitrarily made impossible. Central planning agencies and ministries particularly emphasized procedure and formality at the expense of flexibility and responsiveness. Local governments were in touch better with reality and concerned more about performance and outcome in local economies. It had been proven by experiences of the 1950s and 1960s that once a less controlling strategy was adopted there would be a shift of authority from central planning agencies and ministries to provincial governments. To a large degree, local governments usually helped to break down the centrally planned vertical integration, and helped to implement a pragmatic economic strategy. [15]

Budget Separation

The reform of financial relations appeared at the center of the overall reform of the relationships between the central and local governments. Financial reform focused on the separation of both the responsibilities and the budgets of the central and local governments. The financial reform, in essence, was an effort to divide one "big account" into many smaller ones. Specifically, the reform granted greater and greater authority and autonomy to local governments and made local financial responsibilities and budgets relatively independent from those of the central government. At the same time, the central government wanted to put local governments under tighter fiscal constraints, holding them accountable to balancing their own budgets. Decentralization was the general direction that the reform of the relations between the central and local governments took.

The reform of the financial system began in 1979, and a new financial system was in effect in early 1980. [16] In 1979, the financial reform started with two experimental policies. One was to set a ratio within each local economy (normally province-wide) of revenue remitted to the central government to revenue retained by the local government. [17] This ratio was determined largely on the basis of their respective budget situations in recent years. Under the reform, the local government was supposed to adjust its expenses by keeping its budget balanced. If income in one region increased, the local and central governments shared the increased income proportionally according to the established ratio for that region.[18] The alternative program was first to separate the income that should belong to the central government from the income that was left for the local governments, and then to set a ratio for sharing any increased income between the two levels of government.[19] Only six months into the policies' trial period, the latter of these two options was chosen.[20] The major difference between the first option and the second lay in whether the two levels of government shared the total income or shared the income by separating the sources. The financial reform that was adopted permitted provincial authorities to keep all the profits earned from all enterprises in the areas of jurisdiction that were not managed by the central government, greatly boosting the proportion of revenue kept by the lower-level authorities, in addition to bestowing on their leaders the power to determine how to spend the revenue retained. Apart from that, provinces were entitled to retain their entire tax proceeds from businesses in their areas (with the exception of the industrial and commercial tax, whose receipts were shared with Beijing according to negotiated rates).

A new, revised version of the central government's financial policies was released at the end of 1982.[21] Despite a top-level promise that this set of practices would remain unaltered for five years, a new method was designed, according to the new policies, for allocating finances. The key change wrought by the new method was that most provinces were entitled to draw a larger percentage of the industrial and commercial tax, which in recent years had been a growing revenue stream. The purpose of the reform was to give more incentive to local governments so as to make the budgetary constraint imposed on them more binding. In exchange, the provincial-level governments gave Beijing a share in local tax revenues. These revenues, however, were actually in decline, as the enterprises from which they were derived had been allowed to keep more of the profits they generated and had been enjoined not to raise the prices of their products, despite rising costs.

Financial reform brought about three major changes. First, local governments obtained more sources of income than before as well as responsibility for more aspects of local economies, which in turn meant they had to bear more expenses. Second, local governments were expected to keep their expenses and income in balance and were allowed to keep any surplus for their own use. The reform policies clearly sent signals of encouragement for the balancing of budgets without reliance on the central government.[22] Third, local governments were encouraged to foster the development of local economies and to increase local income. The new system of income sharing, in contrast to the former surrender of all local income, brought a new mechanism that local authorities could count on to increase their disposable income and therefore their expenditures.

Adjusting Internal Relations

The reform of the relationships between Beijing and the provincial governments, particularly the financial relationships, did improve the existing system. Given the importance of provincial governments as the intermediate instrument for transmitting the central government's instructions and implementing its policies, the central government had to rely on provincial governments to mobilize human and other resources in order to realize its reforms. Indeed, the provincial governments were basically branches and extensions of the Beijing government, rather than local representative bodies. The Chinese economy was so huge, particularly in terms of its geographic dimensions and population, that the central government could not easily have directly controlled the local governments without creating a military command system. Also, the sometimes marked differences among regions, with unequal levels of development and more than 50 nationalities, made the provincial governments crucially important to the central government in maintaining harmony and cohesion throughout the nation. In other words, local governments could be especially valuable to the control and governing function of the central government if they could be motivated to be more flexible and responsive as agents of the central government. From this perspective, the early efforts to adjust the relationships between the central and local governments supported the proposition that described the CPE as a "big corporation" with a common interest. The adjustment of these relationships was based on recognition of the incentive problems, and on the prescription to solve them by realigning internal relations. With this adjustment in place, local governments were expected to take better care of the common interest. Further, since local governments controlled potentially substantial resources, the central government was concerned that these resources be used efficiently. Under the old economic system, local governments were tightly controlled by Beijing and had little flexibility or incentive to be more efficient. All these factors determined that in order to improve the functioning of the existing economy, it was necessary to reform the relationship between the central and local governments and to provide more incentive and authority to local governments.

In addition, as will be seen in more detail in the discussion of enterprise reform, the realignment of relationships between the central and local governments was accompanied by reform of the state enterprises. Importantly, some of the authority passed down from Beijing was further passed down to enterprises, instead of being retained by local governments; this was a departure from previous reform efforts in which, as mentioned above, authority was allocated back and forth between the central and provincial governments. This difference implied that the 1979 postreform movement could go beyond what the experiences of the previous decades had suggested.

Lessons from Experience

The efforts to adjust the relationships between the central and provincial governments again exemplified the closed-source approach. Experience still provided the initial guidance in adjusting the relationships in an attempt to motivate provincial governments. Once the reform movement started, the existing relationship obviated the need for change. The real question was not whether, but what changes in the relationships should be introduced. When the need for change grew, the reform's decision makers first drew references and implications from their experiences in the 1950s and 1960s, which in effect constituted the main feasible solution. A closer look at the experiences in adjusting the relationships between central and provincial governments illuminates this point.

There were three rounds of decentralization and reordering of the relationships between the central and provincial governments, and they took place in the 1950s, 1960s, and early 1970s. All centered around the appropriate allocation of responsibility and authority between Beijing and the provinces.[23] Each time, the central government passed its authority and responsibilities down to provincial governments in an attempt to mobilize and organize the economy more effectively. The measures to adjust relationships this time, as discussed above, were essentially those that had been used before.

The focus of previous reforms had been reallocation of control over a large number of state-owned enterprises and the consequent reallocation of financial resources. When the central government had handed over 88% of previously centrally controlled enterprises to provincial governments between 1957 and 1958 and let them collect these enterprises' revenues and profits, the revenue collected directly by the central government had dropped from 40 percent to 20 percent of its total income. The decentralization of the late 1950s was then followed by the Great Leap Forward and a series of other radical economic policies, which led to the collapse of the economy. Then came the recentralization in 1961. In 1964 and 1965, there was another round of decentralization, and Beijing again reallocated authority and financial resources to local governments. Then, during the Cultural Revolution, specifically in 1970-71, the third decentralization took place and more than 95 percent of the centrally controlled enterprises were passed down to local governments, accompanied by a new policy under which local governments were responsible for their own budgets.[24]

The 1979 and early 1980s reform of the capital-provincial relationship was similar to the previous three realignments of the financial system, particularly in allowing some independence in provincial budgeting. This kind of adjustment served the purpose of the central government in its search for a workable balance under which local governments had the incentive and the authority to take initiatives to promote production while still operating under the central government's control.

Like the earlier efforts, this one also failed to develop such mutually balanced institutions. These efforts were not intended to create something akin to federalism or to make local governments independent from the central government. Without exception, all the major initiatives for change came from Beijing. To this end, provincial government officials were appointed by Beijing and were seen as representatives of Beijing, and the nature of the relationship was still determined unilaterally by the central government. The three earlier attempts resulted in a cyclic process of centralization, decentralization, and recentralization, so that in the absence of other profound changes in the relationship, there was no guarantee yet that the decentralization of the first phase would endure. Therefore, even though the decentralization of the first phase was important in introducing limited freedom to the economy during early-phase reform, it was basically on an old track.

Primitive Enterprise Reform

During the early phases of reform, the main context of enterprise reform would seem to have been the allocation of more autonomy and authority for decision making to enterprises and the introduction of new incentive mechanisms in an effort to improve enterprise behavior. Enterprise reform appeared to be more directly related to the behavior of the business world and the efficiency of the economy than did the reform of relationships between the central and local governments. What was similar to agricultural reform and government relationship reform was that enterprise reform was also specifically intended to increase incentives in the system.

What happened to China's enterprises in the early years of the reform movement served as a paradigm for understanding the first-phase reform, which was intended to improve the CPE in its entirety. Early enterprise reform well illustrated the intention of the reform and its experimental approach, as well as the reformers' understanding of the economic system, its problems, and how to solve them. The enterprise reform provides another interesting test for the model of the first-phase form.

Early enterprise reform particularly confronted the issue of the existing human assets in relation to the transformation of the CPE. It involved government officials, managers, and common workers who, while de facto participants in the reform, also constituted a major constraint on the reform process.

Profit-Sharing Experiment

Three parts of enterprise reform merit special discussion. The experiment with enterprise management suggested by the central government on 13 July 1979 and the tax reform of 1983 stood as two significant developments in the first period of enterprise reform. [25] In addition, the experiment to encourage industrial combination across administrative boundaries between ministerial and regional administrations was another major aspect of enterprise reform and industrial reorganization.

As the first major part of enterprise reform, the experiment of 1979, took four years to reform state enterprises: setting up institutions to share profits between enterprises and the state so as to provide incentives for businesses to pursue profits by improving production; raising the depreciation rate; introducing a tax on fixed-asset holdings for the purpose of limiting free-asset holdings (as opposed to previously free investment); and replacing the free use of money and credit with interest charged on all short-term circulating loans and credit.

This experiment was conducted at first in eight selected enterprises in May 1979 and was extended to about 6,600 mid- and large-size firms in 1980. The spirit of the reform was to give enterprises more autonomy in making their business decisions. Apart the principle finance-related measures above, there were others associated with this experiment. Enterprises were allowed to initiate new product development and were granted the right to apply to export their products independently; foreign currency earned in this way was subject to proportional sharing. Enterprises were permitted to use their foreign earnings to import machinery, technology, and raw materials, and to pay for trips outside China for training and business. Moreover, enterprises were allowed, within the limitation of employment quotas, to hire workers according to their own criteria. In contrast, before the reform, laborers or workers had been unconditionally assigned to businesses, which had no authority to decide either the numerical or vocational composition of their workforces.

Almost immediately after the experiment in enterprise management began, it was found that the profit-sharing system had some inherent weaknesses. Among these, the first was that arbitrary and unstable profit-sharing arrangements made it difficult for enterprises to formulate realistic expectations. Second, since the negotiations between government and enterprises on the proportion of profits and the amount of base profit were to occur once every so often, the relationship between the state and the enterprises continued to resemble an administrative governance. Administrative relations were often colored by interpersonal relationships, which might further influence enterprises in their decision making. It was recognized that the profit-sharing mechanism had been irregular and the ratios for sharing profit were usually set arbitrarily; this allowed both more room for government to interfere in business and, conversely, opportunity for enterprises to elude budgetary constraints as long as they could persuade their local governments to be lenient. In late 1980 and early 1981, the experiment of tax reform was tried on a group of enterprises.[26]

Introduction of Taxation

The second major enterprise reform, in June 1983, was the central government's extension of a tax system to most state-owned enterprises that was modeled on that tested since 1980 in about 200 pioneering firms. Primarily, this reform measure replaced the existing profit remittance system with a tax system.[27] According to this program, state enterprises switched from the old system of giving all their profits to the state, as had been practiced in the pre-1979 period and the profit-sharing scheme of 1979-83, to a new system of paying an income tax to the state.[28] In the "Methods for Conversion of Profit-surrendering to Tax (1983),"[29] it was stipulated that all large- and mid-size state enterprises, except for those in deficit, were subject to a 55 percent tax on all profits. According to this policy, the remaining small-size state enterprises were subject to a progressive tax of 7 to 55 percent. Businesses retained what was left. Before this reform, each enterprise and its supervisory body had negotiated a profit "base figure," which the enterprise had to deliver to the state, while the firm could keep some amount between 50 and 100 percent of the profits above that base. Until inauguration of the experiment, state enterprises had essentially operated under one of three categories of distribution relationship with the state. In the first, the state and enterprises shared profits on a proportional basis; in the second, an enterprise submitted its profit in the form of taxes; in the third, which was used for those enterprises that were in deficit and dependent on government subsidies, the maximum subsidy level was set.[30] Thus tax reform was expected to standardize the relations between government and enterprises. As a supplementary but no less important measure, a contingency adjustment tax was imposed on each enterprise, given the fact that unsolved problems with prices, assets, and many other factors put enterprises in a situation of unfair competition with each other. With these existing problems, the contingency adjustment tax was mainly intended to avoid any big interruption of the profit distribution. For example, if an enterprise submitted one million yuan a year prior to the tax reform, and if a 55 percent tax on all profit counted for 750,000 yuan, then the difference of 250,000 yuan would be subject to the contingency adjustment tax. With the introduction of this tax reform, enterprises had less opportunity to conceal profits or to retain what the central government considered excessive funds garnered as a result of highly arbitrary negotiations.

Industrial Reintegration Experiment

Finally, the third major part of the enterprise reform was to encourage enterprises to develop business relations on their own, which resulted in the organizational integration of the industrial sector. In the "Temporary Regulation on Improving Economic Cooperation and Integration" issued in 1980 by the central government, economic cooperation and integration across the boundaries of vertical ministries and regional administrations were encouraged in the name of efficiency, and this industrial reorganization was to be based on free will rather than mandated by the plan.[31] Before the reform, factories located in one community, if they belonged to different industrial ministries, might not have been able to work together, but were confined to working with factories that belonged to the same ministry, no matter what the relative disadvantages were. The central planning system made cooperation possible only through the process of vertical integration.

The reform to encourage horizontal cooperation and integration was a response to a demand from enterprises and local governments, and it was based on their spontaneous practices and experiments. It was obvious that the vertical integration of the CPE created inefficiency of allocation, and there was a strong demand for change. Actually, ad hoc efforts to develop such cooperation across ministries and regions had existed before the reform movement, and these unofficial experiments provided case studies and data for those formulating reform policies.

The reform toward cooperation and reintegration posed a great challenge to the CPE system by breaking down its administrative connections. Instead of directly dismantling the central planning machine, this reform encouraged a gradual breaking away from the CPE from the bottom up. The regulation particularly emphasized that cooperation and integration in production should be outside the limits of vertical and administrative control. As a result, cooperation and reintegration were based on relative advantages (the saving of transaction costs) and voluntary trade. A variety of loose trusts across industrial ministries and administrative regions developed as a result.

Test and Interpretation

The early enterprise reform offers another case for testing the model of "realignment of internal relations" discussed in the previous chapter, and the model helps understand and interpret the early reform. In general, China implemented its enterprise reform from 1979 to 1984 by granting more authority and introducing greater incentive to enterprises within the institutional framework of state ownership and central planning. First of all, granting more authority to enterprises revealed the reformers' understanding of the failure of centralized decision making and the advantage of diversified decision making in business and the economy at large. Granting more authority to enterprises and encouraging industrial reorganization provided evidence. Since the initiation of enterprise reform, enterprises had the authority to make decisions on developing new products, to invest (with limited funds), to sell their extra products where they wished, and to choose their partners. This reform decentralized and diversified decisions regarding business and the economy with the expectation that the quality of those decisions would be improved. A modern enterprise makes primarily two kinds of decisions: internal ones regarding production, and external ones concerning transactions. The enterprise reform that granted authority to businesses and encouraged horizontal cooperation involved the mechanisms of both production and transaction-related decision making.

Moreover, introducing new incentives into enterprises reflected a key aspect of the leadership's understanding of the existing problems and how to solve them. Lack of appropriate incentives was viewed as the source of all efficiency problems with China's CPE. Although there were always some constraints and costs tied to the introduction of a new incentive mechanism, the enterprise reform tried to introduce a new incentive mechanism with minimal costs (especially when compared, for example, to the expense of certain agricultural reform measures). Beijing's decision makers did not want and could not afford to increase deficits to conduct an enterprise reform as it had in agriculture, in which the government enrollment raised food prices from peasants while keeping the same selling prices to urban dwellers by increasing subsidies. Because enterprise reform was a profit-sharing mechanism, entailing a switch from profit surrendering to profit sharing, it would work as long as an enterprise could expand production profitably. The introduction of the profit-sharing mechanism in 1979 represented the start of a series of changes in the relations between the state and enterprises. The state could no longer treat an enterprise merely as a factory that surrendered everything and had no independent interests. With the introduction of a profit-sharing mechanism, enterprises were motivated by self-interest to increase production and efficiency. In addition, profit-sharing reform and the tax reform associated with it were a substantial move toward the institutionalization of the profit-sharing mechanism and a standardized tax system.

Along with the introduction of new incentives and certain budgetary constraints, these early experiences also suggested additional factors that kept the behavior of enterprises from being more rational. The efforts to make independent, balanced budgeting a real and hard constraint failed due to the continued prevalence of government control over the economy and the fact that no one was really taking care of the assets of the state enterprises. Until the question of ownership was clarified and made concrete, budget constraints remained ineffective. Apart from the issue of ownership, three other factors hindered adherence to budgetary constraints. First, as long as prices were controlled, budgeting could not be enforced, since price control could prevent an enterprise from selling its products at equilibrium prices set by supply and demand, potentially resulting in a deficit situation and rendering budget constraints meaningless. Second, as long as the state government still decided what enterprises would produce, the state, and the government, rather than the enterprises themselves, could always be blamed for a deficit. Suppose that the state assigned an enterprise to produce a product that the enterprise would not be able to earn a profit from and therefore did not want to produce. Third, government macroeconomic interference could also be blamed for deficits as when, for example, the cancellation of a centrally ordered project caused losses for contractors and suppliers. The following case illustrates this point. At the end of 1980, the central government found too many projects under construction that were being supported by the government budget. The government issued a decree to decrease the wave of new construction. The subsequent selection of projects to be canceled or terminated was conducted arbitrarily, causing numerous problems to enterprises. In these situations the budgetary constraints would lose their meaning and enterprises would simply ignore them.

Finally, consistent with the still-dominant belief of improving the CPE, early enterprise reform moved slowly toward markets or privatization. Even though enterprise reform had brought some freedom to enterprises and enabled them to pursue their own interests to some degree, it had revealed no intention to relinquish state power over the economy and controlled enterprises. Also, the reform did not conduct any substantial experiment with different ownership models to achieve higher efficiency. This situation, however, was not surprising since the economy's problems were attributed for the most part to radical and ideological policies prior to the reform, not to the institutions of the CPE. Hence, enterprise reform was conducted, in the first phase of the reform movement, under the assumption that low efficiency could be solved solely with improved or new incentive mechanisms.

Specialized Human Assets

Compared to the reform in agriculture, the progress of enterprise reform was more gradual. As the cells of a modern economy, enterprises behave within an institutional complex of division, interaction, and cooperation. Even though the reform of collective agricultural production succeeded by simply dividing the working units and assets of the commune, this technique did not appear promising for the reform of state enterprises. This was because the industrial organizations, transactional relationships, and business decisions that an enterprise had to deal with were more complicated than those of the agricultural sector. Moreover, China did not have much institutional experience with free or private enterprise or with entrepreneurship. The Chinese did not have many experiences to draw on in reforming the enterprise system, in contrast to their background in reforming the agricultural system. The enterprise reform revealed again that issues of experience and people's capabilities to make a new system work related to characteristics of the human assets involved in the reform.

In fact, the human assets inherited from the CPE constituted a major constraint on enterprise reform. As noted above regarding agricultural reform, the institutional memory of family-based production had been a great advantage in initiating, developing, and firmly establishing the new "family responsibility" system. Even though there was resistance due to self-interest and ideology, as well as fear of the unknown and difficulties in dividing physical assets, the transformation from the commune to the family responsibility system was wholeheartedly embraced by millions of peasants. Peasants — the main human asset carrier in agriculture — demonstrated their readiness for the new system in terms of their experiences, skills, knowledge, and the ability to make quick adaptation to it. In contrast, the human assets involved in the enterprise reform — planning officials, managers, and workers — made it tremendously difficult to overcome resistance to the new endeavor. Specifically, officials and reform leaders were largely ignorant about the nature and operation of a free enterprise system; enterprise managers lacked experience and entrepreneurial spirit in running businesses competitively; workers wanted a reward mechanism for better job performance, but were afraid of the concomitant uncertainties as well as being jealous of each others' income increases. All these contributed to increased difficulties and reluctance to transform the enterprise system, and the human assets became a critical part of the constraints facing the reform.

China's human assets had been highly specialized by decades under the central planning system. The central planning system imposed specialized characteristics on everybody. Since the market system differs from the centrally planned system in many fundamental ways, the transition to a market-oriented system was fraught with difficulty. In fact, the mandatory planning system created highly specialized human assets by its political and ideological training, dissemination of deliberately biased information, compulsory assignment according to the plan, reliance on redistribution, lack of open economic competition, and centralized decision-making processes.

As a result, officials knew only how to control the economy with mandatory planning quotas and administrative instruments, and did not know how to help create an environment in which free enterprise could work. Their skills, including how to report, how to listen to and interpret the underlying meaning of their bosses' instructions, how to deal with each branch and unit of the bureaucracy, etc., bore the strong stamp of the planning system. For example, an official would gradually be forced to interpret instructions that sometimes addressed issues in deliberately ambiguous language. In short, they were rewarded for playing according to the rules of a game that rewarded compliance over creativity. They were concerned with how each item of the plan was implemented but did not care about the wider economic impact of their actions. For example, they did not care about overproduction and waste of resources, but they would interfere in production if a quota was not filled, for no matter what reason. They became indifferent to and out of touch with real-world problems to avoid violation of bureaucratic rules and procedure. In sum, the officials of government economic agencies were specialized in maintaining the operation of the planning bureaucracy, in transmitting planning information, and in overseeing implementation of the plan.

Managers were charged with mechanically implementing organizational plans for production but were not allowed to make business decisions on their own and consequently lost the capacity to do so over the years. Even worse, they sometimes did not have a sense of costs and profits, but knew only too well how to win the favor of government officials to advance themselves. Compared to officials, enterprise managers were closer to reality and less bureaucratic. Managers, at least, had the responsibility of putting together all necessary resources and organizing production, but they were selected and trained by the system not to be innovative. The organization of a factory had usually already been set up and just needed to be put into practice. Even the number of employees was assigned and could not be changed. The limited means available to a manager to promote production (if this was a goal at all) were administrative. In specific cases, some capable and creative people might have been selected for many unrelated factors, but the central planning system was only interested in managers' implementing the plan with as little deviation from it as possible. Likewise, under the system, production and transaction decisions were made by planning agencies and the government. For example, it was planning agencies rather than chief managers that determined what to produce, how to produce it, how to source labor and materials, how much to produce, and to whom to supply it. As a result, the managers under the central planning system did not gain experience in making the key decisions of production and transaction. they did not get practice even in deciding how many workers to hire for production. Particularly, there was no competition in the CPE, and enterprise managers lacked experience, knowledge, and skill in free enterprise and market competition. Therefore, enterprise managers under the central planning system were specialized in implementing the quotas and instructions of the production plan and were insulated by the government from decision making in a competitive environment.

Common workers were trained with skills and values benefiting the central planning system. They were educated to trust the government and the party, they were forced to learn to tolerate hardship and bureaucratic procedure, they were trained to implement production assignments and quotas, and they were accustomed to rely on the government for everything from employment to housing. Because of the big-bowl system, everyone earned a relatively fixed income that was essentially independent of job performance. Working and living under this system enjoined a special habit of just doing what was minimally necessary according to one's assignment in the hope of a free ride. Workers also developed a dependence on the government's redistribution of income and benefits, even though they complained about the stagnant living standard (which was in part the outcome of the mandatory redistribution policies). These factors of calculated lethargy and dependence were reflected in their values and skills, which became specialized under the central planning system.

Human Assets Constraint

During the period from the end of the 1970s to the mid-1980s, changes in the enterprise system seemed to pale beside the sweeping changes in agriculture. Even though this era would later be called "the period of agricultural reform," there had been no such designed priority of agricultural over enterprise reform when the reforms were launched. According to the historic communiqué of the Third Plenum of the Eleventh Party Congress at the end of 1978 in which *gai ge* (reform) was spelled out, the focus of reform was to be on economic management systems and business operation methods. The document pointed out that overcentralization was a serious problem in China's economic management system. As a chronic problem, agriculture also attracted a great deal of attention at the meeting, but while emphasizing the importance of promoting agricultural development, it was not associated with reform. Basically the measures proposed to promote agricultural production (except for raising prices on agricultural products) were not very different from the old ones, which were characterized by political campaigns and mass mobilization under the commune system. Even though some isolated and spontaneous experiments of family-based agriculture already emerged in 1978, it did not by any means imply designed priority of agricultural over enterprise reform at the time. In fact, the central government did issue in early 1978 an important document "On Issues of Promoting Industrial Development," in which the profit-sharing measure was suggested.[32] Shortly after the spontaneous experience in family-based production appeared in Anhui Province, a well-organized experiment in reforming the enterprise system was launched in Shanghai, Beijing, and Tianjing.[33] But there is no doubt that during this period the reform in agriculture went much faster and had more substantial achievement than did the enterprise reform. By any token, early-phase reform did not change many of the characteristics of China's enterprise system in the direction of free enterprise. About five years after reform began in 1979, changes in enterprises' behavior, contractual relations and ownership structure, and performance were still marginal. Why did enterprise proceed so slowly?

As a brief answer to this large question, apparently the available human assets in the enterprise and its related systems were too ill-prepared for such a substantial change. The central planning system produced highly specialized and outmoded human assets that needed to adapt to fit the free enterprise system. As analyzed above, officials, enterprise managers, and workers in planning agencies constituted specialized assets whose patterns of behavior, knowledge and experiences, and skills and values all reflected this specialization and were a critical constraint on the evolution toward a free enterprise system. It is true that through experiments and practices with reform these human assets had undergone continual change and some elements of the free enterprise system had emerged, including more competition and independent decision making by managers. But in general, the conservative influence of the highly specialized human assets upon the progress of enterprise reform in its early phase was heavy. For example, when the chief manager of an enterprise wanted to reduce the number of employees to keep its products competitive, workers and government officials would join forces to make it impossible. When a reform to have the market set prices was considered, fear of competition would drive managers to oppose it and try to prolong the old system under which the government-controlled low prices would be guaranteed for state enterprises. When modest reform measures could not change the state-owned enterprises' behavior, reformers lacked knowledge of alternative measures. Even if a new alternative, such as the shareholding experiments in 1983-84, emerged spontaneously, it was not paid much attention simply because of lack of knowledge about the market system and, therefore, lack of sensitivity to it. China's experiences indicated that changes in the characteristics of human assets took a substantial period of time and needed practice to take hold.

Moreover, there was almost no institutional memory of the free enterprise system. Before the communists came to power, China had very limited and underdeveloped capitalist enterprises. Both quantitatively and qualitatively, these capitalist enterprises were far from the dominant institutions in their impact on China's economy. The development of this limited capitalist economy had been completely terminated in the mid-1950s; unlike agriculture, in which there had still been occasional opportunities to return to family-based production after the establishment of the commune system, the enterprise system had never been able to go back to the private system.

Rearrangement of the Planned Economy's Internal Relations: Preliminary Changes

In many aspects, the Chinese economic reform in its first phase was a pioneering attempt to transform a typical CPE. Agricultural reform — the dissolution of rural communes and the establishment of family production systems in their place — provided a successful example of increasing production with virtually the same resources and technology by dramatically transforming the economic institutions of the CPE. Most important, agricultural reform established a strong and illustrative case to break the bonds of communist ideology and to transform, in a substantial way, the CPE. Further, the first phase of the Chinese economic reform movement indicated that such a transformation from a centralized collective system to a decentralized and more individualistic system could not only be successful in increasing efficiency but could also proceed relatively smoothly. [34] Moreover, the efforts to adjust the relationship between the central and local governments and between the government and enterprises did increase the incentives within the economy. The new incentive mechanisms — mainly profit sharing — resulted in increased efficiency, which further illustrated, through the logic of negative proof, the economic losses in the CPE that had been assumed at the outset of reform. By adjusting relations in its economy, China pioneered in encouraging a variety of experiments and spontaneous innovations of organizations and institutions, thereby paving the way for future reform.

The early phase of reform did not succeed in transforming much of the CPE into a market economy, but it provided a solid ground and steady momentum for reform to proceed. It appeared to be important for reform to reinforce itself before it was widely accepted. The early reform movement built up a solid stream of benefits to the whole society by revitalizing the economy, and some of the reform measures gradually led enterprises and individuals to learn to adapt to the changing economy. For example, as the prices of agricultural products went up as part of agricultural reform, production increased and shortage was alleviated. With the ensuing steady stream of benefits came greater acceptance of readiness for further change, despite some initial shocks. In this regard, the early reform fortunately created a strong momentum that enabled later reform to enter phases that would pose more challenges to the CPE. To some extent, the reform in the period 1979 to 1984 was a prelude to the market-oriented economy to come.

During the first period of reform, the Chinese economy was, in essence, still a CPE. It was indeed true that the early reform and economic liberalization brought vast new dynamics into play in the long-stagnant economy and caused steady improvement in performance. It was also true that the portion of economic activities covered by the market had grown rapidly. In addition, some of the early reform was continued in the second phase and eventually led to more fundamental changes in economic institutions. Nevertheless, given the major characteristics of China's economy — very minor market coverage, dominance of the central planning mechanism, intact state ownership structure — the system in China was still a CPE. The operation of the economic system was still based mainly on administrative mandates, and a free economy had yet to be institutionalized. Primarily, changes were made to introduce incentives to individual members and organizational units of the CPE in order to improve it, and the initiation of reform was based on the understanding that what was wrong with the economy was the fault of a radical and orthodox economic development strategy. Changes in the economic system were not made to abandon the central planning mechanism and to introduce a clear concept of ownership; rather, in this phase of reform, as we have seen, central planning was still firmly maintained as the main mechanism for allocating resources and was in the dominant position in relation to the market mechanism. The state greatly influenced decisions on business operation and economic development, and state ownership, albeit vaguely defined, still remained the primary institutional foundation for ultimate control. There was no institutional set-up that served to assure property rights, nor was there an institutional barrier that prevented the government from seizing property, as certain political needs arose, or from imposing state ownership at will.

While economic reform in its first phase indeed led to changes in the CPE, it only succeeded in creating, up to 1983-84, a new species of CPE. Reform measures by then (short-term land lease granted to peasants, profit sharing between the state and enterprises, planning price adjustments by the state) could not be seen necessarily as part of a market-oriented reform, since there were few new institutions outside of the CPE to expand and develop. A market-oriented economy would demand more solid development and growth of such institutions, including clearly defined property rights and an independent legal system, which comprise the basic elements of a market economy.

Internal Relations

The first period of reform could be seen as a continuous realignment of authority and responsibility in the hierarchy of the CPE. In order to create incentives in the CPE system, the Chinese reformers tried to forge new internal relations within its frame by rearranging authority and responsibility. The reform in the relations between central and local governments, between government and business, and between the state and the peasants were the most important rearrangements in the hierarchy. The experiences of the Chinese economic reform's first phase are basically in accord with Kenneth Arrow's observation that "among the most widespread of characteristics of organization is the prevalence of authoritative allocation."[35] Viewing the national economy as a big corporation, its problems as lack of incentives, and its cure as rearrangement of internal relations, China's early reformers essentially treated all the reform issues as if the economy were an organization. Indeed, in this big "organization," the early reform did change its many characteristics, particularly in its authoritative allocation. Specifically, this included more freedom for peasants, more autonomy for enterprises, and more independence for local governments. Thus, the realignment of internal relations in China's CPE during the early reform was reflected in its reallocation of authority and responsibility.

Behind the redistribution of authority and responsibility lay changes in the reward mechanism. Based on their understanding of problems caused by the lack of incentives, the reformers apparently accepted the assumption that the welfare of an economic system would increase if each of its units enhanced its efforts to pursue self-interest and increase efficiency. The overall realignment of internal relations served to introduce incentives into the system and establish new reward mechanisms. The ultimate interest of the economic system was to be achieved with various reward mechanisms for individuals and organizational units. From a certain viewpoint, China's early reform could be seen as an effort to rearrange its internal relations, thereby allowing each individual and unit in the organization to pursue its own interests while enhancing the common interest of the CPE.

Finally, although the economic reform of 1979-84 was a reform within the CPE framework and bore similarities to the adjustments in the 1950s and 1960s, if it is seen only as another cycle of centralization and decentralization in the CPE, its substance will be overlooked. There are three factors that should be considered in measuring the changes brought about by the early phase of the reform. First, the reform took place immediately following the radical upheaval of the Cultural Revolution and was, in this historical context, remarkable as a dramatic and highly significant turning point. Second, the reform was, in effect, open ended: the "touching stones" approach permitted the reform process to break the bonds of both experience and theory gradually. This approach came into its own in the second phase of reform, during which it opened up to, and was enriched by, experiences from beyond China's borders. None of the previous adjustments in the 1950s and 1960s had ever taken this approach. Third, while concern for adhering to the principles of the CPE was still important in shaping the policies of reform, efficiency emerged as the driving force behind institutional change, selection, and innovation. Policies were evaluated on the basis of the perspective of efficiency motivation rather than for ideological or political reasons, which now functioned as the constraints, not the genius, of economic policy, and this represented a landmark change.

The experience of reform strengthened confidence in the chosen approach to reform: "touching stones while walking across a river,'" as Deng declared in 1984 after five years of reform, "our confidence has increased."[36] Further, the success of the early reform movement validated and reinforced the concern for efficiency in the selection and development of China's economic institutions.

Notes

1. The most common movement to boost agricultural production was the so-called "Learning from Dazhai," which was set up as a model of collective production. Dazhai was the name of a village in the county of Xiyang, Shanxi Province. Such movements were usually compulsory and very much pro forma, as dictated by the planning bureaucracy.
2. Armen Alchian, and H. Demsetz, "The Property Right Paradigm," *Journal of Economic History* 33 (March 1973): 16-27.
3. During reform, peasants in certain areas still chose collective production systems. Some of these organizations in rural areas had already evolved into something like businesses, which had the advantage of reducing transaction costs through specialization, the rational allocation of skills and technology, and the efficient use of assets. This kind of rural enterprise allowed peasants to enjoy sharing the risks of production as well as economies of scale. Moreover, it also created some opportunity for entrepreneurship to develop from within the existing rural economy. (Jiangsu and Shandong Provinces provided some interesting cases of this kind of rural production.) In general, however, these mixed economies represented a very small part of the rural economy after agricultural reform. Furthermore, such collective production was not the same as what took place under the commune system and really constituted another form of organization, since decision making was localized and took cost factors into account.
4. Purchasing prices of these different products set by the state might differ as a part of the incentive policies of that time. The price for responsibility grain was the lowest. The price of contribution grain was higher, but still lower than the grain's market price,
5. The cost of labor is generally referred to as the opportunity cost of labor. If there is no major alternative work to do, the cost of labor is at least equal to the cost of overall consumption. For example, if a man is hired to do some work in a field, even though he may just stay at home otherwise, he is going to receive at least his meals in payment for as long as he continues to perform that work.
6. Zhou Taihe 1984, 171-73.
7. "On Issues of the Current Agriculture Policies (1982)," in *Collection of Documents on Economic Reform 1977-1983* 1984, 159-66.
8. In the Chinese Revolutionary History Museum in Beijing there is a brief record about this incident. The 26 December 1988 *Beijing People's Daily* carried an article on page 7 written by Wang Lixing entitled, "The Time after Mao Zedong," which provided additional information.

9. Zhou Taihe 1984, 173.
10. Ibid., 185-87.
11. *Almanac of China's Statistics 1986*, 167.
12. "CCCP's Decisions on Accelerating Agricultural Development," in *Almanac of China's Economy 1981*, 102.
13. Zhou Taihe 1984, 174, 102-6, 271-73.
14. The establishment of the Soviet-type economic system took place from 1953 to 1957. The Great Leap Forward started in 1958 and officially ended in 1960. The early 1960s economic adjustment occupied the period from 1961 to 1965. The Cultural Revolution spanned 1966 to late 1976 and early 1977.
15. The vertical integration determined by the central ministries usually curbed horizontal contacts, transactions, and integrations, which would obviously have weakened a ministry's control. Early in the reform process, the bureaucracies often joined together to block the reforms that led to more freedom for enterprises.
16. "Temporary Regulations on Implementing the New Financial Management System of *hua fen shou zhi, fen ji bao gan*," in *Collection of Documents on Economic Reform 1977-1983* 1984, 813-14. The name of this policy used very uncommon wording. Since any direct interpretation could be misleading, the original pingying Chinese is used here in an attempt to avoid misunderstanding.
17. "Local economies" refers to the economies under the jurisdiction or control of local governments. Local economies make up only some of the economies housed within certain geographic administrative boundaries: the others would be the economies under the control of the central government.
18. "Regulation for the Trial of Financial Management Connecting Income and Expenses, Sharing Total Income, Clearing Budget in Proportion and Keeping Same Ratio for Three Years (*shou zhi gua gou, quan er fen cheng, bi li bao gan, san nian bu bian*)," in *Collection of Documents on Economic Reform 1977-1983* 1984, 804-5. This regulation was issued by the State Council on 13 July 1979.
19. "Regulation for the Trial of Financial Management Identifying and Separating Income and Expense, Clearing up Budget at Each Level" (*hua fen shou zhi, fen ji bao gan*)," in *Collection of Documents on Economic Reform 1977-1983* 1984, 806-7. This regulation was issued by the State Council on 13 July 1979.
20. The reform of 1980 was called, in Chinese, *hua fen shou zhi, fen ji bao gan*. For details see "Temporary Regulations on Implementing New the Financial Management System of *hua fen shou zhi, fen ji bao gan*," in

Collection of Documents on Economic Reform 1977-1983 1984, 813-14.

21. "CST's Announcement on Improving the *hua fen shou zi, fen ji bao gan* Financial Management System," in *Collection of Documents on Economic Reform 1977-1983* 1984, 841.

22. Further, provincial officials were granted new authority to adjust the tax rates imposed at their levels of jurisdiction, and a group of "extrabudgetary funds" (money that local authorities could gather that did not appear in their budgets, so escaping state government inspection) expanded dramatically after 1979. These funds were drawn from industrial, commercial, and agricultural surtaxes, the profits of collective enterprises, and fees for administering free markets among other sources. They had existed from the early 1950s but had never before reached anywhere near these proportions. According to central-level reckoning, extra budgetary revenue in recent years may have amounted to the equivalent of about half of total budgetary revenues.

23. Zhou Taihe 1984, 78-80 for the adjustment in the 1950s; 120-25 for that of the 1960s; and 134-47 for the changes in the early 1970s.

24. Ibid., 71-72, 137-41.

25. "Regulations on Expanding Autonomy of the State Enterprises," in *Collection of Documents on Economic Reform 1977-1983* 1984, 128-29. "Report on National Meeting of *li gai sui*," in *Collection of Documents on Economic Reform 1977-1983* 1984, 908-15.

26. "Finance Ministry on Experiment of *li gai shui*," in Selected Enterprises," in *Collection of Documents on Economic Reform 1977-1983* 1984, 863.

27. This measure was called *li gai sui*, which could be translated as "converting profit submission to taxation."

28. Prior to this tax reform, most of China's state enterprises were operated under the following system: the profits from the majority of their products, which were usually regulated under the state plan, were surrendered to the state; the profits from surplus products were shared between the state and an enterprise. Sometimes the system worked in such a way that enterprises surrendered their planned profits and shared with the state their extra profits.

29. "Temporary Regulations of Income Tax on the State Enterprises," in *Collection of Documents on Economic Reform 1977-1983* 1984, 916-18.

30. Usually, those enterprises in deficit prior to the tax reform had received a fixed subsidy from the government and the subsidy would be adjusted if they performed better and reduced their deficit. In order to introduce incentives to these enterprises to improve their performance, they were permitted to keep their subsidies after they earned some profit; only

when their profits exceeded some set amount would the subsidies be discontinued.

31. "The State Council's Temporary Regulations on Promoting Lateral Economic Cooperation," in *Collection of Documents on Economic Reform 1977-1983* 1984, 207-8.

32. "CCCP's Decision on Issues of Promoting Industrial Development (draft)" (extract) in *Collection of Documents on Economic Reform 1977-1983* 1984, 171-75.

33. The experiment in these three cities was described in chapter 1 and in an earlier section of this chapter.

34. Efficiency is a theoretical concept and doesn't always correlate with practical experience New terms relating to budget, profit, and productivity, need to be used. There is, in other words, no universal measure of the efficiency of economic activities in reality. A smooth conversion of a centrally planned system to a market system might depend on, apart from the timing and coordination of policies, behavioral and institutional memory. The Chinese reform process appeared to reveal that such a conversion would be easier if there were some relevant experiences that could be invoked.

35. Arrow 1974, 63.

36. Deng Xiaoping, "To Construct Socialism with Chinese Characteristics," in *Selection of Important Documents Since the 12th Congress* 1986, 515 (30 June 1984).

4

Analyzing Reform Since the Mid-1980s

Departure From the First-Phase Reform's Path

As Chinese economic reform proceeded into its fifth year or so —
about 1984 — some of the basic elements that had characterized the
first phase of reform began to change significantly. While first-phase
reform did indeed bring some vitality into the stagnant economy, most
of the long-term, serious problems remained. Except for agriculture,
the reforms had not yet produced any dramatic turnaround in
production performance or living standards. Meanwhile, though the
success of agricultural reform posed a challenge to the reform
movement's policymakers, questions arose about the basic beliefs of
reform and the understanding of why and what to reform. Specifically,
the dominant belief of the first-phase reform in improving the CPE
could not stand in the face of the new reality; the old concern of
preserving the CPE made less and less sense as more evidence showed
that most people benefited from economic freedom and the
opportunity to make their own decisions. In terms of reform approach,

too, looking for guidance only from within China's own experiences became increasingly important.

Events since the mid-1980s have substantiated the departure from the earlier path of reform. At this time, China's reform set out more clearly toward a market-oriented economy, and the major parts of the CPE started to disintegrate. Price controls were gradually lifted and the market set prices. These new efforts to reform the price system obviously differed from earlier price-related reform efforts, which had been corrections to the distorted price system designed to achieve a set of prices that better reflected costs. In terms of enterprise reform, the new focus was no longer on what kind of authority should be granted to enterprises or on how to share profits between government and enterprise, but on how to withdraw government controls from business and to develop true free enterprise. In terms of the market's share of control over economic activities, 50 percent of resources and products were allocated by the market at the end of 1988.[1] At the same time, the private economy, which operated outside of central planning, already counted for 36 percent of the nation's industrial production. By late 1992, it is estimated that the allocation of about three-quarters of resources and products will be through the market.[2] From the perspective of the market's function in the economy, its substantial control over the economy was in sharp contrast to the supplementary role it had played earlier in the reform process.

In addition, by the mid-1980s, the improvement in China's overall economic performance brought more enlightened thought on development strategy and the actual meaning of reform.[3] Performance statistics generated by the reforms posed an incontrovertible challenge to the old ideology and thinking habits in the selection of economic situations and development strategies. Adding to the sense of the CPE's failure, evidence of the initial success of reform, particularly in agriculture, taught decision makers and the general populace a lesson about their choices that most of them had not fully comprehended at the outset. The essence of the lesson appeared to be simple: that people would be better off, as would the whole economy, from greater freedom and more diversified policy decisions. All of these developments indicated that fundamental changes underway in the overall economic system would take leave of the CPE. This led to the emergence of the second-phase reform. These changes were reflected in changes in the dominant belief about economic reform, the approach to reform, its chief concerns, and the overall understanding of what needed reforming and how to do it. I will now turn to the paradigm for analyzing Chinese economic reform in its second phase, beginning with its dominant belief.

The Shifting Reform Belief

The dominant belief of second-phase reform is hard to define with a static concept because it tended to shift. What is clear was that the direction of these shifts was increasingly in favor of the market. In other words, the dominant belief of reformers was increasingly comprised of acceptance of the market as the goal of reform. But the crux of the dominant belief for the second phase needed to be widened to include consideration of existing economic institutions.

Attributing Failures to Central Planning

Importantly, this dominant belief reflected not only an awareness of the fundamental failure of the existing economic system, but also the attribution of that failure to the centrally planned economic system. During the first phase of the reform, as discussed in chapter 2, the failure of the Chinese economy had been attributed to the radical and ideology-oriented strategy of economic development. The first phase of economic reform was based on faith in the CPE and on the specific belief that a realistic and pragmatic strategy within its framework could solve the existing economic problems. In contrast, during the second phase of China's economic reform, the failures in the economy were attributed to the institutions of the CPE. Specifically, while early reform severely criticized the ideology-driven economic strategy, its dominant belief was still to improve, not to dissolve, the central planning mechanism and to keep state ownership intact. The reform in the second phase, in contrast, actually tried to abandon, in a gradual way, the central planning mechanism and to transform the existing ownership system.

Even though the dominant belief of the second phase — the intention to abandon the CPE totally — was not declared publicly, the actual reforms in areas of the economy were plainly leading to a market-oriented economy. The Chinese economic reform movement since the mid-1980s included two major processes: first, shrinkage of the planned coverage corresponding to expansion of the market coverage of the economy; second, shrinkage of the state-owned economy corresponding to expansion of the private economies. It was indeed a fact that for most of the period, development of the market and of a free enterprise system was not officially spelled out as a part of the goal of reform. However, this apparent ambiguity simply revealed the special complexity of the Chinese reform: it as not theory or goal guided but rather, as I call it, a historical movement toward economic liberation — without a banner.

The Evolving Definition of Economic Reform

Before discussing the dominant belief further, it would be well to study the definitions of China's economic reform, which have been evolving ever since it began. Essentially, there has been no unanimously accepted, clear-cut, and stable definition of the reform in Chinese economic literature. It is possible, though, to gain a clear picture of the development of the economic reform and a good understanding of the dynamic concept of economic reform. In general, the evolution of definitions of China's economic reform falls roughly into either two or three major stages, depending on whether the second stage is divided. The three stages can be described as follows:

First stage: 1979-84. In light of the obvious failure of the economy and widespread dissatisfaction with it after more than ten years of upheaval during the Cultural Revolution, Chinese economic reform focused on improving and renovating the centrally planned system. As stated previously, reform was presumed to be an internal rearrangement for self-improvement within the centrally planned system rather than a departure from it. Specific reform efforts during that time included recovering material incentive and profit measures, transferring more authority to local governments from the central government, and developing a limited and confined market for agricultural products and other small commodities.[4] The actual reforms reflected, to a large extent, the basic understanding that if workers and managers at different levels of the economic hierarchy could be (appropriately) motivated by introducing new incentive mechanisms that recognized their interests, then the planned economy could be greatly improved.[5] Reform was seen as serving the purpose of improving the efficiency of the centrally planned and state-owned economy.

Second stage: The definition of the economic reform seems to be the most ambiguous during the period 1984 to 1986. The overwhelming success of agricultural reform resulted in an emancipation of ideas on economic reform and suggested a breakaway from the previous understanding of the subject. The dissolution of rural communes had marked a major departure from the old system; in particular, the new governance structures of long-term contracting and leasing (as will be discussed in more detail later on) between the government and farmers set an example for reform that began to transform economic institutions and the economic behavior of agents and businesses without immediately resolving the ownership question.[6] During this period, it seemed there was nothing in the orthodox theory of socialist economy that could not be challenged. In more complex and uncertain reform situations, a variety of experiments were conducted across regions and economic sectors in an effort to transform the centrally planned economic system. However, the effect of rural reform on urban reform (1984 to 1985) was not much more than an emancipation of thought, given that urban industries are much more complex and interdependent. Calls for improving socialism could be heard, but they were no longer dominant. As options diverged and the future course of reform for the overall economy became more uncertain, the definition of economic reform became more ambiguous and controversial. This second stage of defining economic reform was primarily transitional and can be merged with the next stage.

Third stage: Economic reform had been defined primarily in relation to the market since 1986, in part due to lessons learned from agricultural reform. Chinese economic reform at this time involved the dismantling and remaking of economic institutions in general, with strong contributions from a younger generation of economists than had heretofore been involved, and an ever-widening array of experiments and debates was underway in both microeconomic and macroeconomic fields. In this period, Chinese economic reform mainly focused on resolving the problems of state-owned enterprises and on development of the market.[7] In this period, officially, the mission purpose of reform was defined as "to establish a socialist commodity (market) economy," which was referred to by the principle that "government regulates the market and the market guides business." Even though the market economy was explicitly announced as the goal only in late 1992, in many policy and theory papers, the phrase "market economy" had been clearly used in defining reform issues.[8]

Ambiguous Identification and Clear Action

Returning to the issue of dominant belief, it is interesting to note the reform movement's ambiguity on the subject of its definitions and goals. This confusion is probably best reflected in the widely used term "socialism with Chinese characteristics" used by Deng in 1984 and which was often quoted as a vague explanation of the goal of reform.[9] This "socialism with Chinese characteristics" was never clearly and publicly defined. "Chinese characteristics" referred nebulously to China's large population, geographical dimensions, multiple nationalities, diversity in level and type of economic development among regions, and developing-nation status in general. At first, the vague term "socialism with Chinese characteristics" appeared to preserve the empty principles of socialism and to allow nonsocialist economic activities. In 1987, an even more ambiguous concept of a primitive-stage socialism was raised in line with "socialism with Chinese characteristics" during the Thirteenth Party Congress. Zhao Ziyang, the general secretary of the party, specifically laid out at the congress the central government's guidelines for work in China's "primitive-stage socialism," which emphasized the importance of economic reform, productivity growth, nonisolationist policies, and a market economy.[10] Ambiguous words for the reform were also intended in part to avoid the frustration of "unnecessary" controversies over ideology. It was not until 1992, when, after Deng's swing earlier that year, the shyness about using the market concept disappeared. The phenomenon of there being no clear-cut definition for economic reform also reflected the complexity of the uniquely peculiar Chinese tact for handling political conflict in which both sides fought over the issue of defining the economic reform while giving the appearance of not actually fighting. It is also worth mentioning that the terms in use sometimes depended largely on a top leader's preference, revealing that such an issue as defining the reform was sometimes just a matter of "word play." It is worth bearing in mind that, given the circumstances of Chinese politics, the conventional interpretation of such terms could be misleading; what often deserves more attention is what actually takes place.

Theoretical and verbal ambiguity in the official definition of the reform, however, did not necessarily prevent reform practice from moving in a rather clear direction. It is possible that the spontaneous development of economic institutions drives certain changes in an economic system and takes a reform direction that might not be readily apparent. Many phenomena and incidents during the reform were new and there was not much experience or knowledge about them. The pitfall is that people tend to generalize an ongoing event as simpler than it really is: an unfolding event usually exposes only limited aspects of itself, and this is compounded by people's limited capacity to perceive, take in, and interpret the information available to them. Instead of making the world easier to comprehend, the enormous growth of human knowledge in the modern world spurs humans to try to understand the world with a more comprehensive way of thinking that is closer to the nature and complexity of reality, which itself often *is* vague. On the issue of the ambiguous definition of the Chinese reform, keeping such a profound social and economic movement open ended may have helped the Chinese overcome both the physical and mental difficulties throughout the process.

Meanwhile, facts and records provide a means of assessing the development of reform. Some of the actual changes during the reform years were significant: China evolved from a typical CPE in 1978 to an economy in 1988 with essentially all of its agricultural production based on the family and half of its industrial production already covered by the market. [11] In addition, the share of the private industrial sector in the Chinese economy as a whole was growing rapidly, with an annual rate of 2 to 2.5 percent. [12]

Getting to Understand the Market

Evidence for a substantial change in dominant beliefs can be found in the leadership's understanding of a market economy. In the early years, the concept of market was introduced with the clear reservation that the market economy was only supplemental to the CPE. Chen Yun, for example made this point explicit in his comments in late 1981 on newly emerged market activities.[13] In 1982, in a major central government report presented by Hu Yaobang, the Chinese economy was still officially called a "planned economy on the basis of public ownership."[14] But in the later phase of the reform, the market economy was claimed to be the "necessary condition" for modernization that "cannot be skipped and jumped over" (this appeared for the first time in an official document presented by Zhao Ziyang in 1987).[15] Compared to making economic management and business operation systems the major target of reform, as the early reform movement had done, the later reform focused on altering the state enterprises and the price system. By late 1987 and early 1988, the Chinese economy was being described as a "socialist market (i.e., commodity) economy.[16] In other words, the dominant belief of the economic reform reflected the perception of a market-oriented economy as an acceptable and necessary change. By 1988, China was close to claiming to be a market economy with certain socialist characteristics. Although the term was still ambiguous and could be interpreted in different ways, by emphasizing the aspects of either the market or plan, the concept of the market economy was in effect used in policy documentation. About four years later, after certain periods when the process of acceptance halted mainly due to the politic situation, this issue appeared to be finally resolved in 1992.

Further, a substantial change in dominant beliefs could be seen in the "open search" approach to new economic institutions. As most of the direct experiences with the CPE and the efforts to adjust the system were exhausted after the first phase of reform, the reformers turned for study to models from other economies. More important, as the economic reform turned toward the CPE system itself, the value of past reform experiences, which were based on the attempt to improve the CPE system, fell dramatically. Therefore, the new dominant belief resulted in a corresponding need to change the approach to reform that would be appropriate to the search for a new economic system. The new approach to reform, as will be discussed in detail in the following section, differed significantly from the earlier one and reflected the evolution of the dominant belief.

Convincing Facts from New Experiences

The formation of the new dominant belief was influenced mainly by the fresh experiences gleaned from reform practices. There are two points that need to be made clear: first, no particular source of ideas seemed to lead to the breakthrough of belief in economic reform. Second, reform practices created new experiences that provided numerous facts to make decision makers and other people involved change their mind about reform. First of all, briefly speaking, due to limited openness and the inherited characteristics of the human assets, constraints on the availability of information and the human ability to interpret that information combined to prevent the reform decision makers from effectively accepting new ideas and turning them into policy. "Human assets" here specifically refers to those associated with reform decision making. The inherited characteristics of human assets emphasize the attributes of this group of people, who still harbored prejudices against the outside world, along with habits of control and domination. By the mid-1980s, the goal of the reform had become controversial, and there were ongoing debates on its interpretation. Particularly, the overall environment for intellectual inquiry and policy analysis in China did not change so much as to permit free discussion even limited just to nonpolitical issues. Even though they were by and large pragmatic compared to the former leadership, the reform leaders' knowledge and experiences constituted a formidable barrier against new information about the capitalist economy. For them, to a large extent, only facts drawn from their own experience seemed to be convincing. Indeed, it reveals an unfortunate aspect of this story that the development of the economy and the choices of millions of people were still largely in the hands of a few.

Second of all, the new experiences with reform practices produced an endless source of evidence that influenced decision makers as well as the populace in building up new beliefs and accepting new ideas. The more deeply the centralized system was reformed, the more profoundly its problems were exposed, so that more and more benefit was likely to be seen in further reform. Satisfaction was short-lived, and new demands for an economic entity independent from any government interference emerged and grew. As reforms toward more autonomy proceeded, enterprises, managers, and workers kept adapting themselves to the changing economic institutions and learned to make decisions in the midst of uncertainty. After the adjustment of some of the planned prices to market prices, and the benefits of market-oriented reform became foreseeable, the question was raised as to why the government had to preserve overall price control rather than letting the market set all prices. Various practices, both designed and spontaneous, provided convincing evidence of the advantage of market price controls. Because of price incentives, even limited as they mainly had been to a certain portion of total production, the shortages that had been endemic in the economy were alleviated by the mid-1980s. Some free markets already emerged silently all over the country and demonstrated the effect of the market on economic development.

The experience of Wenzhou, for example, attracted the attention of the nation in the mid-1980s for its economic success due to a much less controlled and less planned economic system. Wenzhou is a district in the southeast of Zejiang Province; Wenzhou had been one of the poorest areas in the province prior to the reform, with almost no modern industry and an especially backward transportation system. Since the economic reform at the end of the 1970s, the local government had implemented a less interventionist policy, with little control over production and price. In Wenzhou, private businesses quickly overwhelmed the state-owned businesses and most prices were determined in the market. As the result, Wenzhou developed the largest free market in consumer commodities in the country by the late 1980s and maintained an annual growth rate of about 20 percent.[17] Experiences like Wenzhou's delivered a message that when the government imposed less control over production and price, the economy performed much better.

In the country as a whole, since agricultural reform had delivered the message that emancipation of thought was a critical condition for further reform of the CPE, the practice of reform became a driving force moving the dominant belief forward. In general, all of these reforms together paved the way for the dominant belief to leave behind its first stage and enter its second. Therefore, it was reform practice, rather than ideological preference or a theoretical model, that originally led the transition from the first phase to the second phase of China's reform movement.

In sum, the shift of the dominant belief from improving the CPE to moving out of it and toward a market-based economy can be attributed to the new experience of reform practices up to the mid-1980s. These reform practices, based on a variety of designed and spontaneous experiments, provided new experiences for and comparisons between the old and the emerging economic systems, taught new knowledge about living and working in a more decentralized and diversified economy, and built up a new capacity among government officials, enterprise managers, and people in general to seek reform and adapt to new economic institutions.

The metamorphosis of the dominant belief was reflected in changes in the approach to reform and its chief concerns. Following are discussions of these.

"Touching Stones While Walking Across a River": Approach 2

China's economic reform in the second phase for the most part still employed the approach of "touching stones while walking across a river." Although there were several attempts to design a grand blueprint to package several major reforms — price reform, financial reform, tax reform, and monetary reform — together (specifically called "integrated reform"),[18] this kind of scheme did not get a real chance to be tried out, and reform continued to proceed in a step-by-step and problem-by-problem manner.

More accurately, China's second-phase economic reform adopted an *open* "touching stones" approach. In appearance, this approach seemed to be the same as the previous one, with both emphasizing the importance of experimentation in arriving at a new policy. But beneath the surface, there existed an underlying difference in the kinds of sources from which they drew their experiences and references.

Open Sources Experiments

Contrary to the "closed source" of direct experience, the reform of the second phase drew upon open and diversified sources, including experiences and theories evolved from other developed and developing market economies and also the reforming East European economies. More varied experiments took place as a result of this eclectic borrowing.

Obviously, the openness and diversification of sources for experiments provided greater opportunity for reform to find solutions to existing problems. This open approach allowed an array of experiences to be conducted as long as some potential value was foreseen; hence, an idea could be tested and developed or a policy design evaluated and adjusted before being fully implemented, and the real-world responses to a potential policy design could be assessed before too many resources were committed to the project. Importantly, the approach of using multiple, simultaneous experiments provided a mechanism to acquire information and detect uncertainties (since flaws could be slow to manifest themselves) and, consequently, to prevent or at least reduce chaos and fluctuation. Interestingly, this approach fostered higher tolerance for diversified and daring experiments despite the proliferation of unaccustomed activities and incidents that sometimes increased the confusion and contradictions entailed in the reform. One of the advantages of the open approach was that it could forestall prematurely negative judgments and thus avoid being detailed by initial uncertainties. Experiences from other countries and other economic systems, no matter how successful they might have been, needed to be carefully examined and evaluated with the understanding that all experiences are colored by their context and timing.

New Pattern of Institutional Selection

Differences between the open and closed approaches lay especially in the environment for institutional selection and innovation. The open approach entailed more alternatives and possibilities and permitted healthy selection and innovation of economic institutions; this brought greater freedom of choice and more tolerance for different ideas, as well as emphasized the importance of breadth of economic experience. This in turn encouraged diversity and differentiation, two concepts basic to a healthy environment of institutional evolution. A constant flow of information from the outside world would create new elements of diversity and differentiation, and would help to counter the forces of convergence and homogenization in the development and selection of economic institutions.

The transformation of the CPE has been a new endeavor for the Chinese. Imagination and innovation in the reform process were inevitably influenced by experiences and retrievable knowledge, and subject to certain limitations of reach. By introducing experiments and knowledge from outside China's system, they expanded those limitations on imagination and innovation. In the search for a new economic system, the open approach is faster than the closed approach and faces fewer pitfalls due to blindness. The experiences from and knowledge about other economic systems often provide a sense of direction, rather than a duplicable design, in reforming and selecting economic institutions. Such a sense of direction is often critical to the speed of the search for a new economic system. While institutional selection emphasizes spontaneous process, and designed innovation is more akin to imaginative change, they are usually inseparable parts of the evolution (including revolution in certain dramatic cases) of economic institutions. It is possible, indeed, that the closed approach could eventually have reached what the open approach has, but the time and the paths involved would likely have been different, as would, consequently, the costs and outcomes. Some of the others' experiences and knowledge about economic institutions stand out only after extended periods of competition with and selection among relevant species of economic institutions. Some of this long process of competition and selection could be saved by adopting the open approach. Even though the open approach does not mean the simple and direct copy of other economic systems, it does expand the space of possibility in searching for a new system.

Challenges to Human Assets: Old Experiences Cannot Help

The shift from the closed to the open approach took place when China's own experiences and knowledge were no longer very relevant to the reform process. Driven by the success of the early reform movement but constrained by limited knowledge about the market economy, the shift of economic reform from the closed to the open approach was a natural development out of China's determined search for a better economic system. As the economic reform switched from the determination to improve the CPE to the desire to establish a whole new system, China simply did not have the inventory of experiences needed to organize and operate modern industry in the marketplace, let alone the elements of a market system. By that time the agricultural reform had already indicated that the economy would respond extremely quickly to changes in the economic system, and people were eager to bring similar changes to other parts of the economy. But when Chinese economic reform turned its attention from the rural areas to the much more complex urban economy, what the success of the agricultural reform actually meant to other reforms was little more than inspiration. In brief, the reason was simply that the other portions of the economy had little in common with agriculture and many substantive differences. There was no assurance that the same strategy of dividing the collective assets and organizational units would lead to the same success. Particularly, the agricultural economy, unlike the urban economy, had scant institutional memory of the family-based economic system. (The little market economy there had been prior to the establishment of the CPE in China had been confined to a handful of coastal cities.) Thus, there was a clear need to borrow from external sources in carrying out urban reform, and this need was filled by the adoption of an open approach to change. Likewise, the switch from the closed to the open approach also revealed that nonagricultural reforms faced different challenges to the existing human assets in the CPE. The simple formula that the success of China's agricultural reform in the first phase had suggested was to dismantle the mandatory collective organization of the economy and to let each individual or family run production on its own with discrete assets and capital. As has been mentioned earlier, the primary assets were human assets, and in the transition from one economic system to another, the challenges and costs of converting existing human assets to a new system would be much less were there to exist an institutional memory to call upon.

With the open approach, meanwhile, the reform encountered more uncertainty than ever before since the new experiments were not derived from direct experiences and institutional memories, and, in particular, since models from other economies usually were introduced with incomplete information. Limited information and knowledge were formidable obstacles for the reform with this approach, and often this obstacle was hidden and ignored.

A Variety of Thoughts and Experiments

From late 1984 on, various new ideas for reform policies and experiments were introduced. In 1984, Lou Jiwei and Zhou Xiaochuan put forward one of the earliest proposals for price reform.[19] They systematically raised the issue of allocation efficiency and proposed price adjustments as the initial means for establishing a new price system. Basically, Lou and Zhou followed the track of Oscar Lange, who tried to reach equilibrium prices under a centrally planned system by using market information. Indeed, the proposal did not elude the trap of "the competitive solution," as it was called by Hayek, and the "artificial market," as it was called by Mises. Hayek's criticism is pertinent here and is given in Karen I. Vaughn's synopsis: "While the models the socialists were using to arrive at their solution to the pricing problem were not logically contradictory and socialism was not therefore impossible in the sense of being theoretically inconceivable, it was nevertheless practically impossible since the socialist models bore no relation to the manner in which the prices were formed in the real world."[20] Hayek particularly pointed out the fundamental differences in discovering, transmitting, and using information in the pricing processes of a market economy and a centrally planned economy. To Mises, without the entrepreneur, who is necessary to enable the market to entrust the conduct of business affairs to those men who have succeeded in filling the most urgent wants of consumers, economic calculation is impossible.[21] It appears that the Chinese at the time were not much aware of the details of the scholarly debate on market socialism. Given this assumption, Lou and Zhou had already achieved important progress in breaking away from the old idea of taking prices as accounting units in the planned economic system.

From 1983 to 1984, some experiments on shareholding appeared spontaneously with no guidance or endorsement from the central government. For example, in May 1983 an investment company in Baoan County, Shenzhen, tried the experiment of instituting a shareholding system by publicly issuing shareholding cards; in mid-

1984, the Tianqiao Department Store Shareholding Company in Beijing emerged as the first of its kind; in late 1984, the Shanghai Feirue Acoustic Company became the first to issue shares to the public in a professional, standardized way.[22] Serious discussions on policy formulation started in 1985, as shown by a World Bank Report and a proposal by Wu Jiaxiang and Jin Lizhuo.[23] The debate on shareholding issues was clearly interested in exploring whether and how to transform the state-owned enterprises by means of shareholding experiments. Even though the role of the market and its real policy implications were not fully comprehensible, raising the question of shareholding experiments was a substantive attack on the existing centrally planned and state-owned system.

An investigation conducted in 1985 by the China National Institute for Economic Reform suggested that the reform should go beyond decentralization and emphasize the market development while the central planning system still existed. Another investigation by this same body on the development experience of Shenzhen, one of the original special economic zones, suggested in 1988 that, based on Shenzhen's specific circumstances, an experiment should be conducted adopting Hong Kong's major economic regulation system and reforming its own civil service and legal system.[24]

The Group on Agriculture Development observed in 1985 that both reform and economic development were being conducted in an environment of unprecedented flux in economic structures, systems, and values in the overall economy.[25] This study placed China's economic reform within the larger context of economic institutions and the historic transformation of economic systems.

In 1986, Hua Sheng and others proposed an "asset responsibility operating system" in an attempt to reform the state enterprises by connecting reassessment of assets to establishment of economic responsibility and rationalization of enterprise behavior.[26] As a result of this proposal, "asset responsibility operating system" became a new experiment at the time.

Wang Hui, Li Rengyu, and Lui Kaixiang proposed in 1988 acceleration of the development of the legal system to provide protection for the rapidly growing market activities, observing that the development of market transactions and contractual relations in China was desperately in need of the protection of the law. Further, the article put forth the premise that legal order would be crucially important for the future transformation to a market economy.[27]

In these last years of the second phase of reform, economists, including Wu Jinlian, Zhou Xiaochuan, and Lui Guoguang, proposed setting up regulations to protect competition from monopoly, local protectionism, and market coalitions.[28]

By 1987, a series of studies on other countries' economic institutions and experiences was introduced, including monographs on Yugoslavia, Hungary, the Four Small Dragons, Japan, Western Europe, and the United States. These studies were largely responsible for providing Chinese economic reformers with fresh comparative material. Chinese economists and policy analysts conducted these studies on foreign experiences with great enthusiasm in the hope of finding answers to their questions. These studies included: an investigation of the experiment in worker autonomy in Yugoslavia (1985, 1986); studies on the grand reform plan in Hungary (1985, 1986); a study on the German and Swedish economies in an attempt to learn how to protect competition and how to use macroeconomic instruments; and an analysis of the model of manager-dominant enterprise in Japan (1987) (which contrasted with the usual owner-dominant model).[29] At the same time, Western economists were invited to consult with their Chinese counterparts on issues of reform and development. In the early days of the second phase of reform, the Chinese respectfully turned to the West for suggestions concerning the problems China faced. In 1985, for example, ten Western economists, including Nobel laureates and chiefs of the central banks of some of the major Western countries, were invited to China to conduct a joint discussion on the problems of the economic reform.[30]

Special Economic Zones as a New Reference and Testing Ground

The acceleration of the experiment with Special Economic Zones (SEZs) since 1984 also provided evidence supporting the open approach to reform, demonstrating the advantages of flexibility and responsiveness. The SEZs had been developed from the beginning as a market-oriented economy dependent largely on foreign investments and export and, therefore, by 1984 were recognized as examples of the open approach to reforming the Chinese economy. After four to five years of experiments, the four SEZs and their adjacent areas had become the most dynamic and rapidly growing regions in China. Take Shenzhen, the largest of the four SEZs, for example. Shenzhen's national domestic product grew from 270 million yuan in 1980 to 3.3 billion yuan in 1985; its export rose from 11 million U.S. dollars to 563 million U.S. dollars during the same period.[31] The experiments with SEZs were expanded in 1984 to fourteen major cities along the coasts. These fourteen cities included industrialized zones like Shanghai, Tianjing, Gusngzhou, Dalian, and Chindao, and developing cities like Chinhuangdao, Yantai, Nantong, Nipo, and Beihai.[32] Even though the SEZ experiments were restricted to a certain area of each city, this expansion indicated that the opening-up policy had become one of the most important components of the whole reform scheme. Moreover, the spreading out of SEZ experiments to fourteen cities hastened the entry of the Chinese economy into the world economy. The significance of this bold move was in its connecting of China's economic development with the world market and in exposing the existing economic system to more direct challenges from the outside world.

Soon afterward, the major policies of the SEZ were adopted elsewhere inland, and minority provinces began about late 1985 to try some SEZ experiments, particularly in certain regions of the provinces along the Yangtze River and in Xinjiang and Inner Mongolia. The SEZ experiment at the provincial level in Hainan was initiated at the end of 1987 and fully underway by 1988. The unspoken agenda behind the Hainan experiment was to set the island up as a more ambitious experiment in free market economy on the order of Taiwan. Given the physical isolation of Hainan's economy, the risks of failure and damage caused by fluctuation, if they occurred, could best be contained there.

Since the SEZs were open directly to the outside world, they faced immediate challenge and competition from the world market. The experiences of the SEZs showed that the bureaucratic process of the planning system and government control were inherently in conflict with the desire of enterprises and investors for efficiency. (Bribery, of course, helped to alleviate the conflict temporarily, but bribery is itself a loss of efficiency.) Since, for example, investors would take their money elsewhere if the governments or regulatory bodies of the SEZs could not swiftly respond to their demands, SEZs gradually became an open testing ground for new policies and institutions.

One of the seemingly elementary but most important lessons from the SEZ experiment was that the absence of central planning and government control spurred economic development. In general, at least two implications of the SEZs made the experiments astonishing and enlightening. First, opening up to the outside world enabled an economy to develop much faster, even without planned funds from the government, than otherwise. In the ten years from 1979 to 1988, the total industrial production in the first four SEZs increased 16 times, much faster than the national average of 2.3 times during the same period.[33] Second, the economy of the SEZs, which was almost free of central planning and control, illustrated how an economy survived and thrived in the market. Compared with the governments in other parts of China, the governments in the SEZs had the least interference over the economy and business. One of the important features that distinguished the SEZ economies from others was that they were not subject to central planning and price controls.

Lessons of Intellectual Reasoning

The role of the Chinese economists in the reform movement is worth mentioning here in relation to the reform approach during the early period. There was a lack of theoretical exploration and intellectual reasoning concerning the CPE system for a long time before the reform. Economic literature was confined mainly to the interpretation of policy. Very few economists ventured to explore and tell the truth about the economy. Sun Yefang and Gu Zhun were among the few. Their observations were confirmed by some prominent economists, such as Yu Guangyuan, after the beginning of the reform.[34] Sun had insisted on basing socialist planning on the concept of costs and the law of value in the mid-1950s.[35] Even though he did not go so far as to challenge central planning or state ownership, Sun demonstrated his seriousness and courage in pursuing truth as an economist. Unfortunately, he was treated harshly for daring to question the dominant view of ignoring costs in central planning.

Gu made a real contribution to the critique of the CPE. Gu argued in 1957 that the goal state of the socialist economy should be "making rewards to workers directly relating to the profit of an enterprise, and making price the main instrument for signaling production."[36] Gu further speculated that, in the desired state of the economy, "enterprises would spontaneously choose and adjust production based upon profit, price would spontaneously rise and fall, and then the movement of prices would actually provide signals for increasing or decreasing production." Moreover, Gu claimed that the plan should be one kind of forecasting or target-setting tool, and that the mandatory requirements for enterprise under the plan should be reduced. To Gu, independent cost accounting was necessary for the production of enterprises, enterprises naturally responded to prices in seeking advantage and profits, the plan could not replace the market, and the plan should be a forecast instead of a "synthesis of many individual plans." Gu pioneered the discussion of socialist economy on the grounds of the relationship between market price and production and the nature of the plan. Considering the fact that Gu made his criticism against the prevailing orthodoxy of mandatory central planning and that China had then had only three years of experience with the CPE, Gu was remarkably insightful. Paying a high price for his economic thought, however, Gu suffered from political persecution for the rest of his later life.[37]

In more than twenty years, very few economists spoke up for Sun and Gu. There were many explanations for this; among them, the long period of totalitarian political control is mostly to blame. It was true that Chinese intellectuals before the reform were denied the freedom to pursue the truth in an environment where this was encouraged. However, it has to be admitted that the tendency of intellectuals to make compromises might also have played a part. Intellectual reasoning needs liberty of thought and exchange, but it also requires the passion, endurance, and courage to believe in the truth, to pursue it and to speak for it. During at least half of the reform decade, the range of voices from economists and other intellectuals shaping policy reform was regrettably narrow, and the reform movement was the worse for their lack. (Some fundamental problems, such as market and ownership, for instance, were hardly challenged.) Of course, those few who courageously spoke out on these issues — for example, Dong Furen on reforming state ownership and Jiang Yiwei on "enterprise standard" — are remembered.[38] The narrow scope of intellectual inquiry in the first years of reform seemed to have contributed to the closed experimental approach of early Chinese economic reform. This situation changed rapidly as the reform entered its second phase and adopted the open approach that allowed all the experiences and theories from other economies to be studied, borrowed, and compared. Debates among different schools of economic thought, which sometimes became heated during this period, reflected progress in the impact of economists on reform policy decisions.[39]

From another perspective, after being silent or giving up the pursuit of truth for decades, few economists were prepared for such a profound movement to transform the planned economic system. Had they been prepared, some critical issues, such as property rights and market institutions, would have been better and earlier addressed than they actually were. The real situation was that these important issues of reform were not effectively explored during the early reform. In contrast, it was essentially peasants and officials who drew on their limited experiences and who experimented with specific ways of reform. Indeed, economists could never replace those who directly operated production and business as an experiment, but they did have the opportunity to shed the light of economic theory and intellectual reasoning on reform and policy-making. This phenomenon, to a certain degree, also reflected the nature of the human assets inherited at the outset of the reform.

Chief Concerns of the Second-Phase Reform

For the second phase of China's economic reform, the chief concerns appeared to be efficiency and manageability. This was similar in part to the chief concerns of the first phase, in that both were concerned with efficiency. But later reform differed by being more concerned about how to transform the economic system smoothly than how to maintain the principle of central planning. Indeed, as the reform in the second phase moved from the CPE to a market-oriented system, there were broader and more profound challenges to the existing economic system than when the reform had been merely to improve the CPE. These challenges were the source of concerns about the manageability of reform.

Efficiency

Efficiency still appeared to be the prime criterion for evaluating and selecting an institutional arrangement. When a reform policy was discussed, usually the first question would be whether experiments with it had been designed or spontaneous and whether they had demonstrated increased efficiency. As in the first phase of reform, the efficiency concern was the underlying driving force and optimization factor for the transformation of economic institutions. Naturally, the reform of the second phase used efficiency criteria in much more diversified experiments than did the early reform.

Evidence for the efficiency concern could be found in the experiences of Jilin Province with contracting.[40] Jilin was the first province to choose the system of contracting out as its main form of enterprise reform. Before Jilin adopted this reform, its growth rate was below the national average. After adopting the new system, Jilin boasted a rate of growth in its industrial production of 18.1 percent in 1987 and 18.2 percent in 1988, which was higher than the national averages of 24.6 and 17.7 percent respectively. The province attributed its rapid development mainly to adopting the new system.[41] The increase in efficiency made contracting out the dominant reform policy in this province. Because they achieved a higher growth rate, Jilin's policy experiments were highly praised by the central government in 1988 in an endorsement of the contracting-out system for state enterprises all over the country.[42]

Manageability

As the other of the two chief concerns, the manageability consideration described the major constraint for reform policies. Although the reform of this phase adopted an "open" approach that allowed more and diversified experiments to be assessed by the criterion of efficiency, the optimization of economic institutions was conducted under constraints, among which manageability was uppermost. The reformers worried that a new institutional arrangement would put the reform process at high risk due to uncertainty. If a reform was extremely risky, no matter how attractive it was in theory or in terms of efficiency, it had little chance of being considered. It is interesting to note that each reform phase had a distinctly different second chief concern. In contrast to the earlier one that emphasized ideology and orthodoxy, the secondary concern of the later phase emphasized a controlled and smooth process of reform.

Particularly, there was growing attention in the second phase to the aspect of stability. Among many problems that caused concern for stability were inflation and misinvestment. First, since inflation increases uncertainty and causes implicit redistribution in the whole society and among generations, it would have given rise to strong opposition and made the government unpopular. Inflation, therefore, could have become a sensitive political problem and even led to a political crisis. Second, due to poor information processes and the immature behavior of enterprises, there had been problems of misinvestment, which could have damaged the vulnerable process of economic development during the transformation. The inadequate information process undermined the distribution of information, service, and technology, and misguided the behavior of enterprises, which had an underdeveloped ability to process information, make decisions under uncertainty and competition, and respond to the rise of costs and the ultimate threat of bankruptcy. In addition, the newly powerful local governments often tried to push the development of their economies by using administrative means, thereby making things worse. Under these conditions, the new economy would interpret and respond to signs of expansion with less caution than it should have, and investment and production would be misdirected.

This overexpansion without adequate understanding of its consequences caused increasing concern. The newly freed and reinvigorated Chinese economy faced a crucial challenge in making investments with limited resources. Both the private and state-owned economies suffered due to the poor information process and the immature behavior of enterprises. Most scholars concur that a new economy has to experience just such a painful process of learning and adaptation, and that it has to pay for these lessons in economic transformation. The key problem was that had there been some big fluctuation and loss, the entire reform process would have been jeopardized. Again, economic stability could have become a political problem. Therefore, the reform underwent what were, to the Chinese, many unprecedented concerns for the economic reform policymakers.

Specific Illustrations

In this period, two major policy designs failed to be implemented even on a trial basis due primarily to concerns of manageability. The first time this happened was in late 1986, with a proposal designed to combine price, finance, and monetary reform. Immediately before the plan was to be released, worry about the instability that might be caused by price hikes was the major factor in its abandonment. The second instance occurred in the summer of 1988. An unprecedented rise in prices and subsequent concern over social tolerance for inflation wiped away a reform program intended to lift controls on wages and prices. [43]

The adoption of the contracting system in state enterprises all over the country illustrates the concerns of both efficiency and manageability. Compared to the case of Jilin described above, adoption of contracting on a national level involved more political factors. The contracting system had originally evolved as a variant of an early reform to decentralize authority and delegate it to enterprises. After the tax reform of 1983, this type of reform had remained in the experimental stage. At the end of 1986, the strategy for enterprise reform had been to try a leasing system for small (and some mid-size) enterprises, a contracting-out system for medium- and large-scale enterprises, and to experiment with shareholding. The economic situation of early 1987 was not favorable, and the number of enterprises in deficit at one time increased 40 percent while the state's budgeted income dropped 2.3 percent the previous year. However, as more and more enterprises chose the contracting-out system, industrial production picked up vigorously in the latter half of the year.

By the end of the year, production, rather than declining, increased over 10 percent and the contribution to the state budget increased 6.7 percent over the year before. [44] These increases in production and profit clearly demonstrated the efficiency advantage of this practice. Since state budget problems could always be translated into social and political issues, the improvement of the budget situation would strengthen the determination of national policymakers to stay with such successful measures. Moreover, rapid moves to privatization caused reformers to worry, not only about confrontation with conservatives, but also about maintaining economic stability. There were fears that more rapid reform would result in fluctuation and shock. Consequently, given the contracting-out system could increase efficiency and maintain manageability, it was not surprising that over 90 percent of all Chinese had adopted the system by the end of 1988.[45]

Economically Rational Enterprise

Immediately after the success of the agricultural reform, enterprise reform reemerged as a priority. The first proposition of the second-phase reform involves enterprise reform and states the decision makers' understanding that it is critical for economic reform to shift its focus from decentralizing authority to developing the institutions of economically rational enterprise.

Before proceeding with a discussion of reform, it would be well to define the term, since its meaning evolved significantly from the first phase of reform to the second. Earlier, the state enterprises made up an overwhelming majority of all enterprises.[46] But in the second phase, private and other nonstate enterprises accounted for a growing portion of the whole industrial sector. (The term "enterprise reform" as used herein refers exclusively to state enterprises unless otherwise specified. Where necessary, nonstate and private enterprises will be explicitly distinguished from state-owned enterprises.)

Government Against Rational Enterprise

Reform practices gradually made it clear that no matter how intelligent and rational a government might be, its actions to exercise control over an enterprise would prevent the enterprise from making decisions on the basis of economic rationality. Although the reform of the first phase had reduced much of the government's control, enterprises were still far from free to make responsible decisions and commitments on such issues as investment, wages and salaries, quantity of output, or prices. Moreover, apart from these apparent restrictions on enterprise decision making and performance, enterprise managers and executives always had to take it as their implicit but principal work to curry favor with various offices of the government bureaucracy. Most of these offices had no inherent interest in improving enterprises' economic performance, and so each might stand in the way of an enterprise's attempt to get the certain permit required to introduce any change. Some of these offices might even have influence over the personnel arrangements of businesses' top executives. All of these government liaisons introduced noneconomic factors into the enterprises' decision-making processes, aside from the fact that their decision-making power was already very much constrained. Most of the noneconomic factors would be in direct conflict with businesses' interests, which often had to be compromised. Questions were raised about this problem from the beginning of the reform movement, and it was gradually recognized as one of the key issues of reform. Dong Furen and Jiang Yiwei were among the economists who kept to the fore in the early days of reform. Dong observed that state ownership prevented enterprises from behaving rationally. Jiang speculated that "the state organization (including both the central and local governments) should be separated from the economic organization (i.e. mainly enterprises)." Over time, terms like "economically rational enterprises" were used more and more, and were absorbed into the reform policies mainly during the second phase of reform. [47]

What is an "economically rational enterprise"? The term refers to an enterprise that inherently seeks its own interest, which could include profit and expansion of market share. In fact, the term as used in the reform's policies and documents was very vague and had never really been defined. To China's reform decision makers, the term seemed to bear no relation to any discussion in Western economics, and no such a relation is assumed. Among the voluminous Western writers on the subject of economic rationality, Herbert A. Simon's term "intentedly rational, but only limitedly so"[48] is chosen as a good approximation. The term "economically rational" hence incorporates the element of intent to behave in this way. Questions such as In the end, whose interest is the guiding factor in determining rationally? The manager's, the workers', the state's. the people's, or, vaguely, that of the enterprise itself? will not be addressed here.

From the perspective of reform policy, to be "economically rational" an enterprise must be able to seek its own economic interest in the market. Used in reform policies, the term "economically rational enterprise" didn't rule out possible connections between the state and the state-owned enterprises in certain owner-manager relationships or other clearly defined, similar relationships. In these kinds of cases, a manager would represent the government in exercising its right of ownership. Indeed, during the second phase of reform the most important work for such a representative was to select the manager of a state enterprise.

In brief, it was recognized that the government should withdraw from managing enterprises and let managers run enterprises in an economically rational way and all the efforts to reform the state enterprise system were devoted to establishing institutions to enable this to happen.

Moving from Granting More Authority to Liberating

Like the emphasis on decentralizing authority from the central to local governments that had characterized the first-phase reform, the enterprise reform experiments in the later years of the decade were directed toward finding ways to pass full authority down to enterprises. It had seemed that even though local governments could make better use of information and be more responsive to changes in the economy than the central government, there was the unresolved problem that the interests of the governments were not always the same as those of an economically rational enterprise. It was clear to the reformers that the proper differences in the roles of government and enterprise necessitated their separation from each other. A government exists with various political and social functions, while an enterprise develops as a result of economizing on the use of resources in production and transaction. Although the state conceded that government control of production prevented enterprises from being economically rational, even after granting greater authority, in the first stage of reform, the state kept its hand in the enterprises' decision-making processes by treating enterprises as part of the big corporation. Granting more authority to the state enterprises did mean a marginal withdrawal of government control and led to some improvement in performance, but it did not solve the rationality problem of state enterprises. Conversely, it posed a question to the reform decision makers and managers: Why did the government withdraw from an enterprise only marginally without delegating full authority to those who ran it?

Some material on the proposition of enterprise reform can be found in the reform policy of "separating government and enterprise" promulgated in 1986. Even though decentralization of the CPE motivated lower levels of the planned hierarchy to promote production and improve efficiency, there was no level in the hierarchy whose genuine interest and rationality in production and efficiency would be the same as or could replace those of enterprises themselves. After the early efforts to decentralize authority to provincial and city levels, an official reform policy from 1984 sought to pass full management authority to the state enterprises' top managers and to separate the government from the enterprises' business. The policies to separate government from enterprise represented a major jump from the typical understanding of decentralization in the first period to the understanding of reconstructing enterprises in the second period. The reform in the second phase, in effect, departed from the understanding during the early reform that the economy was a giant corporation represented by the state. It was now recognized that the economy was composed of many entities with independent and occasionally conflicting interests. [49]

This policy principle of separating government and enterprise can be seen in the widespread testing of contracting-out, leasing, and shareholding in Chinese enterprise reform. Enterprise reform simply attempted to establish a clear asset and property relation between the state and the enterprises. Profit sharing, the dominant effort in the early period of reform, was replaced by the much more institutionalized efforts of contracting and shareholding, which were based on a relationship between the government and enterprises. This was especially true of contracting out and leasing, which appeared to limit the participants in the relationship to the owner and the manager. The importance of the separation of government and enterprise lay in the attempt to make an enterprise a real economic entity and empower it to make its decisions on the basis of economic rationality. Even though the understanding of the separation was vague such as with regard to contractual relations and ownership structure, it was a great step forward in building economically rational enterprises.

Briefly speaking, as the major component of enterprise reform in its second phase, the practice of contracting-out was an effort to shape a relationship between the state and business in which the owner (i.e., the state) and the chief manager established a joint commitment, the chief manager agreeing to a goal of profit and certain other objectives, including asset requirement, and the state granting him full authority to operate the enterprise.

It should be noted that the government-enterprise relationship has so far not obtained the degree of separation spelled out in the reform policies. As will be discussed in chapter 5, the reform of the state enterprise system had a long way to go, even when some measures of privatization were considered. The core of the issue centered on how to define ownership and overall contractual relations vis-à-vis the state enterprises, as well as what kind of institutions would be developed to realize ownership and contractual relations recognized by the law.

Development of the Market as the Center

We now discuss the second proposition, which pertains to the understanding among reform decision makers of the market in relation to reform during the second phase.

The proposition for market development was this: China's economic transformation could be seen as a process of developing a market. This induced behavioral adaptation in all members of the economy and related institutional adjustment and innovation throughout the system.

The reform to develop the market system did not have its own descriptive term (as did agricultural reform and enterprise reform), but it was an indispensable part of many reforms. Strictly speaking, market development constituted not the reform of an existing system, but rather the creation of a new system.

No Longer a Supplement

From the mid-1980s on, a series of experiments and new measures made the function of the market no longer supplementary to the plan, and revealed that the reform was, in fact, centering around market development. Three of these periods indicated this change. First of all, during 1984 and 1985, a reform of the price system was announced and tried. Passed at the Third Plenum of the Twelfth Party Congress in late 1984, the Decisions on Economic System Reform formally spelled out the price reform policy and predicted that "the price reform is the key to whether the whole economic reform would be a success or a failure."[50] From the beginning of price reform, as this document reveals, the leaders realized that price reform would have a strong impact on economic issues (wages, taxes, finance, banking and monetary systems, and all agricultural and industrial production). From 1985 on, experiments and new price reform measures continued, and the influence of the market on the economy as a whole grew steadily.

Second, the government gradually lifted its control over the distribution of major natural resources and production factors. In the past, natural resources and production factors (including coal, steel, wood, cement, and electricity) had been among the most tightly controlled commodities and were distributed solely by the government according to the central plan. In the mid-1980s, the government reduced its control and allowed them to be sold by producers and distributed on markets.

Third, as private enterprises continued to grow dramatically in this period, their economic activities came to constitute a substantial part of the overall market activity. Most of their products were not really under the plan's control and entered the market directly. With these changes, the market in effect became the major allocation mechanism in the economy.

Adjustment and Adaptation Facing the Government

It was gradually understood that the government should be only a participant in the economy and that it should let the market be the main, efficient mechanism of resource allocation. In contrast to the early reform movement, which had focused on internal relations, the central government had much less to do with the development of market mechanisms and market institutions in the second phase. The government indeed still played an important role in the transformation by lifting and eliminating the remaining controls on prices; reducing its intervention in the economy; and accelerating the development of a legal system to protect exchange, ownership, and its transfer, as well as by organizing more resources for legislation, judiciary facilities, and professional training. The government, however, was neither so influential nor so decisive in some other processes of the transformation: Enterprises needed to learn how to make decisions under uncertainty and how to make a profit in the face of competition; enterprises had to learn to make a credible commitment and to develop mutually beneficial contractual relations; and individuals had to adapt themselves to the fluctuations of prices and commercial strategies related to profit seeking. In addition to all this, the government had to adapt itself to the changing economy and its institutions, and to learn to stay away from business decisions and activities. Of course, yielding its power and authority was one of the most difficult things for the government to do. Specifically, in the process of economic transformation, the government had to learn to respect the rights it had recently granted to firms and enterprises, and to use economic instruments instead of administrative mandates to pursue the health and interests of all members of the economy at large.

Difficulties that faced the government while learning how to apply the economic instruments supports the proposition. Since the government had never used noncompulsory instruments in the economy, it had little knowledge about how to apply them. The problem could be seen from two perspectives: on the one hand, the government had to make the new instruments; on the other, it needed to be constrained by economic institutions compatible with the market economy. It is true that efforts had been made to use some macroeconomic leverage (such as money supply, interest rates, and taxes) in place of the existing command instruments. (The command instruments usually included freezing loans and credits, setting ceilings on purchase and acquisition amounts, fixing prices, stopping projects by administrative order, and installing mandatory permit requirements for certain economic activities.) Nevertheless, the new nonmandatory instruments took time to be put in place and to be really effective. Before the government gained the necessary knowledge and experience with the nonmandatory instruments, it would often predict the consequences of using the instruments with a built-in bias embedded in the uncertainty typical of inexperience.

The development of effective nonmandatory instruments also called for institutional changes within enterprises. Particularly, clearly defined property relationships and asset constraints were required for the instruments to function. Generally, the switch of nonmandatory instruments for mandatory ones depends on the development of both the instruments and the economic institutions which will respond to them. In China, apart from lack of experience with the new instruments and the underdeveloped institutions of enterprise, the interests of and responses from the government bureaucracies and the remaining planning hierarchy had to be accommodated. Resistance to the nonmandatory instruments from the bureaucracies had always been a difficult problem. However, what might seem to be a possible solution for reducing the resistance — that is, the demolition of the existing government bureaucracies — did not likely result in fundamentally new government behavior. The reason was that the existing human assets and actually available instruments could not be expected to produce, overnight, a government that fit a market economy.

Reform practices revealed that development of the market challenged the government, the existing planning institutions, and every participant in the economy. The government and its officials faced the task of learning to adapt in the face of these changes and challenges.

All Human Assets Facing Renewal

What is often ignored in studies of China's economic transformation is that, like the government and its officials, individuals and enterprises also faced the need for adjustment and adaptation in patterns of behavior and thought. Apart from the change contained in the new decision-making processes, in which enterprises had greater responsibility than before, enterprises also needed to learn how to be a part of a market economy and how to compete and cooperate on the basis of self-organization and legal regulation.

Evidence of this can be found in the negative repercussions of the growing incidence of free exchange in the market. In the course of reform, economic development often brought with it the phenomena of decreased accountability for certain economic activities, crises of confidence in transactions, and confusing expectations in investment. Fly-by-night firms or individuals posed a threat to normal economic activities anywhere, and even worse, the responses to the hazard behavior and outcomes were often individual retaliations of an "eye for an eye" type. In some cases, those who suffered from irresponsible activities even transferred the hazards and damages to innocent parties. Compensation for loss and damages was sought mainly on an individual ad hoc basis instead of through an institutional mechanism that was widely accepted.

One can also find evidence for the proposition in the phenomenon of the explosive growth of contract disputes. Leaving aside the motivating factor of self-interest, thousands and thousands of disputes were caused by a lack of basic knowledge about free contracting — from searching for trade partners to document drafting — an absence of the habit of truthfulness, and a shortage of experience in handling contingency issues and making compromises when interests were in conflict.[51]

In conclusion then, enterprises, individuals, as well as the government and its officials, all had to adapt their behavior and institutions to cope with the development of the market, which was at the center of the country's new institutions and which accomplished the transformation of China from a centrally planned economy to a market system by means of an incremental process.

Transition Through a Two-track System

Based on the concepts of enterprise reform and price reform, the third proposition lays out how to initiate the transformation — realization of a new economic system against the background of a still centrally planned system. A new economic system was to be built with reformed people and institutions from the existing economy. As the reform continued, the economy was expected to perform better and to improve life. Apart from the expectations of change and the accompanying uncertainty in relation to the collapse of that expectation, the existing institutions and their related human factors also contributed to the possibility space in which the reform was conducted.

The proposition of a "two-track" system is this: While elements of both the centrally planned and market economy coexist, two-track policies of economic reform represent an effort to make an incremental and controlled transition to a market-oriented economy.

The Two-track System

"Two-track" policy was the general term for the policies that led to the coexistence of both central planning and market mechanisms. One of the two tracks was for central planning and the other for the market. Specifically, there were both planned and market prices for goods and services, planned distribution and market allocation of resources, and government-controlled state industries alongside private industries. At the core of the reform's set of two-track policies were price policies.

The market price track developed as a result of introducing new incentives and dynamics into the CPE. The roots of this aspect of the two-track economic system can be traced back to the very early reform movement. As peasants were allowed to sell their products on the market and enterprises to sell their extra products or new products on their own, this second price structure emerged. As private economic activities were allowed and encouraged, they operated outside the central planning system and gradually developed into a substantial part of the overall economy.

Although free exchanges and market activities existed even prior to the reform, particularly for agricultural products, they could hardly have qualified in any sense as a parallel economic system or a major mechanism. It could certainly be argued that before the reform there was to some extent a two-track phenomenon. A black market for certain commodities that were in short supply and a limited free market for extra agricultural products did exist back in the 1960s and 1970s, but these phenomena existed only in the exchanges of a very few categories of products and were usually limited to extra agricultural surplus.[52] Moreover, these two-track phenomena oscillated as the government launched, one after another, racial political movements against "capitalism" or the market economy.[53] In general, before the reform came to life, whenever the CPE performed especially poorly, the government needed help from free exchange, but ultimately the market and free economy were seen as "black" and illegal. The two-track system only emerged with economic reform; it eventually became a dominant institutional setting in the reform's second phase.

A Means of Transition

The two-track economic system was a special transitional system of the gradual Chinese reform. If the reform had taken the path of simply installing a market system in place of the CPE, there would not have been any need for two tracks. When the reform movement adopted the strategy of introducing market institutions into the economy and keeping the central planning system, the two-track system was interpreted and accepted from several perspectives. First, it was treated as an outcome of incremental reform, based upon the assumption that through the process of transformation the central planning institutions would gradually shrink while the market institutions grew in importance. Second, it could be argued that a two-track system was inevitable if the aim was the spontaneous development of the private market economy through gradual reform instead of a one-step transformation from a CPE. This presumed that a gradual reform would automatically allow spontaneous economic activity to occur to a greater extent and, at the same time, that the formal central planning institutions would be dissolved step-by-step. Another assumption would then follow that the centrally planned system and the market system would offer fundamentally different information processes and incentive and coordination mechanisms, which would result in different patterns of behavior and interrelations in economic activities. Third, the two-track system could be explained as the result of a compromise strategy to avoid confusion and conflict during economic reform by trading a slowdown in some reforms for continued progress in others. With various opinions on the rationale for the two-track system, debate focused particularly on the two-track system and price reform.[54]

Controversies in the Compromise

The two-track system aroused ever more controversy and debate, taking precedence over discussion of other issues both in China and among outside observers. As with many other reform issues, the subjects of these controversies and the emphases of these debates shifted constantly, as the reform practices exposed more information and deeper problems. Nevertheless, the focus of various ideas in the debates was on how to treat the contradictions and compromises embedded in the system, as well as how to assess the costs and benefits of making the compromises.[55] Some of the issues raised were vital and, among them, three will be discussed briefly.

The first of these was the debate between "adjusting first and then lifting control" and "simply lifting control." The former attempted to reduce the shock and uncertainty of price reform by gradually raising the planned price to the market price, which was assumed to be roughly measurable. The latter mainly argued that equilibrium prices could not be found, given the institutional constraints.

The second debate was between the schools of "grand plan" and those of "small but quick steps." Grand planners intended to seek a comprehensive design for price reform, combining financial, banking, and tax reforms. Those who favored small but quick steps doubted that anyone had the ability to design an "all-around" reform. In general, trying to determine the relationships among different aspects of reform appeared to be critically important in the second phase when the overall planning system was under attack. At the same time, it should be realized that implementation of an artificially designed all-around reform would have to be more dependent upon the still-extant planning bureaucracy. But this dependence upon the existing bureaucracy would be costly, because it at least could be used to excuse or justify maintaining the existing bureaucracy. Moreover, the expectation of a policy effect based on this dependence was often unrealistic.

The third debate was on whether priority should be given to reconstructing enterprises or to price reform. It later evolved into a disagreement between those who felt that "enterprises will not respond to prices as expected before becoming new businesses" and those who argued that "enterprises cannot truly compete without real prices."

No matter what differences there were among these views, they all presumed that the two-track system was inherently related to the strategy of incremental reform. Further, it was realized that there would be a price to pay for the strategy of a two-track system, and that the convergence to the market track should be sought as soon as possible. What the conditions for this convergence would be and whether certain compromises would be reasonable was, of course, always controversial.

To summarize, the promise of economic reform through a transitional two-track system lay in the dynamics of the situation up to that point: most expanded or newly developed economies operated apart from central planning, while the plan covered mainly what it had before. The dynamics of the two-track transition could in turn be described as the continuous and relatively rapid growth of the private economy, the freeing-up of more activities from central planning's control, and the convergence of planned prices to market prices.

But the two-track system was inherently a contradictory double-edged sword. It created pressure and new conditions for reforming the old system at the same time that it sheltered and perpetuated the old planning mechanisms. For example, when the reformers had tried to introduce competition into the economy, the two-track system had actually institutionalized and strengthened some state enterprise monopolies, some unfair positions favorable to the state enterprises in the market, and barriers to free market entry and exit.

Generally speaking, each of the three propositions relates to one of the most important aspects of China's second-phase reform. The proposition of enterprise reform is about the new focus, after the success of agricultural reform, transforming the existing system, and about the change in which aspect of the state enterprises were to be reformed (shifting from granting them more authority to granting them substantial autonomy). The second proposition raises a completely new task — market development — for reform. The reform to develop the market represents the critical difference from early reform, which had been intended to improve the CPE within the system. The third proposition is about the transition during the second phase, specifically how to establish a market system in that particular situation. The mechanism by which the transition was accomplished in this period was a two-track system that allowed adaptation of institutions and human assets to the new system. But the two-track system, like any compromise, has drawbacks.

As an aside, during the second-phase reform, decision makers were much more influenced by reform practices and a wide range of information processes than they had been in the first phase, when they had made decisions on initiating reform measures and experiments largely on the basis of their own limited experiences. In the second period, however, spontaneous institutional developments, experiences and theories from other economies, intellectual reasoning, and academic studies provided an array of sources for reform initiatives. The forces of reform in this period were the private economy (as opposed to the state economy), local governments (as opposed to the central bureaucratic agencies), and the outward economy, including the special economic zones and most of the coastal economy (as opposed mainly to the inland economy). Even though this model is discussed primarily from the standpoint of the reform leadership's still fairly centralized decision-making process, it largely reflects the new diversity driving the reform in the second half of the decade. In other words, given the fact that a variety of more diversified forces and factors influenced China's second-phase economic reform, the model is drawn to represent this reality.

Notes

1. Gao Shangquan. "The Ten Years' Economic System Reform in China," in *Almanac of China's Economy 1989*, II.40.
2. Huang Yunchen, et al. "Forecast of Chinese National Economy 1991 and 1992," *Reform Information* (Chongqin, China) 8 (1991).
3. It was generally agreed that the progress of reform was mainly driven by the success of economic development and the improvement in the living standard. However, there were other factors which might also have contributed to the transformation of economic institutions and to the transition from the first to second phases of reform in particular. For example, political factors in 1983 and 1984 would be interesting to assess in this regard. The victory of reformers on the issue of "antispiritual pollution" could likewise be contributed to the successful acceleration of reform from the agricultural sector to the rest of the economy. (The "antispiritual pollution" campaign was a political movement against Western influence on China and the Chinese economy. The origins of the movement were complex and not easily explained in a few words; in principle, it posed a serious political challenge to the reform and liberalization policies that had begun in 1979.)
4. Most of the measures had also been tried in the 1950s and 1960s to revise and improve the centrally planned system. The connection of

reform to previous efforts to revise the centrally planned system is discussed in the second chapter. These reforms, however, were often controversial in the early years of reform, as they were in conflict with the old ideological doctrines and interests. During agricultural reform, for example, many officials of the communes and local governments were very much concerned about the direction of the reform — departing from collectivism and creating potential income discrepancies. Moreover, those who had been privileged under the old system often challenged the reform in one way or another.

5. This will be further discussed in the following chapter, particularly in the sections on dominant belief and chief concerns.

6. In this period, peasants received land contracts on a 30- to 50-year basis, which differed from the earlier contracts of 3-5 years. This kind of extension of land contracts constituted a substantive change in economic institutions.

7. The dissolution of the commune system and the adoption of family responsibility could be seen as "history's most massive privatization — that of the farmlands of China, where over 800 million live" (Reason Foundation 1990, 34), on the grounds that peasants, after turning over contracted amounts of products to the state, now had the right to use and dispose of the outcome of production. In many areas, land could be subcontracted by peasants to peasants. Nevertheless, to some economists, the most critical point in identifying property rights structures is whether the title to land can be transferred.

8. Enterprise reforms in this period included selling small-size state-owned enterprises, and leasing and contracting out seemed to be the preferred choices. It was not clear whether the short- or long-term contracting out of state firms would be a transition to private ownership — in other words, an evolutionary process leading to a market economy. Meanwhile, as the share of market pricing kept growing, there were several attempts at reforming the price system, through the introduction of a market price mechanism in contrast to the earlier search for equilibrium prices under the central planning system.

9. At the Chinese Communist Party's 14th Congress in October 1992, the goal of the reform was spelled out as socialist market economy. The explanations and definitions in its documents indicate that the market was accepted as the core of the new economic system. For more information see the *People's Daily* (overseas edition) 21 October 1992.

10. Deng Xiaoping, "Toward Constructing a Socialism with Chinese Characteristics," in *Selection of Important Documents Since the 12th Congress* 1986, 511-15.

11. Zhao Ziyang, "Marching Forward Along the Socialist Road with Chinese Characteristics," in *Almanac of China's Economy 1988*, II.1-20.
12. Gao Shangquan, "China's Ten-year Economic Reform," in *Almanac of China's Economy 1988*, II.38-46.
13. Huang Yunchen, "Forecast of the Chinese National Economy 1991 and 1992, *Reform Information* 8 (1991).
14. Chen Yun, "Several Opinions on Economic Policies," in *After the Third Plenum — Selection of Important Documents* 1982, 1057-60.
15. Hu Yaobang, "Creating An All-round New Situation of Constructing Socialist Modernization," in *Collection of Documents on Economic Reform 1977-1983* 1984, 66.
16. Zhao Ziyang, "Report at the 13th Congress of the CCP," in *Almanac of China's Economy 1988*, 1-4.
17. Zhao Ziyang, "March Forward Along the Socialist Road with Chinese Characteristics," in *Almanac of China's Economy 1988*, II.1-20. "Commodity economy" was used in the party's documents to substitute for the term "market economy" before 1992.
18. In academic debates and economics literature there were numerous declarations that a market-oriented economy was the goal of reform. An economist, Wu Jinglian, even wrote a letter in the spring of 1988 to Zhao Ziyang, the general secretary, suggesting that the term "market economy" might be useful in policy documents. For more details, see *Reference (Economics)*, vol. 4 (1988) (People's University Press).
19. For additional details, see the section on Wenzhou, Zejiang, in the *Almanac of China's Economy* for 1985, 1986, 1987, 1988, and 1989.
20. Wu Jinglian, et al. 1988, 6-13.
21. Lou Jiwei and Zhou Xiaochuan, "On the Direction of China's Price Reform and Related Model Methods," *Economic Research* 10 (1984).
22. Friedrich A. von Hayek. "Socialist Calculation: The Competitive Solution," *Economics* May 1940: 125-49.
23. von Mises 1951, 137-42; 1966, 705-10.
24. See Gao Shangquan, "Experiences of Share-holding System in China," *China Economics Reform* 3 (1992).
25. The World Bank, "China: Issues and Proposals for the Long-term Development (Abstract in Chinese)," *The Economic Daily* (Beijing) 8 November 1985. Wu Jiaxiang and Jing Lizjuo. "Share-holding: An Idea for Further Reform," The Economic Daily (Beijing) 3 August 1985.
26. The Investigation Group of China National Institute for Economic Reform, "Reform: the Challenges and Opportunities" *Economic Research* 11 (1985); The Investigation Group of China National Institute

for Economic Reform, "Market Development and Institutional Innovation," *Reform and Development* 8 (1988).

27. The Group of Chinese Agriculture Development Study, "New Economic Development Stage and Agricultural Development," *Economic Research* 7 (1985).

28. Hua Sheng, He Jiachen, Zhang Xuejun, Luo Xiaopeng, and Bian Yongzhuang, in The Group of Chinese Agriculture Development Study, "Reconstruction of the Foundation of Micro-economy," Economic Research 3 (1986).

29. Wang Hui, Li Rengyu and Lui Kaixiang, "On Creation of a New Economic Order During Reform," *China: Development and Reform* 7 (1988): 1-10.

30. Wu Jinlian and Zhou Xiaochuan 1988; Lui Guoguang 1988.

31. Investigations were conducted in 1985 by a group of economists from the Chinese Academy of Social Sciences and in 1986 by a delegation form the National Institute for Economic Reform. Both Yugoslavia and Hungary were studied. A delegation from the China Economic Reconstruction Committee, under the State Council of China, paid a visit to Germany and Sweden in 1985. For more details, see: He Guanghui et al., "Economic Management of Germany and Sweden," *Foreign Economic Management* 1 (1986). A delegation from the National Institute for Economic Reform investigated the Japanese economy.

32. The diagnostic conference in the summer of 1985 was held on the ship *Bashan* on the Yangtze River. Attendants at the conference from the Chinese side included professors, policy analysts, policymakers, and aids.

33. The full list of the fourteen cities established in 1984 is: Tianjing, Shanghai, Guanzhou, Dalian, Chindao, Chinhuangdao, Yantai, Lianyungang, Nantong, Nipo, Wenzhou, Fuzhoi, Zhanjiang, and Beihai.

34. Yu Guangyuan, "Economic Scientific Study Should Be Particularly Encouraged," in *Retrospect and Outlook of the Chinese on the Chinese Socialist Economic Theories* 1986, 1-13.

35. Sun Yefang, "To Found Planning and Statistics on the Law of Value," *Economic Research* 6 (1956).

36. Gu Zhun, "On Commodity Production and the Law of Value under the Socialist System," *Economic Research* 3 (1957).

37. Gu was not allowed to pursue his work. From 1962 on, he therefore turned his time to translation and, as further proof of his foresight, he introduced Schumpeter's *Capitalism, Socialism and Democracy* to Chinese readers. This brilliant economist died miserably in 1974, never having abandoned his unyielding search for and belief in truth.

38. Dong Furen, "On the Issue of China's Socialist Ownership," *Economic Research* 1 (1979). Jiang's "enterprise standard" will be discussed later, however, it basically suggested that enterprises are the only bodies that make decisions on production and business operations.
39. For example, two articles by Hua Sheng (Hua et al. 1988) and by Shi Xiaomin (Shi et al. 1989) reflected in part this debate.
40. "Jilin Province," *Almanac of China's Economy 1989*, VI.48; and "Jilin Province," *Almanac of China's Economy 1988*, VI.45. The coverage of the contracting-out system in Jilin's industrial enterprises was about 96 percent in 1987 and 1988.
41. The Chinese State Council's Center for Economic, Technological, and Social Development, "General Report on the National Economy," in *Almanac of China's Economy 1989*, II.1: and The Chinese State Council's Center for Economic, Technological, and Social Development, "The Chinese Economic Situation in 1987," in *Almanac of China's Economy 1988*, II.1.
42. "Jilin Province," in *Almanac of China's Economy 1989*, VI.47-52; and "Jilin Province," in *Almanac of China's Economy 1988*, VI.45-49. Coverage of the contracting-out system in Jilin's industrial enterprises was about 96% in 1987 and 1988.
43. Jilin's experiences even drew Zhao Ziyang's attention, and a special investigation team went to Jilin just to document its experience with contracting. (A report of this investigation appeared in *China: Development and Reform* 3 [1988].)
44. Gao Shangquan. "Ten Years' Economic Reform in China," in *Almanac of China's Economy 1989*, II.45.
45. "Economic Reform in China in 1988 Finance and Tax Reform," in *Almanac of China's Economy 1989*, III.4.
46. Before the reform, there was basically no private enterprise (except for a very few family businesses, which were not allowed to hire workers). During the early reform, private industry had emerged and grown rapidly, but as yet counted for a very tiny part of the economy. By the end of 1984, private industry produced 0.2 percent of the nation's industrial products. For more data, see China's Statistical Annual 1986, p.273. The term "industrial products" is based on China's statistical terminology. Its direct translation is "total value industrial products."
47. Dong Furen, "On the Issue of China's Socialist Ownership," *Economic Research* no. 1 (1979). Jiang Yiwei. "On Enterprise Standard," in *Models of Socialist Enterprises* (Beijing: Economic Sciences Press, 1989), pp. 20-46. Dong's article originally appeared in *China Social Sciences* (Beijing) no. 1 (1980) after most of it had been published in *Economic*

Management (Beijing) no. 6 (1979). Also see "The Decision on Economic Reform by the CCCCP," in *Selection of Important Documents Since the 12th Congress* 1986, 558-87.

48. Simon 1961, xxiv.

49. "The Decision on Economic Reform by the CCCCP," in *Selection of Important Documents Since the 12th Congress* 1986, 558-87. From 1984, there was a common understanding that separation of government and enterprises was at the core of enterprise reform.

50. Under the central planning system before reform, the government planned, controlled, and implemented all industrial transactions; the movements of grain, cotton, oil, and other agricultural products for industrial use; the flow of rice, flour, vegetables, meats, and oil to city residents; and the allocation of all natural resources and labor. Some exchange of agricultural surpluses did take place in small towns and suburban areas, where the state plan did not really reach. Another kind of exchange also took place in rural areas by way of country fairs, which were normally held two to six times a month. In areas that did not have a long tradition of country fairs, peasants might sell here and there from time to time along the roadsides. But even in rural areas, most exchanges were through the state-run trading organization, which was called *gong xiao she*.

51. "The CCCCP's Decision on Economic System Reform," in *Selection of Important Documents Since the 12th Congress* 1986.

52. See Wang Hui, Li Rengyu, and Liu Kaixiang, "Establishing New Order in the Economy," *China: Development and Reform* 7 (1988).

53. Zhou Taile 1984, 105-9.

54. Ibid., 132-33.

55. Hua Sheng and others (1988, 1989) and Shi Xiaomin and Lui Jirui (1989) brought two interesting and different perspectives to some of the debates. The critical battlefield of price reform was the factor market. Since the reaction to the raising of factor prices was hard to predict, the problem of redistribution was hard to handle. Importantly, what kind of shock a substantial price reform would cause the whole economy was difficult to anticipate. Beginning in 1985, to gain some experience in the effect of price reform on production factors — particularly on the lifting of price controls on steel, cement, and electricity — various experiments were conducted.

Apart from price adjustments, there were also efforts to lift price controls by 1984. In terms of industrial products, price controls over goods such as bicycles, sewing machines, tractors, and recorders were partially lifted during this period. In terms of agricultural products, further experiments were considered, as a series of bumper crops caused prices in the free market to decline in 1984.

5

The Second-Phase Reform: Moving Toward the Market

Chinese economic reform entered into its second phase sometime around 1984, and from 1984 to early 1989 both its policies and practices moved toward a market system. From mid-1989 through 1991, efforts to introduce new reform experiments and policies decreased dramatically or ceased altogether, and some existing reform policies were actually halted. But, interestingly, most of the reform practices that had been in place before 1989 continued, independent of support from the central government. Beginning in 1992, a certain degree of coordination between new reform policies and actual reform practices has reemerged after the political upheaval of the late 1980s.[1] Generally, during this economic period, problems were attributed not simply to the radical ideological strategy, as they had been in the first phase, but to the central planning system. More diversified and spontaneous efforts at reform, as compared to the mainly centrally promoted route in the first phase, propelled the economy to move to the market system in this period.

147

Incremental Changes and Cumulative Effects

Dismantling the centrally planned economy (CPE) and introducing the market through incremental change has been one of the major characteristics of China's economic reform. Many factors related to this method of gradual change; among them, China's experimental approach and particular human assets seemed to be the most important. When reform proceeded incrementally, it was legitimate to ask whether it would lead to substantive changes in the CPE or could stop halfway. Further, questions arose such as how incremental changes could continually take place and how institutional changes would occur during the process. All in all, questions about the progress of steady and continual changes reflected the interest in seeing what kind of effects incremental changes could create and why.

A. *No Stable Halfway Point*

Why did the reform enter the second phase not continuing to realign itself with the internal relations of the CPE but rather departing from the CPE and moving in the direction of a market-oriented economy? History offers evidence that the problems of the CPE had been recognized back in the 1950s and 1960s, and that efforts had been made to revise it, but only this latest reform, particularly after 1984, eventually departed from the CPE and journeyed toward a market-oriented economy.

The open approach of "touching stones while walking across a river" was a critically important factor for the reform when entering its second phase and diverting from improving the central planning system. Leaving aside the entangling issues of ideology and orthodoxy, this approach entailed the search for, selection of, and improvement of economic institutions on the basis of pragmatic experimentation with an open information process. With this open experimental approach, an institution or an economic relationship was no longer judged by the standard of ideology or someone's will, but rather by comparing the economic effects of various alternatives to it. When consequences of different economic institutions could be compared, the inefficient and economically irrational ones would lose their reasons to exist.

In terms of institutional comparison and selection, variety and diversity were crucial and were made possible by the open approach. When the closed approach was applied, lack of variety and diversity limited the meaning of comparison. Without variety and diversity, the outcome of a selection could still be inferior. Had China's approach to economic reform continued to be a closed one, some superior alternatives might have been excluded, and reform efforts might have wavered at a halfway point. The country's experiences with cyclic centralization and decentralization in the 1950s and 1960s provided evidence for this. Instead, this approach inherently anticipated and dealt with the selection of economic institutions from amidst more possibilities, even from among floundering options, which allowed the complexity of behaviors and institutions to be revealed to a greater extent than they would have been had the reform been based merely on ideology and theory. The point is that neither theory nor existing knowledge anticipated or explained every aspect of such fundamentally new processes of transformation. Often, the exclusion of certain alternatives was related particularly to prejudice and ignorance, which could prevent comparison and selection.

Moreover, developments in information technology and international relations provided a favorable climate for an effective, open, experimental approach to reform. The reform process took place in a new era of information technology typified by explosive growth in available information and much freer communications than ever before. Particularly, the exchange of information was occurring in an international environment less hostile to China than previously. Rapidly growing communication with the outside world helped to expose to the Chinese their obviously backward situation, which gradually led to disillusionment about the existing CPE. For those who were aware of or sensitive to rapid progresses in the world, the massive flow of information inspired a search for ways to reform the existing system. And for those who tended to stick to the old way, the new information process left them less and less room to hide or defend the profound crises in the economy. More important, under the impact of new information technology and increasingly international communication, China in general not only came to see what was wrong with its economic system, but also, fortunately, to recognize the opportunity at hand. Further, the less hostile world environment made the information China was receiving more constructive and reduced the barriers in the minds of China's decision makers and common people. The relatively favorable state of world politics and security in the late 1970s and 1980s permitted the Chinese to engage in reforming their economic system primarily on the basis of economic rationality and the long-term interest of the nation.

The natural and omnipresent human quest for progressive economic institutions came to play an increasingly important role in institutional comparison and selection by means of the open information process. As the bonds of radical politics and ideology were loosened, rational human choice emerged as a force that matured as more information flowed in and experiences with reform accumulated. In turn, this continual improvement in the quality of China's assets gained momentum, creating demands for a better standard of living and challenges to existing institutions. Under these circumstances, it would have been against human nature for the reform process to have stalled before promising alternatives had been exhausted in the attempt to find more satisfactory economic activities.

A further question posed by the second phase of Chinese economic reform was whether the CPE could survive in a market-oriented economy. There is no need to go back to the fundamental differences and conflicts between the central planning and market systems. The long debate on market socialism mentioned earlier offered many insights into this temporary solution. The actual process of reform was even more revealing.

First, the Chinese reform comprised a feedback and learning process. As the reform movement developed, it exposed more problems with the CPE; at the same time, the success of the reforms continually proved the necessity of further reforms. In effect, the reform practice and experiments promoted the development of new ideas and new concepts for improving the economy. Moreover, the reform continued to provide new hope and potential reward for further development. The evolving economic system became particularly dynamic through this cycle of feedback and adjustment. Second, the newly developed or newly freed economies offered sharper and sharper contrasts, in terms of economic performance, with the old state-dominated economy. As the state economy and private economy operated with large discrepancies in efficiency, the state economy, in order not to disappear in the competition with the private economy, had only two possible chances for survival: either to exist on subsidies from the government or to become a new enterprise system. In the long run, the costs of subsidizing the huge and deteriorating state economy were not affordable, and from about the mid-1980s there was mounting criticism of the continuing subsidies as more efficient and less burdensome institutions took root and flourished. In other words, the state economy, with only one practical chance for survival, had to compete with the private economy. Third, the central planning mechanism, which operated on the basis of mandatory administrative orders, was basically understood to be an economic failure. On that point there was little argument, and people, the decision makers included, had less and less interest in saving it. It appeared obvious that any such attempt to retain the CPE would be based only on ideological prejudice instead of on any convincing benefits, and it became gradually accepted that the dissolution of the mandatory CPE was only a matter of time. Thus, the answer to the question of whether the CPE could survive in a market-oriented economy was that it could not.

Reward Stream and Incremental Change

By the mid-1980s incremental change had brought about an indisputable decline in the mandatory controls of central planning and a corresponding influence of the market mechanism on the Chinese economy. Such gradual changes in China's economic institutions seemingly lacked drama or obvious or theoretical attraction, but incremental reforms permitted economic institutions to be modified in a way driven by the economy itself. What kind of mechanisms were behind these incremental changes deserves discussion here.

With the experimental approach and constant feedback process, positive rewards and a growing flow of benefits directly contributed to continuous experimentation with further incremental changes. The rewards brought by the first phase of reform led to recognition of and great enthusiasm for the ongoing reform and the direction it was taking among reform leaders and the people alike. Positive evaluation of experiments eventually emerged from these rewards and benefits, and it often determined continuity and adjustment of an experiment or a policy. The experiences of the reforms in the first phase were mostly tentative but often positive, and this contributed to the momentum in the economy and in society for further departures from the old system. The flow of benefits offered in return a signal to continue the ongoing reforms and transformation of economic institutions. When the economic reforms, like many other kinds of organizational and institutional changes in China at this time, were gradually proceeding amid doubts and criticisms, the whole picture of reform was difficult to accurately comprehend; as a Chinese phrase says, "You cannot see the real face of the Lu mountain just because you are on it."[2] Whenever certain correlations between a reform and its outcome could be perceived and some improvement in economic performance could be even provisionally attributed to the reform, evaluation and appreciation of the reform would take place. This explains in part how the meaning and significance of incremental reform could well become, quite suddenly after a certain point in time, enlightening, inspiring, and convincing.

As the benefits of a new system kept flowing in, and before its advantages got close to being exhausted or its negative impact accumulated sufficiently to halt the movement, there was no internal mechanism to stop it. When some part of the economy prospered from the introduction of market institutions, another part would no longer be satisfied to continue under the inefficient CPE. Unless there were sufficient noneconomic reasons influencing the selection of economic institutions, economic reform would inherently tend to arrive at its own balance of advantages and disadvantages, The noneconomic factors that interfered in the process of selection for economic institutions came mostly from the government, and they ranged from the imposition of an arbitrary decision to the installation of regulations over economic activities, returning to political totalitarianism by imposing the government's will over that of the people. Without exception, these noneconomic factors hindered the development of newly won freedom. The noneconomic reasons to halt an economic reform included worry about growth of private wealth, mental acceptance of price discrepancy in a market, high risk, and uncertain costs due to lack of knowledge and experience. Even though there always existed one or another such reason, none was deemed sufficiently serious to stop the reform movement within the period covered by this study. If a move back to political totalitarianism were to have been chosen and the reform stopped, it would present the most dramatic challenge to the political regime itself, since all its credibility would be called into question. On the matter of the possibility of reversing the economic reform process, Harding observes that "a return to collective agriculture would be extremely unpopular in most parts of the Chinese countryside, and the central government lacks the political resources to impose such a system on an unwilling population."[3]

As incremental changes accumulated by the mid-1980s, validation of some of the elements of early reform — decentralization, diversification, and liberalization — became strong. At the same time, the stream of positive rewards kept driving the economy in the direction of the market.

Cumulative Effects and Changes in Human Assets

The accumulation of incremental changes resulted in remarkable changes in the country's economic institutions. China's economic reform brought progress in almost all major aspects of the economy, solidifying the direction of the economic liberalization movement. Because changes were incremental, each change in an economic institution might not appear to be dramatic. But as they accumulated, certain substantial and even qualitative differences in the economic system emerged.

Agricultural reform illustrates this point. Since the reform began, agriculture had achieved unprecedented steady development, and the decline of rural living standards was reversed. The establishment of the family responsibility system and the dissolution of the commune took place in about five years. Agricultural reform experienced a gradual process of comparison and selection among various alternatives, including small groups of families, dividing work among families instead of dividing land, as well as various family-based experiments. The outcome of agricultural reform made it clear that the centrally planned system in the form of the commune system hindered economic development and growth in productivity The success of the agricultural reform also benefited urban residents by supplying them with abundant agricultural products, and it helped convince the country's decision makers and people alike of the necessity of further reform in other fields. Agricultural reform conveyed a strong message that the economy would not only not collapse, but would perform much better under a reform program. As agricultural reform proceeded from the end of the 1970s to the mid-1980s, a welter of concerns was raised; most of these, however, arose from misperceptions related to the old orthodoxy, dismay due to lack of confidence in and knowledge of the new system, and from political resistance due to fear of losing existing privileges under the old system.

By the mid-1980s, developments had demonstrated that not only did the new agriculture system perform much more better than the former commune system, but also that these worries were groundless. Due to agricultural reform and the establishment of new incentive systems, the share of the agricultural sector in the overall economy increased dramatically and almost every peasant family benefited from the reform to the family-based system. The new agricultural system opened vast opportunities for every individual and family, offering neither less arduous labor nor open-handed largesse, but rather the challenges of utilizing everyone's full potential and learning from new adventures. In sum, accompanying incremental changes in economic performance and institutions, people developed new understandings of the old centrally controlled and the new family-based systems, a new sense of the human capability to make decisions and take responsibility, and new skills and learning abilities. Therefore, the outcome of the agricultural reform included, apart from an enormous increase in production and improvement in quality of life, and a new system of family-based production, profound changes in human assets.

The steady accumulation of small-scale changes in other economic institutions also prepared the way for breakthroughs in both institutions and human assets. In the case of enterprise reform, it had first started in 1979 in just eight enterprises as an experiment granting very slightly augmented authority and instituting a sharing mechanism with respect only to surplus products. It had then gradually spread to enterprises across the country. When this proved successful, more authority and freedom were granted to participating enterprises. After these incremental measures, the enterprises started to respond to market information and to seek profit as an important goal. The seemingly slow changes allowed enterprises to learn to seek efficiency and to shift their strategy from fulfilling assigned quotas to achieving rational economic goals by making use of existing assets and capital. Through this gradual reform, all human assets, including managers, technicians, and skilled labor, were under continual but self-imposed pressure to evolve toward a market economy.

Development of the Market Institution's Elements

Although by the end of this period a substantial portion of the Chinese economy's activities and resources were still under the control of the central planning system and the government, the CPE in China was gradually dying. From a dynamic perspective, the central planning system covered only part of the economy, and thus the planned economy provided a factor of continuity during the transformation. As a mechanism of both allocating resources and operating production, the central planning system not only gradually lost its dominance in the economy but also declined consistently in its degree of coercive interference in planning and controlling the economy, serving more as a guide than a commanding force, even among the state industries.

Moreover, as the government continued to reduce and then lift controls over the economy, spontaneous development of the elements of a market economy gained importance as components of the economic transformation. As discussed above, in the first phase of the reform it was primarily the government that initiated and conducted the reform, measure by measure. In contrast, the second phase was characterized by a strong trend toward spontaneous development of market institutions due to continued decentralization and economic liberalization. Spontaneous development of market institutions also included conscious and unconscious adjustments in patterns of behavior and in the processes of decision making, forcing people to learn new behaviors and practice new ways of thinking as they "learned by doing."

In this phase it became clear that institutional change was the essential factor contributing to the increase in production and the growth of social wealth, recalling an observation made two hundred years ago by Adam Smith: "When the crown lands had become private property, they would, in the course of a few years, became well improved and well cultivated."[4] The market was no longer viewed negatively but was called upon to allocate an increasing share of the resources and to coordinate economic activities. In placing greater reliance upon the market, people learned to live with modern divisions of labor and cooperation, to adjust production on their own, and to compete under uncertainties. Moreover, liberated from the bonds of the commune system and free from other forms of mandatory economic institutions, people burst out with immense energy and enthusiasm for creating individual wealth and developing the economy with the "invisible hand."

In some of the areas that had been major battlefields in the first phase, the economic reform of the second phase essentially institutionalized the existing measures (namely those aimed at dismantling the CPE). Specifically, the family production system in agriculture was consolidated, mainly by extending the terms for leasing land; the economic relations between the central and local governments were further decentralized; and a system governed by legal regulation and legal principles began to develop to protect free economic activities, property rights, and transfers of those rights.

Institutionalization of Family-Based Agriculture

In the second phase of the reform, there were solid efforts to institutionalize the new agricultural system. These efforts focused on developing long-term asset relationships based on families and private individuals and on development of the market. Based on the so-called Number One decree of 1983, the central government issued another two Number One decrees in 1984 and 1985 to institutionalize the efforts and policies of the agricultural reform of the first phase. Land leasing contracts were extended typically from three to five years in the first phase to about thirty to fifty years in the second phase.[5] The long-term land leasing system introduced a more stable scheme of rewards and incentives than had the short-term system in terms of expectations for production and decision making, and the behavior of the peasants adjusted accordingly. Additional changes included purchase contracts to replace planning quotas on agricultural products, subleasing of land by peasants, and free-market pricing for most agricultural products.[6] Specialized technological services (e.g., pesticide and farm-machine maintenance) and cooperation on the basis of the family production system also developed rapidly. Basically, most of the specialized technological services would be efficient only when a certain economy of scale was reached. When the communes were dissolved and the land distributed to each family, the scale of average agricultural production decreased dramatically. Had certain forms of cooperation to provide such specialized technological services not developed to fill the vacuum created by the loss of the collective production of the commune, the new family-based agricultural system would have been in jeopardy. The development of specialized technological services along with cooperation among families during the second phase provided the family-based production system with economies of scale and the advantages of specialization, thereby contributing to the consolidation of the new institutions in the agricultural sector. In addition, as the family production system provided more and more surplus agricultural products to sell, new organizations and mechanisms for market transaction emerged, developing as a result of demand generated by the new economy. Market organizations in agriculture developed and expanded rapidly, with tens of thousands of trading centers and specialized marketplaces, specialized and seasonal transportation businesses, and information services.[7]

The agricultural reform, by its nature, started a historical movement of privatization. Indeed, the privatization took place under strict conditions, the most important constraint being the contractual relation of land leasing. Under the new agricultural system, land was owned by the state and not by the peasants. Therefore, peasants could not sell or transfer their land to others. But two points need to be made concerning the profound differences between institutions in the first and second phases, and the understanding of the property rights issue in agriculture.

The agricultural system in the second phase distinguished itself from the first phase significantly by its long-term contractual relations. The short-term land lease contracts that had characterized the early phase of reform exposed peasants to the possibility that the new agricultural policy might be rescinded and that the peasants could not count on enjoying the future rewards of their effort and investment in production. Under the short-term contract system, peasants could not establish their long-term expectation to realize and collect all the outcomes and rewards due to their work and investments. Some short-term expectations emerged in response to the two-year land contract system, and resulted in losses in long-term productivity of the land. One example of the behavior engendered by short-term leasing is that peasants stopped using manure and other organic fertilizers (which take a long time to affect crop yields but have the benefit of protecting the soil) and only used chemical fertilizers, which have a quick effect. Under the short land-contract system, peasants tried to fully realize, collect, and maximize the rewards and benefits from their temporary land. Stimulated by misguided incentives, peasants tried to extract everything movable or squeezable from land that would not be theirs tomorrow. In other words, under this short-term contract system, peasants not only tried to take away all the outcome of their efforts from the land, leaving nothing in the land, but also tried to squeeze out what was not a result of their efforts. This kind of behavior would soon have destroyed the soil and exhausted the land. Hence, land contracts in the second phase had thirty- to fifty-year terms, which made appropriate expectations and behavior possible. When the term of the land contracts was extended, peasants treated their land — from cultivation to irrigation, soil protection, and amelioration — just like their own.

Although privatization of land is a major attribute of any property rights structure in agriculture, it is not the only attribute. Without privatizing land and fully establishing private property rights, the system did not allow peasants to transfer their land, but the new family-based agriculture system enabled peasants to dispose of their products and income, and provided the institutional setting for peasants to establish a definite relationship between their work and its outcome.

Judging an economic institution in transformation is a matter of distinguishing the growing new institutional elements from the old ones. It is important to identify the growth and development of new institutional elements, particularly of property rights, apart from those that only look like old structures of the system. In his article "Toward a Theory of Property Rights," Demsetz speculates, "Property rights are an instrument of society and derive their significance from the fact that they help a man form those expectations which he can reasonably hold in his dealings with others.... A primary function of property rights is that of guiding incentives to achieve a greater internalization of externalities."[8] To Demsetz, property rights lie in institutions that are instruments through which people can develop expectations and realize rewards internally. The key to understanding the property rights issue of China's agricultural reform is seeing the institutions upon which that expectation is based and to what extent one's return on work and investments can be realized. Further, according to Furubotn and Pejovich's analysis of property rights, there are three aspects to the issue of property rights: the rights to use the asset, to appropriate returns from the asset, and to change the asset.[9] The new family-based responsibility system satisfied two of these three criteria. Under the long-term land contract system, peasants planned the use of their land, put their labor and other production factors into production, and bore the costs and benefits. On the one hand, this long-term land contract system on the basis of family production was not a system from which full private property rights would be derived; on the other hand, it definitely was not a commune or state property rights system. It was, therefore, a mixed property rights system. A deeper purpose of these discussions of property rights is to arouse the public's attention to carefully examine the property rights issue within the reality of the reform and the given historic context. Although many of China's institutional developments and innovations were unconventional in traditional economic terms, they did bring about profound changes in behavior and economic outcome. The institutional issues that unfolded from the transformation of the CPE into a market economy deserve closer scrutiny than they have received. This privatization movement in agriculture had origins in the first-phase reform and really started in the second phase when the land-lease contracts were substantially extended.

Differentiation of Human Assets Made Two Groups of Peasants Stand Out

It is also interesting to note that two groups of peasants improved their lives and increased their income faster than the other peasants. One of these two groups consisted of the former production team leaders; the other group was those entrepreneurial peasants who had always risked criticism to sell their goods and services on the black market even under the commune system and who had chafed most under the old system.[10]

Generally the team leaders and commune officials were better connected than other peasants, and the networks inherited from their previous positions often gave them special advantages under the new system. But more important in general was the high quality of their human capital, which made their adaptation to the new system smooth and rapid. Most former team leaders and other officials in agriculture had been selected from capable, skilled, and experienced peasants in the village.[11] They were better informed and more knowledgeable about the world outside the village, particularly after they had had more opportunities than other peasants to know the world outside their villages through their positions, which had necessitated attending meetings and traveling to learn about others' production experiences. These two factors — being more experienced in production and having access to more information — made former team leaders better prepared human assets for the conversion from the commune system to the new family-based agricultural system.

In the other group, the entrepreneurial peasants had been trying to break the bonds of the commune system in order to work on their own. They had often taken leave without pay and saved time in which to produce their own goods to sell on the black market. Working on their own was reasonably more productive than working under the commune system, and they had earned more, but they had constantly been harassed by officials in the commune. Sometimes they had had to find excuses for their activities in order to avoid or alleviate pressures on them. When the commune system was dissolved and peasants started to work in family units, they felt their liberation most keenly. Among all peasants, this group was most ready for the new agricultural system and faced the fewest obstacles in the conversion of human assets. It is logical that this group of peasants, together with the group of team leaders and officials, enjoyed a more immediate increase and faster growth in income than did the majority of the other peasants.

Limited Further Decentralization

The decentralization of authority from the central to local governments continued in the second phase of reform. Experiments on the financial relationships between central and local governments continued by way of separating the sources of income on the basis of tax classification.[12] The continuing decentralization resulted in an experiment that was popular for a brief period: passing authority one additional step down to large cities, instead of simply to the provincial level. The purpose of this was to reduce further the influence of the planning hierarchy and to provide a better system of organization and a broader base of experimentation for the reform in another effort to hasten disintegration of the existing hierarchy of the CPE.[13] Looking at it from another angle, the decentralization to the city level could be seen as one more step in the "realignment of internal relations" within the CPE and reflected the continuation of the early direction of the reform. The problem with this kind of decentralization was that enterprises would still have been under the aegis of the government and, although city-level governments might be more responsive and less bureaucratic than higher-level governments, they were still governments. As the problems gradually focused on the institutions of state ownership and central planning, less emphasis was placed on the decentralization from a higher-level to a lower-level government.

The decentralization started in mid-1984, when a special meeting on reforming the city management system was held in Beijing. Before this meeting, the first experiment had been initiated in Chongchin, Sichuan Province, in 1983. By 1988, over seventy cities were selected to conduct the same experiment.[14]

The Development of a Code of Laws

The development of a code of laws for the economy was another major aspect of the efforts to institutionalize the reforms, but pursued its own course. As the economy was increasingly liberalized and ownership became possible, the economy desperately needed legal protection for the rights derived from ownership, for the transfer of ownership, for the enforcement of contracts, and for resolution of disputes. A legal system became critically important for free economic activity and market operations. The legal problems in relation to the new economy were concentrated on disputes over land-leasing contracts, disputes over free-trade contracts, disputes over joint-venture relationships, and deception and fraud in transactions. An enormous number of contract disputes were taken to court for resolution. In the eight years from 1980 to 1987, the amount of litigation over disputes concerning economic contracts increased by about one hundred fifty times. The developing legal system gave equal status to all enterprises, peasants, and government offices, abandoning the unequal hierarchical status assigned them by the central planning system and protecting their rights in the new economic system. It was true that the government often put itself above the law, but it was also true that a growing number of government offices, high-ranking party officials, and state-owned enterprises were brought to court as defendants and prosecuted for their liabilities, even on criminal charges.[15] The institutionalization effort with regard to the legal system was reflected in part by the development of official legislation. China began to implement an economic contract law in 1980 to meet the needs of the economy under the reform. However, the first Economic Contract Law didn't go into effect until 1982. In 1985 and in 1988, the Law was substantially revised to respond to the dramatic changes taking place in institutions and behavior. As the economic institutions changed and a variety of new economic activities arose, there was a continuing demand for more comprehensive and appropriate laws to provide effective protection in the freer economy. Given that the issue of property rights did not exist in a centrally planned and state-owned economy, contract law was unnecessary. In effect, economic disputes in the CPE were resolved through administrative coordination and mediation. Particularly, since under the CPE any property belonged to the state and individual interest was supposedly subsumed by the common interest, no one cared about the gains and losses of different economic units. Moreover, not only the law and legislative process, but also the judicial system and law enforcement forces, took time and practice to mature. Although it proceeded in a more incremental way than most of the other aspects of the reform, the legal system developed rapidly in the second phase of the reform.

Integration into the World Economy

Starting in the early reform era, integration of the Chinese economy with the world's became another major goal of reform policy. Opening its doors to the world and conducting the SEZ experiments from the very beginning of the reform movement were signs of the reformers' wisdom. The process of integrating the Chinese economy into the global economy could be described as a series of experiments related to the SEZ, and in the second phase of reform the main function of the SEZs was officially altered from "special export zone" to "experimental field of reform policies." The SEZs provided a special source of experiments for the open "touching stones" approach. The ideas of free trade and "small government" were exported to mainland China from the SEZs.

Most important for the economic reform, the policies of integrating the Chinese economy into the world economy were largely used to dismantle the central planning system. The bureaucracy of the central planning system had always insisted on following existing procedures so as to keep its control over the economy. From 1984 on, the reform of industrial integration and reorganization consistently exposed the bureaucracy of the central planning system to attacks arising from the demand for simplifying or eliminating bureaucratic procedures and government control. Specifically, foreign trade-oriented enterprises, both domestic and foreign-funded, filed numerous complaints about the bureaucracy's inefficiency in handling applications and performing its management function. These enterprises often criticized the bureaucracy for its excessive control and blamed it for missing opportunities for competition in the world market. Constant criticism and complaints led to the elimination of some of the planning offices and related procedures. In addition, the economic integration forced the Chinese to follow international conventions of doing business and observing market rules. In an aggressive international market the threat of being excluded pressed the Chinese to adjust their economic system to world competition. By the end of 1988, most of China's provinces had adopted the policies for the SEZs in some way.

Dramatic Expansion of the Private Economy

During the second phase of reform, the nonstate and private economy was the most active part of the Chinese economy and became a powerful competitor of the state economy. "Nonstate and private economy" is a term used to distinguish the emerging sectors from the rest of the economy, that is, the state economy. The nonstate and private economy included privately owned enterprises in both the urban and rural areas, foreign fund-related enterprises, peasant-run collectively invested enterprises in villages and small towns, and the enterprises originating in groups of urban working people.[16] The reform did not convert many of the state-owned businesses into privately owned ones, but brought an economic liberalization that stimulated unprecedented growth of the nonstate and private economy. Compared with the period from 1979 to 1984, when the nonstate and private economy was at first tolerated and then gradually encouraged, the period from 1984 to 1988 witnessed the nonstate and private sector starting to compete with the state economy and making a major contribution to employment, revenue for the government budget, economic growth, and exports. Among many indicators, a comparison of the sectors' growth rates is perhaps the most convincing: During this period, the annual GNP growth rate of the private industry was about 30 percent.

In the early days of the reform, policies to encourage the nonstate and private economies were mostly intended to alleviate the huge pressure of unemployment. A document released by the central government in late 1981 was representative, officially welcoming and encouraging the nonstate and private enterprises to develop.[17] The main purposes were made clear: to find a solution for the problems of unemployment in urban areas, and to tap the pool of surplus labor and capital that was in the hands of the peasants. The development of the nonstate and private sectors in the early days of reform reflected both the rising economic concerns of pragmatic policies since the late 1970s and also the increasing demand for flexible policies to allow some free economic activities. The nonstate and private sectors were not subject to state planning control and were less exposed to government interference.[18] Particularly, while the state-owned firms were still under the supervision of government and tried to fulfill quotas remaining from the state plan, these newborn nonstate enterprises were already operating under conditions of market competition with an overwhelming profit-seeking motive. The nonstate economy learned to survive and profit in competition from its very first days, and its components were driven by self-interest and therefore more active in identifying and defending the rights and interests their ownership entitled them to. The state economy and the nonstate and private economies differed primarily in the areas of growth rate, efficiency, and competitiveness. These differences in economic performance would further translate into a shrinking state economy and expansion of the nonstate and private economies. Thus the economic transformation proceeded.

Perplexed Reconstruction of Enterprises

Enterprise reform presents possibly the best view of the complexity and differentiation in the whole process of China's economic transformation. When agricultural reform accomplished its profound institutional change from the commune system to the family-based system, it inspired many other reforms. It was soon understood, however, that the success of agricultural reform would not be easily achieved in enterprise reform. As has been said earlier, collective agricultural production succeeded by simply dividing work units and the assets of the commune and replaced it with the institution of family responsibility. This kind of reform, however, did not appear promising for the state enterprises, which functioned by means of a sophisticated division and coordination of each and every unit. The characteristics of interaction, interdependence, and frequent transactions involved in enterprise reform differed substantially from those of agriculture. Particularly, few of the available assets were prepared for the change from a centrally planned enterprise system to a free enterprise system.

Two Schemes to Tap the Property Rights Issue

In its second phase, one of the principal features of Chinese economic reform was the construction of enterprises in an attempt to clarify the property relationships between them and the government. The experiments of enterprise reform in this period included selling small enterprises and leasing and contracting out the state enterprises. At first, as part of the continuing reform from the first phase, enterprise reform in these years was accompanied by an important change: whereas the strategy previous to the second phase had been to pass down authority from the central to the local governments, the strategy now was to pass authority directly to the enterprises and to try to solve problems from the perspective of property rights. Gradually, after a period of experimentation, it was understood that the essence of enterprise reform was related to ownership, and that the authority structure was ultimately derived from the ownership structure. Later enterprise reform took on the task of resolving the problems of state ownership and asset relationships. The efforts to reform the state enterprises in the second phase of reform could be categorized into two schemes. The first was to separate the government from the operation and decision making of enterprises and to make it the representative of state ownership, whose only function was to choose chief managers of enterprises. When a chief manager was chosen, he would be given full authority to run an enterprise for a certain contractual period.

The second scheme was to privatize the state enterprises. As the more profound reform, privatization would be more attractive as a means of solving the incentive problems of the state enterprises. Privatization, however, appeared to require more knowledge and institutional support from China's economy, which, having been a CPE for decades, lacked the experience and support that a capitalist economy could have provided. In any case, enterprise reforms in the second phase differed from those of the early reform by breaking away from the idea of "realignment of internal relations" and by targeting the problem of ownership and property rights. If the goal of enterprise reform was to privatize the state enterprises, privatization under the centralized planning system still differed significantly from privatization in a market economy. In a market economy, such as Britain's, the government acts as the owner and generally confines itself to choosing the chief managers, leaving the daily operation and business decisions of enterprises to them. But in a CPE, the government not only played the role of owner and chose the managers, but also planned what, how, and how much to produce of goods and services, as well as from whom inputs came and to whom outputs went. Therefore, the issue and situations involved in the privatization of a CPE and a market economy are not exactly the same.

Contracting-out System to Create Real Managers

One example of the first scheme was the reform of the contracting-out and leasing programs, which were in a dominant position in the enterprise reform of the second phase. Contracting out the state-owned enterprises was intended to keep the government from interfering in the enterprises' daily business and operations, and therefore to cultivate agents who were solely responsible for their decisions in a market environment. The reform of the contracting-out mechanism was conducted since 1987 in such a way that a committee representing the state openly selected from a pool of candidates the chief manager, who signed a three-year contract. By the end of 1988, over 90 percent of the state-owned enterprises had adopted the system of contracting out. In 1987 and 1988, a competition mechanism was introduced into the contracting-out and leasing programs. In some areas, candidates were requested to offer their bids for a contract. On a nationwide base, about 35.5 percent of contracts were granted through this bidding process. In Jilin province, as high as 79 percent of the state enterprises were contracted out through competitive bidding. In addition, a pledge mechanism was put in as an experiment to insure against risk. The pledge included a personal pledge from those who had bids and a collective pledge from all the employees. The personal pledge was usually a certain substantial amount of personal property pledged against the risk of business failure under contract. Among all the contracting out nationwide, about 25 percent was let on the basis of a pledge mechanism.[19] The leasing programs were basically similar to the contracting-out programs and were mainly applied to small enterprises.

The contracting-out and leasing programs reflected, as efforts to solve the problems caused by state ownership, an incremental two-step approach to reform. The problems faced by the state industries in capitalist economies such as in Britain where daily operations of the state-owned enterprises are basically left to managers or agents. In contrast, the problems for the state enterprises in the CPE included not only those of principal-agent relations based on state ownership, but also the relentless interference of government in their daily operations. As discussed above, it was generally agreed that government's direct interference in enterprises would degrade their ability to make economically rational decisions; the reform was thus intended to separate the government from the enterprises. This separation was twofold: first, separation of the government from the daily operation of the enterprises; and second, separation of the government from the ownership relations of the enterprises. The first part of the separation obviously was not a necessary condition for the second part. Combining the first and second separations, if possible, would be a one-step solution for the removal of the government from the enterprises. The one-step solution might have included selling the state enterprises and introducing a shareholding system. In general, however, a one-step privatization would need more favorable conditions than simply the first step of separation of the government from the enterprises. The primary conditions for considering privatization, of major enterprises in particular, would include reasonable competition in the market,[20] ability and institutions of pricing before there was a market, buyers, regulations, and entrepreneurship. Some of these conditions matured as the reform proceeded; others needed more time. In this situation, the contracting-out and leasing programs were partly to realize the first part of the separation by introducing a contractual relation under which the government was to stay away, during contract periods, from interference in the daily operation of enterprises. It was true that in many industries contracting-out and leasing programs were only a transitional reform. The problems of state ownership would still exist after contracting out, and the state ownership would continue to hamper the managers' behavior.

In addition, the contracting-out and leasing programs were chosen as a result of compromises arising from concerns about efficiency and manageability. From the perspective of efficiency, which was usually an immediate and short-term consideration, contracting out and leasing were usually conducted with modest requirements for some improvement in efficiency of production and operations. From the perspective of manageability, contracting out and leasing appeared to cause fewer uncertainties, given the minimal experience of the Chinese with the market economy, than would one-step privatization.

In the reform process, uncertainty was often translated into the concern of manageability. However, this kind of general understanding did not conflict with another aim of reform: to privatize enterprises in service and industry directly. As will be discussed further below, the experiments in selling state enterprises and introducing a shareholding system had been conducted even before most of the state enterprises adopted the system of contracting out, and these experiments were continued even when contracting out was chosen as the chief system (in 1987 and 1988). In sum, the system of contracting out was chosen as a result of the concern about immediate and short-run efficiency, institutional acceptance, and preparedness in terms of the pace of reform and the overall strategy of enterprise reform.

It is noted that the state enterprises was employed also to save those enterprises in deficit from going into bankruptcy or continuing to be subsidized. Merging took place in the state economy during the mid-1980s. The merges often happened in such a way that profitable businesses simply took over those firms that had been in deficit for years or even had negative assets. According to a report based on data from twenty-seven of China's provinces in 1988, 2,856 enterprises merged with 3,424 other enterprises.[21] Reintegration[22] took place competitively in an attempt to increase efficiency, to reduce uncertainty, and to enhance survival ability.

Shareholding System to Transform Ownership

Under the second major scheme, enterprise reform simultaneously sold small state enterprises and instituted a shareholding program. Such one-step enterprise reform was conducted on an individual basis instead of as a policy. Specifically, in the cases of small state-owned factories and shops, in which the pricing of assets and the establishment of clear ownership structures were relatively simple, privatization was adopted. Moreover, the fact that such small businesses did not pose a threat of monopoly would usually make privatization easier to consider. First, from 1985 on, small enterprises, particularly those in service sectors as well as some in low-profit or deficit situations, were sold to private parties. Second, some important experiments in shareholding were conducted. Although some spontaneous efforts to create a shareholding system started in 1983 and 1984 in a few areas, this spread to medium and large enterprises only after 1986. By the end of 1988, according to the statistics of twenty provinces, there were about 3,800 enterprises experimenting with shareholding. Among them, 85 percent of the enterprises were sold to employees, 13.5 percent were held by other enterprises, and 1.5 percent were sold to the public.[23]

Shareholding experiments became increasingly attractive in the later years as the practice of contracting out proved flawed due to the persistence of state ownership. One of the major problems with contracting out was still the matter of owner representation. Local governments, which were usually responsible for formulating a contracting-out committee, did not work under any mechanism that protected the owner's interests. Another problem was arbitrariness in the process prior to contracting out and prior to the assessment, which left room for the government to interfere and for managers to get away from the strict constraints of responsibility and liability.

The enterprise reform in the second phase focused on the separation of the government from the enterprises and on the issue of ownership. Both one-step privatization and two-step separation were put into practice in an effort to reconstruct Chinese enterprises. While the two-step separation policy — the contracting-out system — was the main route of enterprise reform, a variety of experiments related to state ownership took place in the process of searching and then preparing for reform solutions. The progress made by enterprise reform in the second phase, in essence, was the adoption of a strategy to separate the government from the business operations of enterprises, creating relative independence for enterprises, allowing them to compete on their own in the market, and promoting the growth of a new generation of entrepreneurs. For most of the state-owned enterprises, this kind of a two-step separation reform worked as a transition to eventual withdrawal of government control over enterprises and appropriate privatization of the state enterprises.

A Perspective from Transaction Costs

From the perspective of transaction costs, the practice of enterprise reform suggests special avenues of speculation. Economic reform inevitably caused changes in contractual relations between the government and enterprises in the direction of efficiency; whenever the existing system hindered this evolution, there were demands for further reform of the system.

Many industrial and organizational relations were embedded from the relations between the government and enterprises. Reducing transaction costs constituted an important and constant motivation to adjust and reform the existing economic relations. When the contractual relationship between the government and enterprises obviously prevented from making timely, competitive decisions, certain parts of this relationship would be subject to demand for adjustment. When the mandatory employment system, which determined contractual relations between enterprises and workers, could not create a sense of responsibility or the efficient use of labor, these relations faced challenges. Gradually the issues of property and asset ownership, too, were inevitably involved. When vertical integration and the centralized, planned control of industry inhibited efficient cooperation directly between enterprises and maintained artificially high transaction costs, a dissolution of vertical integration and bureaucratic control was called for. Initially, problems of high transaction costs were solved on a contingency basis and contractual relations were adjusted in line with these cost savings. Institutional adjustment based on individual cases built up substantial cumulative change in the overall economic system. Several cases sometimes caught the policymakers' attention and led to changes in policy and regulation and, hence, to broader institutional changes. The steady reduction in transportation costs offers an interesting explanation for the incremental reform of contractual relations. As economic freedom grew, the effort to reduce transaction costs and to search for more efficient governance structures increasingly influenced economic reform and evaluation of the economic system. Oliver E. Williamson offers a brilliant observation on economic institutions in general: "Transactions, which differ in their attributes, are assigned to governance structures, which differ in their organizational costs and competencies, so as to effect a discriminating (mainly transaction cost economizing) match."[24] This observation sheds light on the reform of China's CPE.

Development of the Market Through a Two-track System

The Two-track System Emerged as an Outcome of Incremental Reform

In the second phase, many specific reforms proceeded along a two-track system. Two-track policies had already existed in the first phase of reform, but they prevailed only during the second phase. Basically, in the first phase of reform, economic activities free of central planning emerged and developed as a result of new policies formulated to alleviate the problems in the planned economy. As part of its effort to introduce new incentives to enterprises, the government started in 1979 to allow enterprises to sell their extra products themselves. In consequence, although planned production and distribution continued to dominate, a small but expanding share of products and resources were priced and distributed outside of the planning system. This share grew dramatically during the second phase from a minor portion to a substantial portion of total resources and products. Although the extra products were part of total marginal products, the signal of incentive was imperative. The market pricing mechanism eventually came to cover most products. At the same time, the nonstate and private economy became a substantial part of the overall economy. The Chinese economic system could now be characterized as a two-track system. Importantly, the two-track system was attributed to the incremental "touching stones" strategy. While the complexity of transformation was overwhelming and the related uncertainty high, the parallel tracks permitted the central planning system to play acceptable roles in the operation of the economy and to change itself gradually, while experimenting with the new institutions of market economy. The choice of the two-track policies and development of this system seemed to reveal implicit risk aversion in the overall strategy of the Chinese reform movement.

The two-track system provided a dynamic process that kept the existing system working while transforming it into a new system. This dynamic process included evolution of the goal of the reform (discussed in chapter 1) as well as evolution of the economy and its system. Importantly, the two-track system was not a static coexistence of planned and free economies but rather a transitional institution that allowed the free economy to grow and the planned economy to adjust itself under competition. As long as the government gave up its control of choosing economic institutions, the mechanism of institutional selection would work during the transition. Institutional selection provided the direction of the dynamic process. The history of the two-track system demonstrated that the advantages of a free economy over a planned economy entailed a dynamic process of transition. The economic activities that were not under the central planning system grew relatively faster and, during the second phase, became a substantial part of the Chinese economy. Since the two-track system allowed comparison of and competition between the free economy and the CPE, the market economy gradually replaced the planned economy.

Coping with Uncertainty

The two-track system provided a path of transition by helping to reduce some of the difficulties in the reform process and by paving the way for a smooth transformation. There are two interesting aspects of the two-track policies and system that are worth exploring. The first one is related to the smooth adjustment of supply. In the early days of the reform, the effort to allow enterprises to sell their increasing surpluses on the market helped to send out signals to consumers that they should adjust demand. Compared with the alternative of a one-step lifting of price controls, the two-track policies allowed the market to provide a pricing mechanism and to alert enterprises to adjust their production in accord with these indicators. The key point is that although at first only a small portion of a product was priced on the free market, the information borne in the market prices influenced production as a whole. The mechanism, specifically, was that the allocation of all new resources and investments was influenced and directed by prices. China's steel industry will serve as an example. In the early days of reform, steel was in short supply as a result of its state-imposed price. Every steel-consuming enterprise fought to buy steel. When lifting price controls on steel was discussed, the government worried that it would cause too much redistribution among industries and the collapse of some of them. But the old planned price was too low to allow the steel enterprises to increase production. Facing a policy dilemma, the government put a two-track policy into effect: steel manufactured under the central plan would continue to be sold at the planned price but, importantly, any extra amount produced would be allowed to go to market at a 100 to 150 percent higher price. This was a strong signal for the enterprises to increase production. Even though there was still a price control on steel, the production of raw steel and rolled steel increased over a period of ten years by 86 percent and 110 percent respectively.[25] Ten years later, with the dramatic increase in quality as well as output, most steel products were priced according to the market and the planned price was gradually adjusted to the market price. Thus, once an initially small amount of surplus product that was in short supply entered the market and was sold at market price, it spurred a huge boost in production of those goods.

Institutional and Human Assets Preparation

The second key to understanding the two-track system is institutional preparation and selection. Importantly, the two-track system provided broad opportunities for developing the basic elements of market institutions, which included managers' being able to make decisions of competition and uncertainty, development of the structure of a competitive market, contractual relations based on free choice and voluntary cooperation, and entrepreneurship. There was an implicit danger that policymakers would want to choose a certain style of reform based on one theory or another and try to design an optimal path and institutions accordingly. Since the previous thinking about the optimization of the economic system still remained, there were always tendencies to ignore the importance of process in establishing new institutions, as well as the importance of the environment of institutional evolution.

Given the context of culture, history, and economic development, the best path for China's transformation lay in consideration of a variety of alternatives and timing options. The success of reforming China's economy appeared to have taken place through various processes instead of any single process. The primary context of the Chinese economic reform was two thousand years of self-sufficient agriculture with little exchange, three decades of central planning, and the fact that, as late as 1987, 59 percent of the Chinese labor force was illiterate, semiliterate, or had received no more than five years of formal education.[26] This was the environment into which the Chinese launched an unprecedented transformation by choosing the incremental two-track transition method. Moreover, the two tracks should not be seen as an attempt to delay any significant reform. In fact, the ten years of reform not only liberated eight hundred million people from the communes, but also rapidly and fundamentally transformed the Chinese economy to one largely dependent on market forces. Most of the major institutional changes and selections were related to the two-track process. This underscores the importance of the existence of different experiments and the possibility of selection and innovation on the basis of diversification of economic institutions.

Two-track Price as the Core

As a major constituent of two-track reform, the two-track price reform shifted from essentially adjusting prices in order to improve the planning system to gradually lifting price controls in order to establish a market system.[27] As the share of products sold at market prices kept growing, the market was no longer a supplementary mechanism in allocating resources, but became a major mechanism operating simultaneously with the planning mechanism. As markets provided a reference for planning prices, the two price structures clearly began to converge. It merits mention here that it was the market, instead of "calculation," that drove this convergence.[28]

In general, the transition by means of a two-track system implied that the institutional elements of a market system could not have been converted from the CPE; instead, a process of institutional development was necessary. Even if government control over the economy were to have been lifted in some fields, the vestiges of government control would still have existed for a certain period of time, and enterprises and individuals would still have remained associated with the government in many respects. The point is that the market would not immediately have assumed the place of the central planning mechanism, which had operated for decades in an environment devoid of entrepreneurship and competition.

Problems and Contradictions

The ten years of Chinese economic reform did not go unchallenged. Problems, both economic and political, hampered the reform, and within the ten-year period there occurred three mandatory economic contractions (1981-82, 1985-86, and 1988-89) and three instances of political retrenchment (1983-84, 1987, and 1989-90). Some of the economic and political events were connected, but others were not. Behind these fluctuations were some problems inherently related to the economic reform.

Inflation

The first threatening problem was high inflation. From 1984 on, complaints about inflation had been growing and, particularly after 1987, placed a great deal of pressure on the central government. At its peak in 1988, the problem began to threaten the continuity of some major reform policies and even the continuity of the top leadership.[29] Inflation caused uncertainty and tension, discrepancies in the distribution of income and wealth, and confusion in investment, issues that the reform was not able to address either carefully or successfully.

Corruption

The second major failing was corruption, which was related to both equity and efficiency. Government officials and their associates took advantage of their positions in the government to gain access to scarce resources in shortage and to low price quotas, which were a legacy of the CPE. Most government-controlled resources and goods were priced much lower than equivalent commodities in the market and were distributed by the government through quotas, so that there were two prices for many identical items. Since market prices for resources and goods in shortage could be as high as two or three times their controlled prices, some government officials and their associates benefited from the difference between planned and market prices. In addition, permits and quotas issued by the government were sold and resold on the black market by those who had special connections.

While it was true that such types of exchange might increase the efficiency of allocation by favoring low-cost producers, since access to low-priced resources and quotas came from political privilege and corrupt nepotism, the practice was unfair and intolerable to most people. In addition, the government did not make enough effort to develop other mechanisms, mainly the market mechanism, to improve allocation, which further antagonized people. The two-track system was also blamed in part for the worsening corruption in Chinese society. The two-track system created new privileges due to the price advantages and continuing central control, and these were seized upon by the bureaucrats and political officials. Such new privileges were easier to translate into economic benefit in a partial market than in a pure CPE; they enhanced the sense of corruption and inequality during the reform process, and increased the hostility felt by the general population toward reform and the reform government.

Infrastructure

The third problem was the government's mistake in underestimating the rising importance of infrastructure in the new economy. During a large part of the ten-year period, and particularly in the early years, irrigation facilities, transportation systems, and the education and medical systems received much less investment than they should have. The core of the problem was that the government was slow to realize and respond to the alteration in the function of infrastructure. More specifically, even while the government controlled fewer and fewer resources than it had under the CPE, it still made investments on the basis of its old function: to take care of every area of the economy, from building factories to arranging transactions. As a result, the government invested much less money in almost every field, including infrastructure. At the same time, as the economy grew rapidly, the need and corresponding demand for improved infrastructure increased dramatically. The slow development of infrastructure created widespread problems, such as traffic congestion, inadequate defense for agriculture in case of bad weather, soaring medical costs, and general inconvenience in the life of the Chinese people.

Ongoing Misallocation of Resources

Yet another problem was the continued misallocation of resources, which was related to delayed attempts to lift price controls. The two-track system was at the root of the issue. The meaning of the two-track system lay entirely in the transitory nature of its role and there had been a danger that it might have been used as an excuse to delay the final lifting of remaining central planning controls. The two-track system, apart from its functional advantages, could have prevented the formulation of unified rules for market activities, hurt fair competition, and insulted low-efficiency producers and services. To that end, any delay in the effort to complete the convergence of the two price tracks would have led to ineffective allocation and use of resources, and it would have greatly increased the negative side effects of the transitional system.

Local Protectionism

Local protectionism was another complication. As local governments came to exert more and more authority over the allocation of resources, they tried to set up barriers to trade and exchange with other regions in order to promote local efficiency and protect local interests. Local protectionism caused three major losses. First, it kept certain areas in China backward and allowed the old system in particular to survive. Since most protectionism occurred in the inland regions, where internal markets were underdeveloped and did not have much competition, local protectionism most often perpetuated backwardness, obsolete technology, and inefficient organizations and institutions. In the long run, it hurt local economies. Second, it allowed local governments to maintain control over enterprises, and thus forced enterprises to depend on the government's support instead of relying on competitiveness. Third, it hurt the development of the market by preventing competition. However, local protectionism was and is a difficult and often complicated problem in China, given the existence of imbalances among regions.

Stagnant Political System

Finally, and most important, the stagnant political system became a major barrier to lifting the remaining government controls over the economy. Under the political system current as of this writing, the government still has the ultimate authority in the economy. In addition to the fact that there has not been institutionalized protection of human rights, property rights and ownership have not been firmly guaranteed and protected. Regulatory policies and even reform policies were used to discriminate economically against certain types of ownership. For example, loan and credit policies treated enterprises unfairly on the grounds of ownership. The granting of loans and credit for business was not based on performance or ability to repay but on whether an enterprise was state owned or collectively or privately owned. The banks, which were solely state owned, tended to provide loans and credit to the state enterprises, often due to connections within the planning bureaucracy, and loan and credit policies were traditionally set in favor of the state enterprises. The reform to dismantle the central planning bureaucracy had been particularly difficult, given its powerful influence over decision making in the reform effort. In addition, the central political control protects the government from effective surveillance by the people, and it allows corruption to disrupt the equitable allocation of resources and to direct public wealth into personal pockets.

Some of these problems could be attributed, to a large extent, to mistakes in politics; others are related more to the fact that the reform was a new venture. After all, many of these problems existed in the shadow of human assets schooled by the CPE and of the uncertainty attending the new undertaking. During the reform movement, even though the government initiated and implemented reform measures, the decision makers and officials were not able to foresee or did not fully realize the outcomes of those measures at various stages. Particularly, as reform proceeded, the total economic system was continually evolving, and this should have been taken into account in formulating and adjusting reform policies. A lack of human asset adjustment to changes in the economy resulted in many policy mistakes, some of which could have been avoided. The problem of infrastructure, for instance, was in this category. Some of the problems had to do with transition, since they were related more to the process of the transformation than to policy mistakes. This kind of problem occurred when the legal order was not yet capable of replacing the old administrative order in the economy. There also happened as a result of the lack of competition and certain necessary regulations in the economy. Some problems presented features of both categories and added more difficulties to decision making in the reform. The pressure of most of the problems could have been alleviated by improving reform policy analysis and, most importantly, by persisting in the reform to a market-oriented economy and a more democratic political system.

Briefly then, the process of second-phase reform was characterized by two factors: an open information process and a transition under a two-track system; it was distinguished from first-phase reform by its pursuit of a market system. The reform's driving forces included more diversified and spontaneous factors in the movement's later years. The challenges to and responses from the human assets represent the most profound element of the entire transformation from a CPE to a market system. By the end of the second phase of the reform, China was well on its way to a market economy.

Notes

1. After Deng Xiaoping's early 1992 trip to southern China, in which he appealed to local leaders to return to the reform and to take even more daring measures to change the existing economic system, it appeared that, after more than two years' hiatus, the Chinese leadership might want to make economic reform a priority again. Deng's campaign also reflected that, under China's existing political system, power was still vested in one supreme leader.
2. In pinyin, this phrase is: "bu shi lu shan zhen mian mu, zhi yuan shen zhai ci shan zhong."
3. Harding 1992, 308.
4. Smith 1937, 776.
5. China Economic Reconstruction Committee, "China's Economic Reform in 1984," in *Almanac of China's Economy 1985*, II.5.)

6. "CCCCP and CSC's Ten Major Policies on Further Development of the Agricultural Economy," in *Almanac of China's Economy 1985*, X.10.
7. By the end of 1988, there were about 71,400 trading centers and marketplaces for the exchange of agricultural products around the country ("China's Economic Reform in 1988 Development of Market System," in *Almanac of China's Economy 1989*, III.22.
8. Harold Demsetz, "Toward A Theory of Property Rights," *American Economic Review* 57 (May 1967): 347-48.
9. Furubotn and Petjovich 1947, 4.
10. "Black market" here refers to the market outside of the government-controlled trading and transaction system, where only the government-run agents and state-owned firms could sell goods and services before 1979. Black markets existed throughout most of the prereform era, but the government changed its policies toward the black market from time to time. Sometimes the selling of goods and services by individual peasants in the black market was encouraged. At other times such activity was restricted, and those who sold their own products through unofficial channels were criticized and harassed. Sometimes, their products were confiscated by local government officials and the sellers were labeled as "capitalist."
11. Despite the fact that some of the officials had been corrupt and skilled in favoritism under the commune system, peasants even at that time had had to be realistic and choose capable people to manage production, which largely determined how much food a village or team had at the end of a year. A Team leader in a village was supposed to be a master of how and when to grow crops, how much labor was required for certain tasks, and what kind of tools and techniques were best suited for which plants. Normally, team leaders were elected every one or two years. If someone in the position was proved unable to organize all the peasants to work under the collective system, another peasant would most likely replace him the nest year.
12. "Finance Ministry on Tax and Tax-return Policies for Import and Export Products," in *Almanac of China's Economy 1986*, X.57-58.
13. "Memorandum of the Meeting on the Experiment in Reforming the Urban Economic System," *Economic Daily* 15 May 1985; "Development of Urban Reform Experiments," in *Almanac of China's Economy 1985*, II.3.
14. "Suggestions on Conducting the Integral Experiment of Economic System Reform in Chongchin City," in *Collection of Documents on Economic Reform 1977-1983* 1984, 673-78; Gao Shangquan, "China's Ten-year Economic Reform," in *Almanac of China's Economy 1989*, II.40.

15. For more details, see: Wang Hui, Li Rengyu and Liu, "On Creating A New Economic order in the Reform," *China: Development and Reform* 7 (1988). In this report on the development of the legal system in relation to economic reform, the disputes in the new economy were analyzed on the basis of an empirical study using the data from 1979 to 1987.

16. Collectively owned peasant enterprises started to appear in Jiangsu and Zejiang Province in the 1970s when some communes or production teams invested their surpluses to form construction teams and factories. This kind of enterprise initially manufactured certain agricultural products, produced small parts for urban state-owned factories, and provided services for the urban community. Particularly in the late 1970s, peasants in these areas felt great pressure from a decline in the average acreage per capita and were forced to find ways to support population growth. When the communes were actually dissolved in the early 1980s, these collectively owned peasant enterprises survived and further developed as more resources became available in the marketplace. These urban collective enterprises were mostly formed in the late 1950s and early 1970s. During the Great Leap Forward, many housewives and retired workers tried to produce something with their skills. They made a variety of small articles, from shoes and furniture to pots and food. Following the peak of the Cultural Revolution, another wave emerged of such collective enterprises.

17. "Decisions by the CCCCP and CSC on Liberalizing the Economy and Solving the Problems of Urban Employment," in *Collection of Documents on Economic Reform 1977-1983* 1984, 634-38.

18. Sometimes, particularly during the early years of the reform, owners of the nonstate and private businesses claimed to have been treated as "second class" citizens and their businesses as "second class" businesses. Primarily, they usually had less access to loans and credit, did not have the quotas of low-priced supplies, and had less guarantee of supplies of products that were being held in reserve, such as electricity and gas. But this was also their most important advantage over the state-owned firms in that the nonstate and private firms did not have to be restricted and controlled by state planning, the chief complaint of the managers of state enterprises.

19. "China's Economic Reform in 1988 Situation and Problems of Enterprise Reform" and "China's Economic Reform in 1988 — Development and Trend Toward Ownership Reform," in *Almanac of China's Economy 1989*, III.4-8.

20. Vickers and Yarrow 1988, 45-63.

21. Ibid.

22. "Suggestions by China Economic Reconstruction Committee and National Economic Committee on Organization and Development of Enterprise Groups," in *Almanac of China's Economy 1989*, IX.17-18.
23. "China's Economic Reform in 1988 Situation and Problems of Enterprise Reform," in *Almanac of China's Economy 1989*, III.5.
24. Williamson 1985, 387-88.
25. Wang Mongkui, "Ten Years' Economic Construction," in *Almanac of China's Economy 1989*, II.31.
26. Ibid., p. II.36.
27. In the period 1979-84, the main target of price reform appeared to be to rid prices of distortion and to make planning prices close to equilibrium prices. The prices of agricultural products were raised first in 1979 and again in 1981. In addition, from 1981, prices of timber and wood products were raised. Price was seen foremost as a factor in introducing new incentive to production while it was still used to control and assign resources. It was a common phenomenon that because of low prices, which could not even cover costs, peasants and enterprises in some industries had no incentive at all to increase production, which led to increased loss and deficit. The distortion of prices influenced not only enterprises' behavior but also local governments' behavior. A local government was interested in supporting or encouraging an enterprise to increase the production of goods that were not profitable. If an enterprise was in deficit, the local government might have to use part of its budget to subsidize it. In general, from early 1979 to 1984, the price reform adopted price adjustment measures, allowing enterprises to sell their extra products in the market, and decontrolling the prices of small commodities. While price adjustments took place mainly as a measure to encourage and promote production, some extra products or marginal products were priced in the market. When price adjustments were used simply to raise prices, there was usually a simultaneous adjustment of wages to cushion the impact on workers.
28. Mises and Hayek were among the economists who severely criticized the model of market socialism offered by Lange and asserted that the imitation of market on the basis of "calculation" was doomed to failure.
29. At the Beidaihe meeting in the summer of 1988, which was originally planned for discussion and examination of the reform program lifting price controls, the top reform leadership was called to task for the program and was blamed for the "mistake of radical and too-fast reform." The reform program was dropped and realignment of power followed.

6

Conclusions

China's economic reform was by its very nature a revolution, fundamentally changing the major characteristics of the country's economic system and driving it away from central planning and toward a market economy. Today, this reform movement is still continuing. In terms of economic institutions, this reform has evolved and gone far beyond any of its original or early decision makers' intentions.

This concluding chapter begins with a discussion of the profound changes that have occurred in China's economic institutions due to the gradual revolution and describes the major reasons for its occurrence. The next topics to be taken up are the relationship between the transformation and the conversion and reappreciation of human assets, and the mechanism of these twin processes. Following these topics will be a discussion of human assets as determinants of transformation. Throughout this chapter, implications of China's incremental experimental approach, its manner of giving and receiving information to and from the outside world, the environment in which the transformation occurred, and uncertainty issues facing the reform will be discussed.

The Gradual Revolution

Although a revolution is seldom perceived accurately at the time it occurs, China's economic reform is bringing its centrally planned system — an artificially constructed mechanism — to an end, and the reform movement already has had a tremendous impact on the lives of over one billion people. A revolution here refers to creation of fundamentally new characteristics of an economic and social system. Since the end of the 1970s, the Chinese have abandoned most of their mandatory controls over agriculture, services, and industries. New incentives have been introduced in areas of the economy through the dissolution of the commune system in agriculture; contracting out, leasing, and shareholding of state enterprises; and development of the private economy. By the end of the first decade of reform, the market was allocating and coordinating more than half of the nation's resources and production. In the last two to three years, another quarter of the resources and products have entered the market, which now allocates about three-quarters of the total. The Chinese economy can no longer be characterized as a centrally planned system but rather as a mixture of planned and market systems. Most important, there is a tremendous momentum moving the economy toward a market system. This momentum is built upon the elemental pursuit of happiness and a better life, which have been illuminated by the decentralization and liberation of the economy since 1979. Although the trail to the market remains to be blazed and more fluctuations of reform may still occur, decentralized and diversified searches for improving economic performance, the rapidly developing private economy, and a new rational underlying the decisions of private individuals and officials alike compose the foundation of a new economic system.

China's reform was, from the perspective of its evolving attributes dealing with transition, a *gradual* revolution. Incremental change was the hallmark of its goals, definitions, and content, in each of the particular reforms undertaken throughout the reform. In terms of the process and progress of reform, there were physically and mentally cumulative effects of change in both specific economic institutions and the overall economic system. Shifts in the constraints and rationale of economic reform also indicated a pattern of gradual change and the impact of the accumulation of such unspectacular, steady changes. On the one hand, the revolution was gradual in the sense of its evolving dominant beliefs, its experimental approach, and its shifting focus on dismantling the old system and developing the new system. On the other hand, the revolution was gradual from the viewpoint of adjusting the planning system while rapidly developing the market. As the development of new economic institutions was highly uncertain and took time to reach normal operating levels, a continuous adjustment of the existing planning system helped to smooth the transformation, reducing fluctuations and enhancing the capability to sustain risks.

The Chinese case demonstrates that incremental reform can achieve revolutionary effects. Throughout the Chinese reform, most economic institutions changed in a series of steps. From its agricultural reform, enterprise reform, the reform of the relationships between the central and local government, and development of the market, we see continual adjustments, adaptation, and innovation of economic institutions. A series of incremental measures accumulated a fundamental change of the economic institutions in China. This explains in part the Chinese economic reform: In *appearance*, it proceeded mostly gradually; in *substance,* it profoundly transformed the CPE into a relatively market-oriented economy and gave it the momentum to continue toward a free-market economy.

Momentum

For the reform to continue, there three structural and institutional factors had to be put in place. First, giving provincial governments independence from the central government creates and leaves room for them to decide whether or not and how to pursue a certain reform. When the central government wants local governments to implement a policy that is apparently against local interests, local governments would, more often than not, say little against it, but also would do nothing really seriously to bring it into effect.[1] After gaining substantial financial independence from the central government in the 1980s, local governments gradually become a major player in the whole game of reform and could create noticeable resistance, explicit or implicit, to any policies and regulations from Beijing that hurt local interests and economies. In the near future, once the remaining special figures, such as Deng, leave, the effectiveness of the central government's authority will further fade. In the long run, local governments will play an even more active role in shaping economic policies and institutions. During the first decade of reform, top reform leadership basically adopted a strategy of advocating and supporting local governments to put new ideas into action and to provoke local governments to challenge the central planning bureaucracies. Even though certain ministries in the Beijing central planning bureaucracy also initiated some experiments during the time, local governments were inherently more enthusiastic in disintegrating the central control.

After the mid-1980s, local governments took the lead in experimenting with new policy measures and institutional arrangements. For example, local governments played a prominent role in pioneering and testing bankruptcy policies in Liaoning Province, contracting out state enterprises in Jilin Province, lifting price controls in Guangdong Province, and reducing controls over border trade in the Inner Mongolia Region. Provincial governments were no longer only mechanical executors of instructions but rather initiators of new reform measures. The special relation between the top reform leadership and local governments in promoting reform and opposing central planning bureaucracies left behind an interesting legacy, in addition to the increased financial autonomy and approval power already granted by the central government. This new legacy, in brief, is that there is more freedom on the basis of *convention* rather than on the basis of formal institutions that local government might use to implement its own reform policies. New patterns of local government behavior emerged and a greater discrepancy between local and central policies was implicitly allowed as a result. Thus, if a similar incident or issue occurs later, a local government, according to precedents, may not need to apply for approval from the center but, instead, may just go ahead and make its own decisions. If the center intends to be more authoritative and demand an approval procedure, it needs to break the existing convention. Suddenly breaking this kind of convention would require imposing special political power and might risk political conflict. Allowing this discrepancy to exist allows local governments to take a more active role in future reforms. This more active role not only can offset the attempt to go back to a centralized system, but also, more important, will aid the reform by increasing the diversity of experiments and institutions, and by providing more appropriate policies according to local circumstances. However, since this allowance is based on convention and tradition, the freedom enjoyed by the local governments varies from one to another and is not guaranteed — it is more often than not related to the individual local leader and is not guaranteed, let alone subject to any political check and balance mechanism.

Second, the continuous growth of the private economy over the state-owned economy steadily erodes the foundation of the CPE. The thriving growth of the private sector not only propels the development and growth of the whole economy, but also directly creates new economic institutions beyond the control of central planning. Private enterprises are by definition in opposition to the CPE. They have constantly confronted the central planning schemes and bureaucracies, and will naturally continue to demand elimination of any remaining central controls in the economy. As this portion of the economy grows, it increases competition in the economy. Private enterprises are competitive not only with each other but also with the state-owned enterprises. Facing the competition, some state-owned enterprises fail to survive while others turn the situation into a challenge to government control over them, arguing that such control prevents them from operating on the basis of economic rationality. To some degree, the outgrowth of the private economy teaches the state-owned enterprises how to compete and helps them to reform their relations with the government in order to survive. The lesson from the fast-growing private economy is straightforward: government's hands-on enterprises reduce their ability to achieve efficiency and to survive in competition. Thus, the development of private economy creates new challenges to the central planning system and further aids the state enterprises in their demand for more rapid reform of the entire planning system and of the ownership structure. In addition, as private and nonstate economy supports and involves more and more individuals and families, any reversal of the economic system would cause more and more economic loss and political opposition. History has provided proof for this: In the summer of 1989 after the Tiananmen Square event, for example, the central government drastically curtailed or cut off loans and credit to private enterprises through banks, which were a state monopoly, but this unpopular action had to be rescinded half a year later because as private businesses reduced their production or shut down their operations in a response, millions of workers and small businessmen lost their jobs; thus, it posed the ultimate political risk to the government. The thriving of the private economy undoubtedly contributes to the momentum of the Chinese economy to move to a market system.

Third, China's opening-up to the world introduces the most pervasive and constructive challenge to the existing economic system. This challenge is embedded in the direct confrontation between the centrally planned system and the market system. As China explicitly seeks acceleration of economic development and growth from trade with the outside world, numerous and constant adjustments of its economic system take place. The central and local governments, enterprises and individuals, are all involved in the adjustments. From the experiences of SEZs and other opening-up experiments, those who stubbornly ignore the need for adjustment or respond to it slowly suffer from relatively sluggish development. The experiences in trading with the outside world reinforce the understanding that controls from the government and planning bureaucracies reduce the flexibility and ability of business to respond to changes in markets. In addition, integration with the world economy increasingly presses the Chinese government and businessmen to set up new rules for economic activity and to reform its institutions to enable the Chinese economy to compete and cooperate with its counterparts in the world.

With recognition of the critical importance of the information process to China's transformation, there are clear implications to support the efforts to maintain a sound flow of information from the outside world. Information from the outside world has been a major source of ideas and references for designing experiments to move toward a market economy. Even in the first phase of the reform, the increasingly friendly international environment contributed to a change of attitude toward both the market economy and the West, which, in return, lowered the barriers against accepting information from outside and taking a more objective view of the problems of the CPE.

In sum, built through the gradual revolution, the inherent momentum to move the Chinese economy to a market economy is particularly embedded in the three new mechanisms: the increasingly active role of local governments in initiating and promoting reform in a way more appropriate to local economies; the thriving growth of the private economy, which not only challenges the state enterprises but also encourages them to be economically rational; the vigorous integration of the Chinese economy into the world economy, which further leaves the existing system in conflict with the market systems and offers rewards for reform.

New Mechanism of Institutional Selection

Underlying the momentum of the Chinese economy to move to a market system is a wholly new mechanism for selecting innovating economic institutions that never existed in the CPE. The new mechanism derived from a new rationale that developed from people's new experiences of reform, information exchange, and new knowledge. Particularly important to forming a new mechanism for selecting innovative institutions is the emergence of economic rationales to replace politics and ideology in shaping economic policies, development strategies, and business decisions. While it is indeed true that China's political structure still interferes in the economy from time to time, causing extraordinary fluctuations in economic development, economic rationality has become a more constant and lasting factor in determining the orientation of institutional changes. No one wants to rule out the possibility of political forces that would bring the economy back to system dominated by ideology and politics, but the direct experiences with the CPE and the sharp contrasts between it and the new market-oriented economy make it extremely hard for anyone or any force to convince a majority of the people to take it. It can hardly be imagined that the general preference for a market-oriented system over the CPE could be reversed without using force, which would be extremely unpopular. If the construction of a CPE at first had been founded on unrealistic expectations and lack of experience with it, then reinstallation of the CPE in the foreseeable future would be totally against the plainest truth, and mean deprivation and a reversal of all the choices made by the Chinese people, which would be far worse than simply forcing people to accept "a good dream" before.

Further, the new mechanism for selecting innovative institutions is also attributed to the replacement of centralized processes with diversified decision and information processes. In the later phases of the reform, diversified decisions and relatively free choices seemed to have been the primary forces continuing the revitalization of the long-stagnant economy. Differing from the early reform, which relied largely on a top-down process, China's reform since the late 1980s has already shown itself to be a process in which local governments, private enterprises, and ordinary individuals play the main roles. Although diversity referred to here is mainly in the area of decision making rather than in institutions, diversity of decision making and diversity of institutions are related in the sense that diversified decisions make diversified institutions possible. With a variety of contractual relations in production and with incentives to use assets and resources efficiently, which rely on diversified decisions, the free-market economy entails diversity of institutions.

In practice, an appropriate institutional arrangement for a given economic activity is tied to diversified effort and decision making, neither of which existed under the typical CPE. Even in the early reform, such diversified effort and decision making were very limited and were supplementary to the central planning decisions. This situation has since changed. Even though certain top leaders still have some power to promote a reform policy, these individuals' roles in the whole process have changed profoundly: at the end of the 1970s their roles were largely to criticize the old system and launch reforms; since the late 1980s, among many reforms in local governments, enterprises, and almost everywhere else, their roles have been to assist with the transition of the entire economy to a market economy. In other words, centralized decisions dominated the early reform, but diversified decisions have been contributing to the reform since the late 1980s. Now, after more than a decade of reform, this diversity not only exists but is growing, constituting a key part of the new mechanism of institutional selection and innovation.

Three Elements of a Gradual Revolution

The occurrence of a gradual revolution is worthy of a more general discussion. In most situations, an economic system must face serious and profound problems prior to a revolution, with the existing mechanisms failing to provide effective solutions to these problems and to recover to acceptable levels of performance. In other situations, this system must be in the midst of a tremendous breakthrough (such as that of technology or war) that suddenly introduces imbalance; both the nature of such a shock and the flexibility of the system in adjusting itself contribute to whether or not a revolution will happen as well as, if it happens, how the revolution takes place. Particularly, emergence of certain abnormal factors, such as an incident or special information, internal or external or both, may directly foment the demand for a revolution and immediately provoke one. In general, a revolution arises out of a system in crisis and this crisis causes responses that lead to the creation of fundamentally new characteristics of the system.

There are several factors that determine why a revolution occurs gradually. First of all, a gradual revolution may take place when a reform is largely conducted using the existing assets of the old system and is not heavily influenced by ideological choices or a purely imaginative perception. When a system is about to be or already is in a crisis, the demand for change or revolution could well be vague in its goal and tend to diverge completely from the existing system. If this demand leads to abandoning most existing assets in the old system, a drastic revolution will occur. Completely abandoning existing assets would be due either to availability of a set of new, less costly assets or to ideological choice or romanticism. If this demand for change is somewhat constrained by reservation of certain parts of the old system and by restriction primarily to existing assets, then a revolution may take place in a gradual manner. Cost would appear to be an important factor in the development of a revolution, and to depend in part on the degree to which the old system's assets could be converted. A gradual revolution only occurs when such a demand is combined with recognition of certain positive functions of the existing system under

certain specific circumstances. Such recognition often arises from
sensitivity to the constraints to which a revolution is inherently subject
that are imposed by the existing system. It is important to note that the
participants of a revolution should be considered part of the existing
system, and that they themselves are also components of the
constraints on revolution.

Second, there are apparently certain positive expectations for a
compromise between two or more conflicting preferences, agendas, or
forces representing them. The necessary condition for such a
compromise would be that a balance exists between the confronting
forces. Each side may have its ideal preference and agenda if it does
not need to work with the other side but, realistically, the best interest
of each side may be saved by compromise. Each side of the conflict
may foresee an immediate loss if the conflict escalates, with
corresponding immediate benefit in compromise. There must be a
measure of shared interest in at least temporary cooperation if a
compromise is reached. In this case, a gradual revolution may take
place as a result of compromise and cooperation. If there is no such
common ground for cooperation and no potential balance of
conflicting agendas, or if escalation of conflict happens to be chosen,
then a drastic revolution could occur if the revolutionary side
dominates the conflict. Miscalculation often buries unrecognized
potential opportunity for compromise, sound calculation being
difficult because of lack of information, communication, objectivity,
and rational expectation.

Third, whether a system allows diversified spontaneous changes to
take place from inside can be critical to the manner of a revolution.
Both diversification and spontaneity are essential preconditions for a
gradual revolution. Once a crisis builds up, there must be various
tensions and conflicts in a system. If the system is very homogeneous,
and each part structurally similar, then its response to revolutionary
signals would often be characterized by unanimity and synchronism.
Being homogeneous, all parts of the system tend to reinforce and
compete relentlessly with each other in one single or a few narrowly
confined directions. As a result of this, certain parts of the structure of
the system would be destroyed immediately with the remainder largely
untouched, and the function of the old system collapses but most of its
components remain intact. Without a certain degree of diversity, a

change in one component in a system tends to cause a chain reaction among like units. This kind of simple chain reaction in one or more closely related directions often aggravates the pain of change and leads to drastic revolution. When a revolution comes to a system of homogeneous components, it often appears to be radical, and destruction of the old system and construction of a new system barely balance. In other words, a system with homogeneous parts would not be able to avoid destruction of the old system and slow development of a new system. In economic terms, when customers are homogeneous, they have similar needs and preferences. Therefore their demands are simultaneous and focused on the same things. If somebody wants something, everyone else also wants it. There is either no demand or a massive demand for something. A demand implies challenges to and opportunities for an economic system. The economic system responds with changes in supply and institution. Since the demands are closely related, challenges to the system would be limited to narrowly confined areas. These narrow challenges then stimulate responses in production in several aspects, and other unchallenged aspects of the system remain the same. Even though the supply side can initiate changes in the whole system, a response in the system may eventually arouse others. Homogeneous customers from the demand side can only initiate a few isolated challenges to the status quo but under a quantitatively drastic appearance. Moreover, since these kinds of demands often become overwhelming, the economic system can hardly adjust itself under certain time constraints to effectively meet the demands. When customers are homogeneous, the price mechanism does not work because it is based on a variation of preferences. The price mechanism creates balances of supply and demand by providing resources to those who have stronger needs and higher preferences for them.

Another important concept, spontaneity of action, relates to inherent demand for and momentum of change. Spontaneous actions in seeking changes usually find their origins in the need for solutions to certain immediate problems. Spontaneous actions respond to a problem differently in accordance with specific circumstances. Spontaneous changes tend to target concrete problems and to set immediate goals for improvement. As opposed to spontaneous change, there are artificially designed and principle-guided actions which are rooted in an attempt to mobilize large social and economic resources to solve some very general problems. Artificially designed and principle-guided actions usually emphasize structural change and ignore change in the mechanism of each component. [2]

Conversion and Reappreciation of Human Assets

Being a revolution in economic system, China's economic reform had to deal with the conversion of various assets inherited from the former CPE. The disposal, reallocation, use, and dissolution of such assets applied to the overall transformation from the CPE to a market economy. These assets included physical assets, like factories, buildings, land, tractors and other vehicles; institutional assets, like industrial organizations, planning bureaucracies and their apparatus, contractual relations among the government, enterprises, and individuals, etc.; and human assets, which directly related to entrepreneurship, the ability of government officials, the quality and skill of labor forces, the habits and behavior patterns of individuals, and so on. These assets bore, more or less, attributes of the CPE, and experienced, to different degrees, changes in these attributes. For example, land was farmed collectively under the commune system and now, after the agricultural reform, land is divided and farmed by individual families; delivery and supply relations among enterprises were designed and assigned by government planning agencies under the former CPE and are now mostly established on a basis of free choice and voluntary cooperation; in the old system, a chief manager of an enterprise simply followed planning quotas and government instructions in production but now needs to cope with the uncertainties of price and cost, and faces market competition and liability for his decisions.

Among all the assets, human assets were at the center of the assets conversion during the transformation. Disposal and reallocation of physical assets and, particularly, efficient use of the assets in a new system, depended on what managers, government officials, workers, and peasants did with them. Disintegration and abolition of previous contractual relationships under the CPE, establishment of new relations, and reorganization of industry all resulted from decisions by the individuals and groups involved. Further improvement and continuous evolution of economic institutions lies likewise in the hands of those who run and work in economic organizations. The transformation of human beings is governed by the quality and value of the human assets in a new economic system, and influences all the choices and decisions regarding the other assets and the reform as a whole.

The conversion of the human assets was made critically important to the transformation by the central planning system's radical specialization of human assets in its extremely artificial institutional arrangements. Conversion of human assets is defined as fundamental change in the specifications of human assets from one economic system to another. In this study, conversion of human assets specifically means changing the human assets, which were highly specialized by the mandatory central planning system, to those adapted for the mechanism of free choice and orderly competition. It is true that each economic system imposes molds and specializes human factors to a certain extent,[3] but the centrally planned system shaped China's human factors in a way that differed from all other economic systems by its pervasive artificiality. This artificiality overwhelmed every branch of economic activity and of life in general, extending from all-round assignments and quota mechanisms, centrally controlled education and training programs, political and ideological training and retraining lessons, to monopolistic control of information and personal mobility.

For example, a child was educated from primary school on to love the party and to recite highly selected party history, and had little access to knowledge of any other society or history other than the party's; in high school, he was taught mathematics and natural sciences, learned to obey instruction, and was trained to have unconditional faith in the party; in college, he was assigned a narrowly specialized field and learned how the centrally planned system worked and how to fit into it; then, after graduation, he was placed in a specific position to be a "screw in the socialist machine."[4] Nonthinking, highly specialized screws were what the artificial, compulsory system produced. Thus, the CPE specialized its human assets in all the aspects of knowledge, skills, values, habits, and thinking that it could.

Apart the well-designed training schemes, working and living under the centrally planned system was another process of specialization of human assets. The impact of central planning permeated everyone's work and life. As a worker, one had to rely on the government for a guaranteed job, a low but stable income, and a narrowly specialized skill. A worker did not have an opportunity to choose occupations, jobs, or skills, and thus had no experience in looking for a job or sustaining the threat of wage cuts and unemployment; but lack of such experience and knowledge made it difficult for a worker to deal with competition and uncertainty in a market system. As an enterprise manager, one only had to follow the instructions of the plan, and did not have an opportunity to make decisions on transactions and investments. As a result, a manager in the CPE had little entrepreneurship and no experience in taking business risks. On the other side, anyone under the central planning system had to accommodate himself to the system. Such accommodation took place constantly and often unconsciously, shaping a special pattern of behavior in the well-designed system. Therefore, both the well-designed training scheme and working as well as living under the CPE were attributed to the creation of specialized human assets by the system. Such were the human assets that the reform confronted. Because of enormous differences in the attributes of human assets between the two systems, their conversion posed a formidable obstacle to the transformation from the CPE to a market economy.

From a different viewpoint, the quality and characteristics of the human assets — specialized by and inherited from the CPE — constituted a major constraint on development and transformation. Many mechanisms that exist in developed market economies do not work in a reforming economy. Institutional arrangements that are set up according to models from developed market economies often misfunction or do not stimulate reactions in another economy as expected; they may even cause a backlash. In situations like this, reform might seem to have stalled. More often than not, this kind of problem relates to the constraints of existing human assets. As the human assets modify themselves, the constraints shift gradually and more effective reforms are both possible and needed.

The quality and characteristics of human assets inherited from the CPE were reflected in many ways, including normal patterns of behavior, cooperation, competition, decision making, and how uncertainty was handled, each different from its counterpart in a developed market economy in the West. For example, when Zhao began to do business on his own, he at first was hesitant about establishing business without government help because he had no credit or collateral (no one had) to get a loan; later he asked his friends Chian, Sun, and Li to join him in the business, but they knew nothing about forms of legal ownership or contractual relationships. After they signed a contract to deliver something to another business, they found they could sell it at higher prices to someone else, and they did. When the original purchaser discovered the problem, it could not find an effective institution to force Chian, Sun, and Li to implement the contract or compensate the him for his loss. One year later, when the manufacturers had earned some money, they found that they could not spend it at restaurants or hotels without being asked, "Who owns this money?" Everyone claimed it, and constant quarrels interfered with production. The partnership broke up, with Zhao taking the special technology, Chian the client information, Sun selling the office assets and pocketing the proceeds, and the still friendly Li begging his former boss in a state-owned factory to take him back and give him a mouthful from the remaining "big bowl." This example reflects that when people first left the CPE, many basic elements of a market economy were not yet in place, including a sense of credible commitment, knowledge of legal rights, experience with fair cooperation and competition, etc.

Combination of Conversion and Reappreciation

China's highly specialized human assets needed practice and time to convert to the market system and to reappreciate their potential value.[5] Without such appropriate conversion and reappreciation, human assets would be largely wasted when a market system was imposed. Closely related to the definition of human asset conversion, reappreciation of human assets refers to an increase in their capability, skill, and overall value in production and other economic activities. In other words, reappreciation of human assets means raising the value embedded in specific human assets in relation to the market system. Waste of these resources leads directly to the decline of economic welfare and individual satisfaction. From another angle, before this specialized asset of human resources was appropriately converted, a new institution might not operate in the way expected. Of course, there is almost no doubt that the central planning system was the most serious cause of the waste of human resources and the low efficiency of the economy, so that any delay in dissolving the old system and introducing the new would only increase the losses caused by the centrally planned system. This does not, however, justify waste and inefficiency due to misguided reform policies when better choices were available given a better understanding of the nature of reform.

Conversion and appreciation of the highly specialized human assets link all the reforms of government, enterprises, and individuals. Had the central planning system been abandoned in one step, and all transactions become free of government control, all the government officials, enterprise managers, labor, and other individuals in the economy would have faced a sharp decline in their value. The preservation of values of the highly specialized assets would have been realized only under certain specific systems, i.e., the centrally planned system. Even though the market system is a more efficient system overall, it may not enhance the value of all specialized assets. In this situation, a decline of efficiency and decrease of production would have followed.

In fact, for specialized human assets to be of value in a new economic system, the Chinese reform experience shows that government officials (not necessarily personnel held over from the previous regime)[6] need to learn to protect the market and to reduce externality of business misconduct without mandatory planning; enterprises and entrepreneurs need to learn to deal with uncertainty and to take responsibility for their own decisions; and individuals need to learn to live in competition and voluntary cooperation.[7] All these are part of the conversion and appreciation of human assets. Without them, the existing resources and assets would be less useful and even detrimental to a different economic system. Although reform is intended to introduce a market system and to increase the efficiency of production and use of resources, the new system may be less efficient if the existing assets and resources become worthless and no appropriate new assets available. Although reform is based on an implicit assumption that such a conversion and appreciation of specialized assets is possible, the tasks take time and practice to accomplish. In this regard, there is a rationale for gradual transformation of economic institutions and incessant conversion and appreciation of human assets.

It can be said that the transformation starts with conversion of the human assets and ends up with reappreciation of them. Many elements of market economy would not entail merely converting the existing human assets, but need also incessant reappreciation of those assets. Totally new knowledge and behavior patterns, for example, would be needed as part of the appreciation process. Actually, the market economy should be seen as a system based on a series of different specialized assets. A large part of the new knowledge would be the outcome of market institutions. There are at least two main categories of efforts in relation to the reappreciation. The first group deals with competition and cooperation. Rules for free competition and voluntary cooperation may be very specific and exclusive for certain market activities. New patterns of behavior, including making binding commitments and taking concrete responsibility for certain decisions, would be necessary for all market participants. The second category relates to making decisions under uncertainty. Price fluctuations are taken for granted in a market economy but still make those in transition from a CPE angry.

Change of rationale for individuals is the most profound part of human assets conversion and reappreciation. Changes in individuals' rationale is revealed in their behavior and decision-making processes. For example, as people gain more experience in a market economy, they realize the importance of binding commitments in free exchange: if one cheats, another can cheat next time, and if everyone cheats, no one derives any benefit from cheating but only pays for it. Experiences can demonstrate this truth, and a new rationale will develop; as a result, people will try to make credible commitments in market activities because it is in their own interest.

Knowledge-Related Uncertainty

Reform itself creates uncertainties and also proceeds in uncertainties. It is not difficult to imagine that this unprecedented transformation in China creates enormous uncertainties facing its reform decision makers, officials, enterprise managers, and people of all walks of life. Activities and decision making range from initiating a new experiment to responding to a new institutional arrangement and are constantly accompanied by high uncertainty as the economy and people are experiencing the profound changes.

Tjalling Koopmans speculated thirty-five years ago that there are two kinds of uncertainty: primary uncertainty, which is of a state-contingent kind; and secondary uncertainty, which exists in "lack of communication."[8] In China's reform, many problems and decision-making processes are related to these two kinds of uncertainty. For example, the economic impact and direct outcome of an experiment would seem to be associated with the state-contingent uncertainty; the interactions between the central and local governments in reforming their relationships often involve the secondary uncertainty embedded in "lack of communication."

Apart from these two kinds of uncertainty, there is that which arises from such human factors as ignorance, inexperience, lack of knowledge, and ideological blindness. In reform, another kind of uncertainty lies particularly in the reaction of the existing human assets in the face of changes of institutions. In reform practice, it relates to attitude toward new economic activities and institutions, bias in knowledge, special ways of thinking, and mental barriers against certain ideas. Since this kind of uncertainty is mostly related to knowledge, I call it "knowledge-related uncertainty." This kind of uncertainty was widespread in almost all decision making during the transformation.

The third kind of uncertainty differs from the two other kinds of uncertainty by being related mainly to human mental state. The long-entrenched central planning system created certain special traits that caused enormous uncertainty. Years of living under a CPE produced misperceptions about the market economy, special attitudes toward life and work, and a different combination of knowledge, skills, and capabilities. Absence of apprehension of competition in work and life in general, lack of knowledge about free pricing, lack of experience in handling uncertainty, etc., were all characteristic of people under the old system. This characteristic of human assets often entails both fear and unrealistic expectations of new experiments and institutions. These knowledge-related factors not only aggravate the feelings of uncertainty but also obstruct clear observation and true understanding, thereby causing further uncertainties in decision making and behavior.

The experimental approach helped to alleviate the third kind of uncertainty and other kinds of uncertainties as well. This approach provided the substance and the environment for certain processes to unfold in a less costly way and to allow the causes of the uncertainties to be understood. The experimental approach particularly allowed the factors of specific circumstances, time, and human assets to be included in the selection, evaluation, comparison, and innovation of economic institutions and their associated processes. This approach permitted people to gain the relevant knowledge and experience directly; this, once accomplished, helped to raise people's readiness for reforms. Implementation of a variety of diversified experiments allowed people to acquire, process, and comprehend the information needed for the reform in a faster and more complete way. The more diversified the experiments, the greater the knowledge gained and the uncertainty reduced. As human asset conversion and reappreciation takes place through the diversified experiments and new experiences, knowledge-related uncertainty fades as a result.

A tolerant and free environment is critically important for this to take place, particularly in the early phase of reform when economic freedom is very limited and the government still plays a dominant role in initiating and supporting reform. If there is freedom of choice, and diversified actions become the dominant force of reform, tolerance may lose most of its sense to reform. Tolerance is needed only when freedom is limited and prohibitive interference still exists. There are two kinds of tolerance: tolerance of a system or, more specifically, of the government; and mental tolerance, which exists in everyone's mind and influences decision making. Here we refer only to the tolerance of a system or government. The importance of such a tolerant and free environment is based on two primary assumptions: first, that existing knowledge offers very limited understanding of such profound transformation; second, that a successful search for new economic institutions or healthy reform of the entire system requires diversification, which makes the evolution of economic institutions possible. The Chinese economic reform essentially supports both of these assumptions.

Human Assets as a Determinant of Transformation

At the start of China's economic reform in 1979, there was no factor more important than human assets in determining the way the reform would proceed and for explaining its reasons. Among the many factors that contribute to development of the reform, human assets are directly related to the reform's origin, the incessant selection of economic institutions, and the effective outcome of reform. This relation is revealed from the behavior and decision making of those who carry out the reform to the constraints under which the reform has progressed. First, early reformers' beliefs on reform were associated with their own experiences and knowledge, upon which the reform's goal and definition were based. The early reform decision makers, a group of pragmatic leaders, drew many implications from their own experiences in the 1950s and 1960s and intended to correct and improve the planned economy. Being largely uninformed about the world outside China and recent developments of market economies, they simply attributed problems in the economy to radicalism instead of central planning, believing in the advantages and superiority of the CPE.

Second, China's approach to its problems and the shift from a "closed" to an "open" perspective reflects the human asset characteristics of reform decision makers and their people. A few years of early reform quickly exhausted their own experiences, and this forced the Chinese to turn to others' experiences and new knowledge for clues on how to conduct the reform experiments.

Third, as reform experiments and practices provided new evidence for both the failure of the old planned system and the advantages of the new market system, basic understanding of the reform gradually changed, as presented earlier in the two groups of reform propositions. As a result, developing the market (the new strategy in the second phase of reform) replaced realigning internal relations within the CPE (the old strategy of the first-phase reform).

China's reform practices indicate that the major characteristics of its human assets evolved during the reform and, consequently, so did the vision, expectation, and rationale of reform. As discussed above, these characteristics relate to people's knowledge, skills, habits, values, and inclination to accept information and to learn. Changes in the major characteristics of human assets led to changes in people's vision, expectation, and rationale of reform.

In the end, the Chinese reform movement proceeded under the evolving constraint of the human ability to initiate changes in economic institutions and to respond to the consequences of changes in its contexts. Moreover, the improvement of the ability depends on practice, gained through a variety of experiments and exposure to diverse sources, experiences, and knowledge of tolerance and a free environment for the evolution of economic institutions, and on an unencumbered information process. The Chinese economic reform revealed that every member of the economy, including individuals, enterprises, and the government, were both part of this constraint and confronted by it, contributed to the slackening of the constraint, and thereby played a vital role in the fundamental transformation of human history.

In the remaining part of this chapter, discussions on the impact of human assets on the transformation focus on four issues: institutional memory, readiness of human assets, two-track transition, and relationships among development, institutions, and human assets.

Institutional Memory

Institutional memory was an important factor for a successful reform. The experiences of pragmatic criticism and experimental revision of the Soviet-type economic model in the 1950s and 1960s influenced the direction of economic reform in the early phase. Evidence for the importance of these memories was offered by the major reforms, including agricultural reform, intragovernmental relationship reform, and enterprise reform. Institutional and behavioral memories are defined as records in direct experiences that can be retrieved. Usually, institutional and behavioral memories are best remembered by groups of people whose current interests are connected to certain past institutions and behavior. In addition, institutional and behavioral memories may be revealed unconsciously and unintentionally. Moreover, these memories are usually personal and not transferable. There is plenty of evidence to demonstrate the influence of memory on the formulation of reform experiments and policies. For example, when land was to be allocated to each family, and the family responsibility system was to be adopted, most peasants responded intuitively to deciding how they would manage the production on this basis. Such intuitive responses did not, unfortunately, always occur in other reform fields, particularly in industrial reform (e.g., shareholding reform) and the introduction of modern market mechanisms (e.g., the stock market).

It is a fact that before the communists took power in mainland China, there was very little modern industry and little experience with the organization of modern capitalism. Peasants, in contrast, still remembered how to grow grain and run agricultural businesses as individual families. For some two thousand years before the commune system was installed about twenty years ago, peasants had been working on a family basis of production. At the time of the reform most of them still remembered the procedures of plowing, irrigation, seed selection and preservation, harvesting at appropriate seasons, storage and processing, and small-scale marketing. As discussed in other parts of this book, even after the establishment of the commune system, peasants in many areas still had opportunities to work on a family production basis. True, it was surely more than coincidence that the reform started in at the same place where peasants had pioneered their departure from the commune model and gone back to family production in the 1950s and 1960s.[9] Even the officials who were primary supporters of such initiatives were those who had been criticized for their "tolerance of capitalism" in the early 1960s.[10] But, when there were few such memories, a new reform policy suggestion met with much skepticism and reluctance during decision making as well as implementation, followed by disorientation, at least at first. In the experiment with shareholding, the stock market, and leasing, for example, people from government policymakers to enterprise managers found it difficult to figure out what the new systems could and should be. In practice, they simply conducted the experiment in the best way they could envision, which then sometimes made it difficult to assess the outcome of the new policy. In general, institutional and behavioral memory helped reduce the uncertainty of reform, provide the crucial factors for spontaneous evolution of institutions, and buttress a smooth and stable transformation.

Readiness of Human Assets

The success of China's agricultural reform revealed a delicate process of institutional selection in relation to existing human assets. The salient factors in this process included applied agricultural technology, information technology, the nature of agricultural production, the inherent transaction processes both within agriculture as well as between agricultural and nonagricultural sectors, recent institutional history, and human and nonhuman assets inherited from the commune system. Among these factors, human assets appeared to be the most immediately relevant in determining the specific circumstances under which reform occurred. In general terms, human assets are the primary input of production in association with agricultural technology; their efficient use is always the constant motivation for institutional change. More specifically, an immediately new agricultural system worked well only if the relevant human assets — mainly the peasants — had some matching characteristics. I add the "immediate" to distinguish a transitional system from the goal system. During the whole process of transformation, an economy may go through a series of transitional systems. Some new systems did not work as in other circumstances simply because they did not have a match in related human assets. For example, in many areas, peasants first divided the commune's land into small groups, which were composed of several families, instead of moving directly to the family responsibility system; this transitional stage allowed those peasants who were not ready to proceed faster to learn from more experienced peasants. Because in a small group each peasant normally assumed more responsibilities than he would have as part of a larger production team, the small group system functioned as a "training" ground in which peasants could adapt by gradually assuming more varied responsibilities. Whether peasants needed this transitional system depended largely on their experiences with family-based production and on whether these experiences were still retrievable. Those peasants who had gotten the chance to return to family-based production in the 1960s could be expected more readily to move to the new system in one step. Peasants in some areas, however, had started to work on a collective basis as early as the mid-1950s and had never gone back to family-based production since; they found this change of institution more drastic and its consequences more uncertain. At this time, institutional memory made a critical difference in readiness of human assets, necessitating some differentiation in appropriate institutional settings during this interim period. In other words, if there is a match between a human asset and an institutional setting, then the human asset with certain characteristics would require a certain specific institutional setting so as to bring out the potential capability of the human asset. In sum, how this new agricultural system worked depends to a large extent on how its human assets are prepared, in relation to new institutions, to engage in certain production and economic activities.

It is interesting to note that two groups of peasants improved their lives and increased their income faster than other peasants. One of these two groups consisted of most of the former production team leaders and commune officials; the other group was those entrepreneurial peasants who had always risked criticism to sell their goods and services on the black market even under the commune system and chafed most under the old system.

Generally, the team leaders and commune officials were better connected than other peasants, and the networks inherited from their previous positions often gave them special advantages under the new system. But more important in general was the high quality of their human capital, which made their adaptation to the new system smooth and rapid. Most former team leaders and other officials in agriculture had been selected from capable, skilled, experienced peasants in the village. [11] They were better informed and more knowledgeable about the world outside the village, particularly since they had had more opportunities to know the world outside their villages through their positions, which had necessitated attending meetings and traveling to learn about others' production experiences. They usually became more open minded and inclined to accept information from outside. These two factors — being more experienced in production and having access to more information — made former team leaders better prepared human assets for the conversion from the commune system to the new family-based agricultural system.

The other group — the entrepreneurial peasants — had been trying to break the bonds of the commune system in order to work on their own. They had often taken leave without pay and hoarded time in which to produce their own goods to sell on the black market. Working on their own was reasonably more productive than working under the commune system, and they earned more, but they were constantly harassed by officials in the commune. Sometimes they had to find excuses for their activities in order to avoid or alleviate pressures on them. When the commune system was dissolved and peasants started to work in family units, they felt their liberation most keenly. Among all peasants, this group was most ready for the new agricultural system and faced the fewest obstacles in the conversion of human assets. It is logical that this group of peasants, together with the group of team leaders and officials, enjoyed a more immediate increase and faster growth in income than did the majority of the other peasants.

Two-Track Transition for Conversion and Reappreciation of Human Assets

China's two-track system served primarily to convert and reappreciate existing assets while introducing new institutions, and contributed to the country's dynamic economic development. The two-track system started with the early effort to increase production by allowing surplus to be sold at higher prices in markets than at the planned prices, mainly as a measure to create incentives. Specifically, by setting certain base amounts of output, determined according to the previous year's performance, the government allowed and then encouraged enterprises and individuals to sell their extra products in markets. The widespread shortages in the economy then drove most market prices higher than the centrally planned prices for the same products, so that high prices and profits further stimulated production. Since the planned base amounts were essentially fixed, an increase in production meant an increase in market coverage.

Under the two-track system, institutional changes were introduced incrementally while adjusting and making use of the existing institutional arrangements. During the gradual expansion of the market, peasants, enterprises, officials, and other individuals learned to survive and succeed in a competitive environment, in effect converting these human assets from the CPE to a market economy. In turn, the ongoing conversion of human assets was reinforced by the obvious benefit of diverging from the CPE, leading to the initiation of new reforms and accelerating the accumulation of institutional changes. Meanwhile, adjusting and making use of the existing institutional arrangements provided immediate stability, which contributed to a sound environment for reform and the conversion of human assets. Gradual conversion and reappreciation of human assets, together with an increase in new economic institutions, spurred both long-term and immediate growth. The two-track system contributed to these incremental processes by utilizing existing assets, providing crucial stability, and introducing new institutions with less risk. In a cumulative process, the two-track transition resulted in a dynamic economic transformation: the market gradually replaced the central planning apparatus as the dominant force in the allocation of resources and the coordination of production; the private economy emerged as a deviation from the CPE and eventually made the inefficient state industries obsolete; and gradual reform of the state enterprises moved toward a revolutionary outcome: the transformation of ownership structure from profit sharing to contracting out, leasing, and shareholding.

However, the two-track approach was not a risk-free game but a system in deep internal contradiction. While it is well recognized that the two-track system made a great contribution to the Chinese economic reform, it also provided an excuse to maintain certain parts of the central planning system or to delay more fundamental reform. Unnecessary and inferior compromises in reform decisions were made in consideration of the two-track system, and as the new economic institutions became competitive with the old ones, the two-track system turned out to provide protection for the old. For example, the supply of artificially lower-priced resources under the centrally planned price system could certainly have provided poorly performing state-owned enterprises a special shelter from competition with free enterprises that purchased at higher market prices. In this case, the two-track system worked in opposition to the reform's intention to introduce competition and the market and against the basic principle of equal competition. In other cases, the two-track system would be used to postpone the final eradication of the central control and mandatory intervention in the economy. Further, the two-track system engendered opportunities for corruption. The two-track system created two prices for a resource or commodity. While gaps between planned prices and market prices existed, as some major resources were still allocated by the government instead of through the market, access to planned prices and the privilege to maneuver the distribution of these resources inevitably created opportunities for corruption. Moreover, the two-price mechanism prevented the market from functioning normally. The lower-than-cost price caused overconsumption and misallocation of resources. Many enterprises competed with each other not on how to lower costs and improve quality but on how to access the lower-than-cost-priced goods. On the other side, it discouraged those who played by the rules of the market.

Therefore, it should be clearly understood that the two-track system is transitional, and its use and termination should be treated with caution. Three points are hereby emphasized: by making use of many of the existing assets of the old system, first of all, the two-track system did help foster a gradual revolution; second, inheriting many attributes of the old planning economy, the two-track system did provide shelters for the old system because it actually justified some parts of the central planning institution; third, as soon as reform momentum toward the market in certain parts of the economy was built up, the two-track system no longer had a reason to exist.

The conversion and reappreciation of human assets was subject to differences among groups of people in pursuing their various roles in the economy. This differentiation was reflected in the process by different speeds of conversion and reappreciation, by relative ease or difficulty of conversion and reappreciation, and by varying requirements for conversion and reappreciation. The variables of the differentiation include what people's vocations had been and would be, specific differences between the former system and its replacement, institutional memories enhancing the values of existing assets, capacity to learn and adapt to the new system, and differences, if any, in the values and cultures of different groups of people. The variables in the differentiation of the conversion and appreciation of human assets also include the overall institutional environment, and social, political, and information processes (information technology and communication methods).

Given the existence of this differentiation, if there is freedom of choice, then dramatic shifts in roles for each individual and group of people will happen. Under mandatory planning some individuals were assigned a job they would not have otherwise chosen. They might be in the wrong place either in terms of their will or in terms of their relative advantages. Of course, the market also imposes certain constraints of its own on them, mostly related to competition and a new give-and-take mechanism (this refers to everyone making his own choice and allowing others to do likewise while, at the same time, taking the impact of many individuals' free choices). This is different from its counterpart in the central planning system in which individuals did not have the freedom to make a choice and had to take what was assigned by the plan while, at the same time, everyone was closely connected to everyone else, paying much political attention to others.

China's overall political system was and still is an important constraint on the conversion and reappreciation of its human assets. Because political reform lagged behind economic reform, and major economic measures had to be accepted and approved by political leadership, the conversion and reappreciation processes were frequently held up. Only once the leadership's knowledge and experiences allowed them to understand and support new measure of institutional arrangement could the economy and its human constituents act on it. In the course of the reform years, too, the nature and quality of the leaders' human assets also changed and even appreciated, and they tended to move along with the reform. But the problem was that if the conversion and reappreciation of the human assets of the whole society and economy had to rely on changes in that small group of people, then the progress of conversion and reappreciation would inevitably be slowed down. This factor contributed to the way in which China's economic reform proceeded.

Development, Institutions, and Human Assets

One of the most challenging and often confusing tasks of Chinese economic reform was to keep a delicate and dynamic balance between vigorous economic development and effective institutional change. In general, economic development inherently demanded compatible institutions; conversely, changes in economic institutions often led, as Karl Marx and Joseph Schumpeter both emphasized a long time ago, to economic progress. This point was fully borne out in the experiences of China's reform. As freedom was introduced into the economy and the ban on criticism of the centrally planned system was lifted, the demand for a new economic system was reflected in a growing number of officially sanctioned experiments and a vast array of spontaneous efforts to search for solutions. However, since the CPE was so highly and artificially structured and its coordination so rigid, simply abandoning it would have led to large-scale unnecessary losses and economic devastation, so this was not a rational choice.

Therefore, we have to be specific in observing the relation between development and institutional changes as to the transformation. For obvious reasons, a proper economic development scheme lays out a sound foundation for the reform of economic institutions. Without a doubt, issues of political feasibility and even possibility would arise out of poor economic performance. But, even leaving aside political concerns, there are evident pitfalls in the attempt to seek a single and absolute solution for the problems of the CPE. The dangers lie in misunderstanding the entire meaning of the transformation, that is, to further China's economic development and individual economic satisfaction by reforming the economic system, not to reform it solely because of its being a centrally planned system. All the reform policies promoting efficiency serve this purpose.

Although it is inevitable that reform would generate some costs, these do not excuse a lowered consciousness of economic welfare or wasteful losses. Decades of central planning created and left behind strange legacies, from mandatory allocation of resources, technology, and information to the quality and characteristics of human resources adapted to the needs of the CPE. Of all these, as has been stated earlier, the quality and characteristics of human resources were the most critical factors for economic development and the transformation as a whole. Human resources, among all other resources, were in most wasteful use and poorest allocation under the centrally planned system. The specialization and quality of human asset of the CPE reflect the long-time inefficient use and allocation of human resource. Without a comprehensive and profound transformation of the human assets, a sound economic development based on the market system was impossible. Physical assets can be replaced, the institutions of a developed market economy can simply be duplicated, but a market economy cannot be run without people, and new people. Such a comprehensive and profound transformation of human assets can take place only gradually. If it is possible to fully replace new physical assets and institutional set-ups, there apparently is no chance to replace the human assets overnight. Because of this, appropriate changes in other assets and institutional arrangements must take place in order to achieve proper economic development. The reasoning is simple: certain specialized human assets make their most appropriate contribution to production only in certain specific relationships with other assets and institutional arrangements. In other words, economic development is contingent upon a good fit among institutional arrangements and all available resources and assets, of which the most central are human assets. In general, the delicacy of balancing economic development and economic institutions is attributable to the complexity of the evolving economic institutions and changing human assets.

In addition, it merits comment that human assets have a strong tendency to select and modify institutional arrangements as long as there is freedom of choice. This point is obvious but, unfortunately, is often underestimated or ignored. From a certain perspective, lack of freedom of choice and the inclination to replace the dictates of the elite with diversified free choice have always been a threat, especially when spontaneous economic change has not become a dominant force of reform.

To the concern of economic development, efficient use of human assets is always the most important issue. Based on Chinese experiences, while political and social concerns in reform decision making varied, efficiency, as an economic concern, always drove the evolution of economic institutions, in both the first and second phases of reform. During the transformation, while attention has been given to the efficient use of nonhuman resources, more efficient use of human resources lay at the center of all the efforts to increase efficiency. One of the most frequently used phrases in reform documents was "to bring into play the initiative of the people,"[12] which, in more or less socialist terms, emphasized the more efficient use of human resources. The reform dismantled the mandatory planning system and made it possible to use human resources efficiently, as reflected in the boom in the private economy that constituted a major contribution to China's development and growth.

In promoting the transformation, reform efforts to develop new institutions succeeded when the institutions could allow appropriate conversion of relevant human assets and provide a sound setting for them to reappreciate. "Appropriate conversion" here refers to the conversion of a certain specialized asset with as few losses as possible. Put differently, given the highly specialized human resources and other factors, finding and choosing the economic institutions that produce a match between institutions and assets would seem to be a prerequisite for successful reform. Two points need to be emphasized. First, the new institutions implied fewer restrictions and more freedom for individuals to make their own decisions and pursue their interests. Second, the new institutions were relevant to certain groups of people's experiences and knowledge, or adjustable for the groups of people. These two points could be found in China's agricultural reform and enterprise reform. The agricultural reform of returning to family-based production freed peasants and was closely relevant to their experiences. The enterprise reform took the way that each minor reform cumulated new experiences and knowledge for another reform leading to a free enterprise system. With such a match between institutions and human assets, individuals were effectively motivated and coordinated to transform themselves and also create more efficient economic institutions. In addition, reform decisions to choose certain institutional arrangements and to make efficient use of human and other resources would be better left to those directly involved. The rationale underlying this is, except for concerns of externality, that efficiency of an economic activity is seen most clearly by those who perform it.

In general, an efficient arrangement of economic institutions for using human and nonhuman resources is related to specific circumstances, including the characteristics of the human assets, the nature and costs of transitions, and available information. Among these, the characteristics of the human assets appear to be critical, because the human assets entail, to a large extent, the form of transaction, how to process information, and the technology chosen. Given the variety of circumstances in reform reality, suitable institutional arrangements for efficient use of human assets are only possible with a mechanism of free choice and spontaneous change, as human assets are the most important resource for achieving economic development.

Notes

1.   Many tactics, which could be generalized as "shang you zheng ce, xia you dui ce" (you upper have policies and we lower have tactics), have been played by local governments against the central government. For

example, one often heard doggerels like "man ban pai" (half step slower — in following the central government) and "ni shuo ni de, wuo zuo wuo de" (you [center] say yours and we do ours).

2. As to the Chinese case, three factors particularly contributed to the occurrence of this gradual revolution. The first relates to the specific pragmatic leadership that initiated the reform. The second is population. The third is variation of economic development among regions

3. Generally speaking, the capitalist market system imposes its influence of molding human factors primarily on the basis of capital and property rights. The landlord feudal system imposed the influence mainly on the basis of seniority and holding of land.

4. Many people were created as models of such a screw to be learned, such as Lei Feng, a Liberation Army soldier.

5. The terms "appreciation" and "reappreciation" are used interchangeably here.

6. By saying government officials, we mean those who work as government officials in the new government during the transformation to the market system.

7. Actually, all enterprises and entrepreneurs, including both private and state-owned ventures, face the problem of learning to survive and succeed in a market economy. No matter what their ownership in the initial stage of transformation, they are inevitably part of the legacy of the CPE. Even though private enterprise and entrepreneurs usually are more enthusiastic in embracing the market than their state-owned counterparts, they still need to make fundamental adaptations in critical aspects (values, habits, and ability).

8. Koopmans 1957, 162-63.

9. As discussed earlier, the most illustrative case is the experiment with family production in Anhui Province in 1959, 1962, and 1978.

10. Many officials in Anhui Province were criticized in the early 1960s, particularly in a political movement called "four clean-up" in 1964, for tolerating and promoting noncommune production systems.

11. Despite the fact that some of the officials had been corrupt and skilled in favoritism under the commune system, the government even at that time had to be realistic and select or let peasants choose capable people to manage production, which largely determined how much food a village or team had at the end of a year. A team leader in a village was supposed to be a master of how and when to grow crops, how much labor was required for certain tasks, and what kind of tools and techniques were best suited for which plants. Normally, team leaders were elected, often under the influence of local governments, every one or two years. If

someone in the position proved unable to organize all the peasants to work under the collective system, another peasant would most likely replace him the next year.

12. Koopmans 1957, 162-63.

References

A Statistical Survey of China 1989. 1989. Beijing: China Statistical
   Press.
After the Third Plenum — Selection of Important Documents. 1982.
   Beijing: People's Press.
Almanac of China's Economy. various years. Beijing: Economic
   Management Press.
Almanac of China's Statistics. various years. Beijing: China's
   Statistical Press.
Arrow, Kenneth. 1974. *The Limit of Organization*. New York: W. W.
   Norton.
China's Statistical Annual. 1986. Beijing: China Statistical Press
Chow En-lai. 1956. *Report on Suggestions for Second Five-year Plan
   of National Economic Development*. Beijing: People's Press.
Collection of Documents on Economic Reform 1977-1983. 1984.
   Beijing: China Finance and Economy Press.
Friedman, Lee S. 1984. *Microeconomic Policy Analysis*. New York:
   McGraw-Hill Book Company.

Furubotn, E. and S. Petjovich. 1947. *The Economics of Property Rights*. Cambridge, Mass.: Ballinger.

Harding, Harry. 1987. *China's Second Revolution — Reform After Mao*. Washington, D.C.: The Brookings Institution.

Harding, Harry. 1992. *A Fragile Relationship*. Washington, D.C.: The Brooking Institution.

Hirshleifer, Jack. 1980. *Price Theory and Applications*. Englewood Cliffs, N.J.: Prentice Hall, Inc.

Hua Sheng et al. 1988. "Ten Years Reform of China: Retrospect, Rethinking, and Prospect." Part I *Economic Review* 9 (1988): 13-17; Part II *Economic Review* 11 (1988): 11-28.

Koopmans, Tjalling. 1957. *Three Essays on the State of Economic Science*. New York: McGraw-Hill.

Lange, O. 1936. "On the Economic Theory of Socialism (I)." *The Review of Economic Studies* 4 (1) (October 1936): 53-71, and 4(2) (February 1937): 123-42.

Liu Guoguang. 1988. *Model Study of Chinese Economic Reform*. Beijing, China: China Social Sciences Press.

Lui Guoguang. 1988. *Model Study of Chinese Economic Reform*. Beijing: China Social Sciences Press.

Ma Hong. 1982. *Facts and Events of Contemporary Chinese Economy*. Beijing: Chinese Social Sciences Press.

Perkins, Dwight H. 1988. "Reforming China's Economic System," *Journal of Economic Literature* 26 (June).

Reason Foundation. 1990. *Privatization*. Santa Monica, CA: Reason Foundation.

Selection of Important Documents Since the 12th Congress. 1986. Beijing: People's Press.

Shi Xiaomin and Lui Jirui. 1989. "Economists Should First Respect History and Facts," *Economic Review* 2: 11-33.

Simon, Herbert A. 1961. *Administrative Behavior*. New York: Macmillan.

Smith, Adam. 1937. *The Wealth of Nations*. New York: The Modern Library.

The Economic Daily, ed. 1986. *Retrospect and Outlook of the Chinese on the Chinese Socialist Economic Theories*. Beijing: The Economic Daily Press.

Varian, Hal R. 1987. *Intermediate Microeconomics*. New York: W.W. Norton & Company.

Vickers, John and George Yarrow. 1988. *Privatization: An Economic Analysis*. Cambridge, Mass.: The MIT Press.

von Mises, Ludwig. 1951. *Socialism: An Economic and Sociological Analysis*. Revised English edition. New Haven: Yale University Press.

von Mises, Ludwig. 1966. *Human Action: A Treatise on Economics*. 3rd revised edition. Chicago: Henry Regency.

Williamson, Oliver E. 1985. *The Economic Institution of Capitalism*. New York: Free Press.

Wu Jinlian and Zhou Xiaochuan, eds. 1988. *The Integrated Design of China's Economic Reform*. Beijing: China Outlook Press.

Ye Jianying. 1979. "Speech at the Meeting on the 30th Anniversary of the People's Republic of China." In *Selection of Important Documents Since the Third Plenum Meeting* (Beijing: The People's Press), 207-248.

Zhou Taihe. 1984. Modern China Economic Reform Editorial Committee. *Economic Reform of Modern China*. Beijing: China Social Sciences Press.

Index

Agriculture
  failures in, 73-74
  production, 6, 42-43
  reform in, 153-55
Alchian, Armen, 68
Arrow, Kenneth, 97

"Big bowl" distribution system, 67-69
Black market, 136
Budgeting
  separation of, 53-54, 78-80

Capitalism, 29-30
Centrally planned economy (CPE), 2-3, 48
  assets inherited from, 196-201
  confrontation with market system, 190
  dismantling of in second reform phase, 148-55
  failures of, 105-6
  and first phase of reform, 21-57, 65-67
  lack of incentives in, 49-52
Chen Yun, 7, 27-28, 44-46, 110
China National Institute for Economic Reform, 118
Closed sources experiment, 35
Code of laws, 161-62
Cold War, 21
Common interest, 45-47
Commune system, 9-10, 67-69

Contracting-out system, 124, 126-27, 167-69
Corruption, 176-77
Cultural Revolution, 7, 25, 27, 30-31, 52, 77, 82, 98, 106

Decentralization, 82-83, 160-61
"Decisions on Economic System Reform," 131-32
Demsetz, Harold, 68, 158-59
Deng Xiaoping, 7, 9, 27, 98, 108, 188
Development, 212-15
Dong Furen, 122, 128

Economic Contract Law, 162
Economic reform
  balance between development, institutions, and human assets, 212-15
  constraints on, 6-8
  early, 21-57
  belief in improving CPE, 27-31
  common interest of planned economy, 45
  concern for CPE's principle, 44
  devastated economy, 23-25
  dominance of central planning, 48-52
  efficiency concerns, 41-43
  experimental approaches, 33-39

223